Cultivating Socialism

GEOGRAPHIES OF JUSTICE AND SOCIAL TRANSFORMATION

SERIES EDITORS

Mathew Coleman, *Ohio State University*
Ishan Ashutosh, *Indiana University Bloomington*

FOUNDING EDITOR

Nik Heynen, *University of Georgia*

ADVISORY BOARD

Deborah Cowen, *University of Toronto*
Zeynep Gambetti, *Boğaziçi University*
Geoff Mann, *Simon Fraser University*
James McCarthy, *Clark University*
Beverley Mullings, *Queen's University*
Harvey Neo, *Singapore University of Technology and Design*
Geraldine Pratt, *University of British Columbia*
Ananya Roy, *University of California, Los Angeles*
Michael Watts, *University of California, Berkeley*
Ruth Wilson Gilmore, *CUNY Graduate Center*
Jamie Winders, *Syracuse University*
Melissa W. Wright, *Pennsylvania State University*
Brenda S. A. Yeoh, *National University of Singapore*

Cultivating Socialism

VENEZUELA, ALBA, AND THE
POLITICS OF FOOD SOVEREIGNTY

ROWAN LUBBOCK

THE UNIVERSITY OF GEORGIA PRESS
Athens

© 2024 by the University of Georgia Press
Athens, Georgia 30602
www.ugapress.org
All rights reserved
Set in 10.5/13.5 Minion 3 by Kaelin Chappell Broaddus

Most University of Georgia Press titles are
available from popular e-book vendors.

Printed digitally

Library of Congress Cataloging-in-Publication Data

Names: Lubbock, Rowan, author.
Title: Cultivating socialism : Venezuela, ALBA, and the politics of food sovereignty
    / Rowan Lubbock.
Identifiers: LCCN 2023043130 (print) | LCCN 2023043131 (ebook) |
    ISBN 9780820357959 (hardback) | ISBN 9780820357942 (paperback) |
    ISBN 9780820357966 (epub) | ISBN 9780820366036 (pdf)
Subjects: LCSH: Alianza Bolivariana para los Pueblos de Nuestra América—
    Tratado de Comercio de los Pueblos. | Food sovereignty—Latin America. |
    Agriculture and state—Latin America. | Agriculture—Economic aspects—
    Latin America.
Classification: LCC HD9014.L32 L83 2024 (print) | LCC HD9014.L32 (ebook) |
    DDC 338.1/98—dc23/eng/20230920
LC record available at https://lccn.loc.gov/2023043130
LC ebook record available at https://lccn.loc.gov/2023043131

In Memoriam
Jeremy Lubbock
(1931–2021)

CONTENTS

List of Tables and Figures ix

Acknowledgments xi

Introduction 1

CHAPTER 1. The Hidden Edifice of (Food) Sovereignty:
A Marxian Approach 23

CHAPTER 2. Capitalist Geopolitics and the Rise of "Continental History":
Latin America's Long Road to Regionalism 49

CHAPTER 3. From Magical State to Magical Region:
The Social Origins of ALBA 72

CHAPTER 4. Spaces of Agrarian Struggle:
Rights, Territory, and Food Sovereignty in ALBA 101

CHAPTER 5. The Political Economy of ALBA-Arroz:
Class Struggles across the "Point and Circle" 132

Conclusion 160

Notes 169

References 175

Index 211

LIST OF TABLES AND FIGURES

Tables

TABLE 1. Peasant, Indigenous, and proletarian organizations and agroecology   41

TABLE 2. Fertilizer (nitrogen, phosphorus, and potassium) consumption in selected countries (annual averages in thousands of tons of plant nutrients)   57

TABLE 3. Tractors used in farming in selected countries (thousands of units)   57

TABLE 4. Intra-ALBA trade in food, by economic category, to analyze regional production chain potentials. Subperiod 2005–11, in U.S. dollars at constant prices (2005=100)   90

TABLE 5. Land distribution in Venezuela, 1997/8–2007/8   110

TABLE 6. ALBA-Arroz, results of Annual Project (2012)   142

TABLE 7. ALBA-Arroz, results of Annual Project (2013)   142

TABLE 8. ALBA-Arroz, results of Annual Project (2014)   148

Figures

FIGURE 1. Institutional structure of the ALBA as of 2009   86

FIGURE 2. Agriculture, value added (percent of GDP), selected ALBA states   91

FIGURE 3. Selected ALBA food exporters to Venezuela (current US$)   91

FIGURE 4. Strategic-relational view of ALBA   98

FIGURE 5. Number of hectares rescued/regularized, 2009–16   111

FIGURE 6. Growth of inflation (average CPI) and monetary base (2012–16)   135

FIGURE 7. Production volumes (metric tons) of rice, corn, and sorghum   144

FIGURE 8. Ratios of surface area (hectares) to yield (metric tons) of rice production   144

ACKNOWLEDGMENTS

The genesis of this book began so long ago that it appears in the mind like an image dancing on the horizon of the sweltering Venezuelan *llanos*; a faint, flickering outline of an object half real, half mirage. I have tried my best to recall the innumerable individuals who have helped me to get to where I am today. Even if I could remember them all, a mere mention in a book's acknowledgments would never come close to repaying the debts I have incurred throughout this journey. Nevertheless, in keeping with academic tradition, I will make a paltry attempt to do so here.

First and foremost, I would like to extend my deepest thanks to the editorial team at Georgia University Press who helped me to write the book I never knew I had in me. Their acute insights, helpful suggestions, kind encouragement, and endless patience allowed me the space to reflect more fully on the story I wanted to tell and how I was going to tell it. Special thanks to the peer reviewers, both of whom gave sharp feedback and thoughtful comments to several drafts of the manuscript.

The first step on my journey began at the School of Social Science, History and Philosophy at Birkbeck College, which provided me with generous financial support throughout the entirety of my doctoral research, from which this book is derived. In a world of crippling austerity and increasing financial strain on students everywhere, I am enormously grateful for having had this opportunity. My supervisors at Birkbeck, Alejandro Colás and Ali Burak Güven, were exemplary mentors. As the project encountered a series of false starts, wrong turns, dead ends, and major reorientations, Alex and Ali were always there to provide a compass for navigating the choppy seas of doctoral research. The Department of Politics at Birkbeck was a wonderful home over those four years of research and teaching and I am grateful for the stimulation and support I received from both staff and students alike, in particular

Kieran Andrieu, Rosie Campbell, Jason Edwards, Marco Arafat Garrido, Dermot Hodson, Callum McCormick, Scott McLaughlan, Sam Mutter, and Antonella Patteri—thank you one and all for your conversation and company. Beyond Birkbeck, I've been lucky to have met, talked with, or otherwise been assisted by a number of scholars: Maribel Aponte-García, Andrea Califano, Asa Cusack, Thomas Muhr, Thomas Purcell, and Mark Tilzey—thank you for your support and advice.

My odyssey in Venezuela would not have been possible without the help of various people. Stephanie Pearce pointed me in the right direction before I even had a plan. Lee Brown was instrumental in organizing my first trip there in 2013. In Venezuela itself, my unwavering *compañero*, Paul Dobson, helped me traverse the weird and wonderful world of Venezuelan culture, politics, and wildlife. My *familia* in Mérida helped make the city my home away from home. América Uzcátegui, Rohan Chatterjee, Jesus Lacruz, Cesar Gonzales, Yani Esteva Tumbarinu, and many more—thank you for the laughs, dancing, and many *cajas*. In Caracas (my basecamp), I was given a literal sanctuary at the Prout Research Institute of Venezuela. Dada Maheshvarananda was a spiritual and political guide, but more importantly he was a source of laughter and harmony in an often-challenging city. At the Prout house, I had the good fortune of meeting and living with some wonderful people: Thales "Nacho" Fortes, Eduardo Hidalgo, Josh Rowan, Cecilia Verónica, Sergio Zaurin, and too many others to name here—they all made their mark on my journey, and I am grateful to each of them for doing so. I would not have been able to see this project to its completion without the kind assistance of Manuel Mauricio Nevada Santana, who tirelessly transcribed my many conversations in Venezuela.

My fieldwork was significantly assisted through the kind cooperation and support of many people, all of whom made invaluable contributions: Ruben Pereira, Miguel Angel Nuñez, Juan Reardon, Francys Guacarán, all the students at the Instituto de Agroecología Latinoamericano Paulo Freire, and the workers at the ALBA factories. *Gracias a todos, por todo.*

Much of the writing for this book was undertaken at Queen Mary, University of London. Enormous thanks go to friends and colleagues at the School of Politics and International Relations, especially Felipe Antunes de Oliveira, Ida Birkvad, Miri Davidson, James Dunkerley, James Eastwood, Clive Gabay, Dan Gover, Kate Hall, Sophie Harman, Rachel Humphries, Laleh Khalili, Nivi Manchanda, Angus McNelly, Diego de Merich, Andreas Papamichail, Patrick Pinkerton, Sharri Plonski, Holly Eva Ryan, Alex Stoffel, Layli Uddin, and Joanna Yao. They have each made their mark on the writing of this book, even if they didn't know it. Special thanks go to colleagues at the Queen Mary Latin

America Network (now the Center for Research on Latin America and the Caribbean), where parts of this book were previously presented.

Given how wrapped up we get in our scholarly lives, it is sometimes easy to forget about our personal networks outside of academia and how important they are in staying grounded (and sane). Harry Styles, John Standfast, Tommy Hartridge, Adam Kangura, Andrew Szederkényi, both Francescos, Mike Sheer, Holly Lubbock, Vivi Webb, Simon Webb, and Maria Deiana—I would have become untethered without you. To my mother and stepfather, there are no words that can express my gratitude for your unconditional love and support. I only wish my father could have lived to see the birth of this book, about which we often spoke. He is sorely missed, by many.

Lastly, and most importantly of all, my deepest thanks go to Giulia Carabelli. If anyone has done more in helping see this book through to completion, it is undoubtedly Giulia. Her emotional support, intellectual guidance, practical advice, and endless love have each in their own way made this book (and me) immeasurably stronger. I will never be able to sufficiently express my gratitude for everything she has done, but I will spend the rest of my life trying.

Parts of Chapter 4 were previously published in *Journal of Agrarian Change*, Chapters 2 and 5 in (respectively) *Globalizations* and *New Political Economy*. I am grateful to Wiley Company and Taylor and Francis (https://tandfonline.com/) for permission to reprint these materials for the present book.

Cultivating Socialism

INTRODUCTION

On December 14, 2004, during an international meeting in Havana between Fidel Castro Ruz and Hugo Chávez Frías—respectively the presidents of Cuba and Venezuela—a new diplomatic agreement was announced that would come to represent perhaps the most radical expression of regional cooperation in Latin America's history. From this meeting emerged the creation of the Bolivarian Alternative for the Peoples of Our America (Alternativa Bolivariana para los Pueblos de Nuestra América, ALBA), a regional institution that positioned itself as an alternative to the destructive forces of global capitalism.[1] Foremost in the minds of Chávez and Castro was the danger posed by the U.S.-led Free Trade Area of the Americas (FTAA), a hemisphere-wide neoliberal project that, in the eyes of ALBA's founders, "would create levels of dependence and subordination without precedence" (ALBA 2004). As an antidote to the FTAA, ALBA aimed to foster a *socialist geopolitics* based on the principles of cooperation, reciprocity, complementarity, and inclusive development (Angosto-Ferrández 2014). While the rise of ALBA was just one expression of Latin America's so-called Pink Tide during the first decade of the twenty-first century, which saw a variety of left-progressive governments come to power in almost every country in the region (Belém Lopes and Pimenta de Faria 2016), it was within the more radical variants of this trend—Bolivia, Ecuador, Nicaragua, and Venezuela—that new state/society relations based on "revolutionary democracy" would eventually coalesce into a project of regional socialism (Muhr 2013).

The evolution of this "posthegemonic" region (Riggirozzi and Tussie 2012) began with the Barrio Adentro program, a bilateral agreement between Cuba and Venezuela that facilitated trade in oil for doctors (SELA 2013). The influx of Cuban medical personnel into Venezuela's poorest neighborhoods filled a gap left behind by middle-class Venezuelan medical professionals who refused to enter the barrios. With a renewed focus on the health sector, the ratio of medical personnel to population went from 1:14.373 in 1998 to 1:1.380 by 2007 (Lubbock 2020c, 158–59). The Petrocaribe energy agreement between Venezuela and a number of Caribbean members of ALBA expanded this philosophy of solidarity and cooperative advantage through the supply of low-cost Venezuelan oil to traditionally energy-dependent states, with the option for deferred payments that would be directed toward regional development policies. Through the circulation of oil wealth, Petrocaribe established a series of infrastructures across the Caribbean, from oil storage and electricity grids to low-cost housing. By 2014 around 432 "social projects" (to the tune of $3.9 billion) had been carried out under Petrocaribe agreements (Cederlöf and Kingsbury 2019). Other far-reaching social policies, such as the *Yo Sí Puedo* literacy campaign brought a network of education professionals to underprivileged communities both within and beyond the ALBA. By 2008 three ALBA countries (Bolivia, Ecuador, Nicaragua) were declared to be illiteracy-free by UNESCO standards, while some 3.64 million people acquired literacy across the ALBA space by 2011. This regional pedagogical network also extended beyond the ALBA territory, bringing the *Yo Sí Puedo* literacy method to over twenty Latin American/Caribbean countries by 2009 (Muhr 2011, 206).

The first phase of ALBA's evolution thus centered on raising the standard of living for its constituent peoples through expansive social policies. Yet it would take a worldwide crisis to kick-start the second phase of ALBA. Four years after ALBA's founding declaration, in 2007/8, the world experienced the worst global food crisis in living memory. A combination of high energy prices, climate change-induced crop failures, and expansive biofuel production within the Global North led to a dramatic fall in global food supply (Mittal 2009, 18–19). With the concomitant increase in prices, the poorest 20 percent of the world's population struggled to cover their basic food needs (FAO 2015). In response to what Chávez called "the greatest demonstration of the historical failure of the capitalist model" (cited in Suggett 2008), ALBA announced a Food Security and Sovereignty Agreement in 2008, underwritten through an ALBA food fund of $100 million dollars, and, the following year, the formation of a regionwide "Grandnational Enterprise" (Empresa Grannacional) that would integrate agricultural production and cooperative development across member states (ALBA-TCP 2009a; 2009b). In seeking to overturn the logic of capitalist agriculture, the agreement proclaimed the goal of achieving "food sovereignty" as a common objective through "strengthening the internal production of each country in a sustainable manner and technical-productive potential can be complemented by a collective effort" (ALBA-TCP 2008a).

By means of this declaration the ALBA elevated a long-standing practice among rural movements the world over. For the past three decades, "food sovereignty" has become one of the defining features of peasant and farmer organizations within the transnational movement La Vía Campesina (LVC) (Desmarais 2007). Each manifestation of food sovereignty is relatively unique, but its underlying principles gravitate around the protection of agrarian livelihoods against the dominance of corporate capital (Trauger 2017). Characterized initially by a stronger emphasis on state-led regulation of national food systems (LVC 1996), peasant movements later transformed the very notion of sovereignty from an exclusive privilege of the state to a set of decentralized powers among rural actors capable of making (sovereign) decisions over the production, organization, and distribution of food (LVC et al. 2001). In challenging the state's exclusive claim to sovereign power, peasant movements have faced enormous obstacles in their struggle to construct new food regimes that better reflect the political demands of food sovereignty, such as secure land rights, cooperative production, and low-input sustainable agriculture (agroecology).

With ALBA's declaration of support for the regionalization of food sovereignty, peasant movements found a rare opportunity to scale up their demands into national and regional contexts. Three of ALBA's largest members by GDP (Bolivia, Ecuador, and Venezuela) had variably proclaimed the path to "socialism in the twenty-first century," as well as incorporating modes of Indigenous knowledge in the form of *Sumak Kawsay* ("life in harmony") and its more institutionalized expression *buen vivir* ("living well") (Cuestas-Caza 2018). These principles, along with more explicit references to food sovereignty, were integrated into new national constitutions that emerged from direct participation and input from peasant/Indigenous movements seeking to roll back the dominance of neoliberal development (Betances and Fiueroa Ibarra 2016; Veltmeyer and Záyago Lau 2021). As well as enjoying greater participation in the crafting of national policy, food sovereignty protagonists also found new spaces of inclusion within the ALBA's Council of Social Movements.

And yet, despite these innovations and opportunities, ALBA's attempt to construct a participatory food sovereignty regime has remained limited and contradictory. While several member states have pursued food sovereignty policies (particularly Bolivia, Cuba, Ecuador, Nicaragua, and Venezuela), these initiatives are largely unconnected with the ALBA institution itself. Even with notable growth in agricultural trade between ALBA states, much of this growth has been concentrated among large-scale capitalist producers; indeed, piecemeal efforts to reinvigorate peasant livelihoods have been eclipsed by the reproduction of landed capital and the broader agro-extractive complexes of which they are a part (Vergara-Camus and Kay 2017). Meanwhile, ALBA's goal of establishing transnational production chains, in the form of *Empresas Grannacionales*, never truly materialized. The only tangible evidence of ALBA's food policies is found in a string of factories within Venezuela producing for the domestic market. And in a bitter twist of fate, Venezuela has recently endured the most severe food crisis in its history.

This book aims to explore the politics of food sovereignty within the ALBA as a means of unraveling the contested and contradictory dynamics of building a participatory food regime at multiple political scales. In one sense, the subject matter of the book centers on the ways in which a number of Latin American states—Venezuela in particular—attempted to cultivate socialism, literally from the ground up. Of course, the "Bolivarian Revolution" in Venezuela, and its regional project within ALBA, should not be read entirely from the vantage point of rural development. Yet the effort to forge a new type of agriculture in Venezuela and an ambitious attempt to regionalize food sovereignty contain a number of parallels with the material practice of *cultivation* itself.

Zygmunt Bauman's concept of the "gardening state" gestured toward the specificity of modern political organization, in which the state organizes national territory much like the gardener brings order to a domestic plot (Bauman 1987, chap. 4). Intrinsic to the practice of the gardening state is the "will to improve," a ubiquitous feature of "modern" politics. The modalities of improvement are diverse, from colonial trusteeship to communist revolution (Li 2007; Hoffman 2011). Whatever form they take, schemes to improve the human condition, as James C. Scott (1998) once put it, tend to contain common ingredients:

> Their intentions are benevolent, even utopian. They desire to make the world better than it is.... They modify processes. They entice and induce. They make certain courses of action easier or more difficult. Many schemes appear not as an external imposition, but as the natural expression of the everyday interactions of individuals and groups. They blend seamlessly into common sense. Sometimes they stimulate a more or less radical critique. Whatever the response, the claim to expertise in optimizing the lives of others is a claim to power, one that merits careful scrutiny. (Li 2007, 5)

This book shares many of the observations and sentiments expressed by Tania Li's portrayal of the willful state. Across a variety of ALBA members, policies centered on or around food sovereignty principles aimed to entice and induce new forms of agricultural work, not only through state dictate but also in concert with peasants that gave expression to state policies through everyday interactions and strategies. However, some policies also elicited radical critique and resistance from those same actors that rural policies aimed to benefit.

This was particularly true with Venezuela, which offers the most radical example of agrarian reform (and its unintended effects). The Venezuelan state did not undertake a uniform approach to its national garden, nor to the project of food sovereignty. On the one hand, the Land Law of 2001, as the first step toward a more ambitious land reform program, recognized the precolonial *conuco* as the country's "historic source of agrarian biodiversity" (article 19, rbv 2001a), while redoubling efforts toward agro-ecological education and training (Domené-Painenao and Herrera 2019).[2] On the other hand, across the *llanos* of Venezuela, the agricultural heartland of the country, one would find large billboards projecting an image of the garden state, often with the line: "*Cultivando la Revolución Agroindustrial*" (cultivating the agro-industrial revolution) (Kappeler 2015, 86). These two approaches to agrarian development were intimately connected, rather than parallel or haphazard approaches. As we will see further in chapter 4, the initial state-led push toward re-peasantization and small-scale cooperatives led to a relative underperformance in the rural sector, requiring a more concerted effort at reconsolidating large-scale production of key staples.

These disjunctures emerge from the complex and often contradictory relationship between the state and grassroots actors of various types. One of the earliest known uses of the political term "grassroots" emerges at the turn of the twentieth century, when U.S. senator Albert Jeremiah Beveridge of Indiana referred to the Progressive Party as an organization "from the grass roots. It has grown from the soil of people's hard necessities" (cited in Rainey and Johnson 2009, 150). Beveridge's choice of words seems apt to the history of grassroots politics, particularly with respect to its chequered relationship to state power. As with the tending of a garden, the gardener (state) may come into mutual balance with the grass (roots). But more often than not, the radically fluid interests between these two sets of actors lead to entirely unanticipated futures. The gardener (state) may have all manner of tools and techniques at its disposal, but it quickly finds that the grass (roots) has its own plans (cf. Ginn 2014). To paraphrase Natasha Myers (2017, 297) grass is, like its roots, entangling.

If ever grassroots politics has become entangled with state power, it is undoubtedly under Latin America's left turn. *Cultivating Socialism* thus aims to shed new light on a well-studied topic, by revealing the ways in which the

Latin American project of "socialism in the twenty-first century" was neither a complete success nor an utter failure but a concrete historical moment in which the cultivation of *el pueblo* (the people) moved through a dynamic synthesis of political forces, from above and below, each striving toward a common goal, yet each entangled in a process of *becoming* (Dussel 2008, 75). As with the cultivation of fields, the story of ALBA's twenty-first-century socialism reveals the fertile growth of new forms of power and organization, the "sticky" nature of socioecological transformation, and periodic reversals as popular power momentarily withers on the vine.

At the center of this story is the struggle over sovereignty itself and the ways in which a variety of actors attempt to (re)claim sovereign power as their own. While food sovereignty (FS) studies has become increasingly prominent over the past few decades, it is only in recent years that scholars working in the field have begun to address the fundamental puzzle at the heart of FS politics: "Who or what is 'the sovereign' in food sovereignty?" (Edelman 2014, 920). As we will see in chapter 1, the current state of the art on the "sovereignty problem" in FS studies comprises attempts to answer this question through a variety of frameworks. This book hopes to contribute to these ongoing conversations through a critical Marxian approach that starts from the class-relational edifice of sovereignty. From this perspective, I suggest that if we want to understand the strategic possibilities for the construction of food sovereignty, we need to understand the very source of sovereign power itself.

What's the Problem with Sovereignty?

Since the high watermark of decolonization in the 1960s, sovereignty has become the universal characteristic of "the international," as a set of rights and duties bestowed upon all states large and small. Underpinning the regime of sovereign equality is the long-held belief that within discrete, unified political jurisdictions the state remains free from external interference and holds undisputed and legitimate power to decide the fate of its territory and the people within it (Hinsley 1986). And yet, it has long been sensed that some states are more sovereign than others. Krasner's (1999) early critique of sovereignty as "organized hypocrisy" foregrounded a subsequent generation of critical scholarship that increasingly called into question both the reality and normative value of sovereignty (cf. Lawson and Shilliam 2009). Yarimar Bonilla's rich history of the Caribbean, for instance, suggests the formation of a "non-sovereign archipelago," littered with military bases, free trade zones, tax havens "and other spaces of suspended, subcontracted, usurped, or imposed foreign jurisdiction" (2015, 10). The late Lauren Berlant went to so far as to claim that the very idea of sovereignty as a coherent practice is a "fantasy," one that collapses under contemporary conditions of radical uncertainty, risk, and disturbance. Instead, they argued, political subjects (whether individual or collective) should be considered decidedly "nonsovereign" (Berlant 2011).

The problems with sovereignty are therefore numerous. But does the hypocrisy of sovereign equality make this global regime entirely vacuous? And does the incompleteness, incoherence, and contingency of sovereignty render this concept a mere fiction? My answer to these questions is no. One of the problems with the above perspectives is the unspoken assumption lurking at the center of their critique: that sovereign power is absolute, indivisible, and permanent. As the logic goes, if we can identify inconsistencies within this absolute principle, then surely the principle itself is ephemeral. I suggest, in contrast, that if we really want to get to grips with this concept, we have to stop taking sovereignty at its own word. Many working within critical anthropology, for instance, have done just that by pointing to the messy and incomplete nature of sovereign power, in which the traditional hallmarks of state sovereignty—the power to punish, discipline, control, and sometimes kill—are inherently dispersed across a variety of nonstate actors (Ong 2000; Hansen and Stepputat 2006; Humphrey 2007; Monsutti 2012). Yet even here, there is a tendency to represent these examples as outliers, or a kind of deviance from the norm of state sovereignty, such as "vigilante groups, strongmen, insurgents, and illegal networks" (Hansen and Stepputat 2006, 296). Alternatively, I find more helpful Sasha Davis's take on sovereignty as inherently sociorelational, which prompts us

> to view power and governance as *that which happens*: as actions performed, connections made, places transformed, and rules of the game that are created and enforced. In this view there are no types of power per se, only relations of power and actions that vie with each other to achieve different aims.... Power, if thought about relationally, is not something one can be free of, and it can never be simply resisted or destroyed—it can only be countered by the production of other actual actions and practices." (Davis 2020, 136)

From this angle, sovereignty is not assumed to be split between the binary of light/shadow, or normal/deviant but is rather understood as a pervasive field of power relations through which people attempt to (re)produce a specific rationale of governance. But what kind of governance gives rise to sovereign power? If all social relations are simply an expression of sovereignty, then the concept itself may begin to lose its specificity. While I do not wish to foreclose the parameters of what sovereignty might be, my own approach to the sovereignty problem begins from the historical materialist problematic of the general and particular, or the ways in which the most general features of human societies—"the physical organization of... individuals and their consequent relation to the rest of nature" (Marx and Engels 1998, 37)—take on a variety of historically specific forms.

Historicizing (Food) Sovereignty

One of the curious aspects of critical scholarship on (food) sovereignty is its historical boundedness, with the implicit assumption that sovereignty is an exclusively "modern" invention (e.g., Jackson 2007; McMichael 2014; Conversi 2016). While the script of modernity certainly places the idea of *state* sovereignty at the center of its universe, Marxian historical sociology has long been interested in excavating forms of sovereign power across a variety of modes of production (Anderson 1974a, 1974b; Wood 2012). While Marx himself had little to say on the topic (Loick 2018, 95–103), he suggestively characterized relations of exploitation as a relationship of "sovereignty and dependence" between socioeconomic classes crystallizing into a set of *rights and duties* (Marx 1991, 927).[3] At the heart of this reading is the idea of *labor* as the mediator of the social and ecological milieu, or as Joshua Barkan puts it, "a means by which the potential of the world was [and is] rendered actual and usable" (2013, 10). With the rise of class societies, the potentialities of labor are no longer entirely owned by those who work but are appropriated by those possessing the (sovereign) *right to exploit labor*.

If the control of labor, and the relations of production in general, are in essence a form of governance, then the question of space and territory immediately enters the frame. As Lefebvre (1991) underscored, every mode of production has its own particular space as a reflection of social production and the symbolic constellations that give meaning to it. From the first instances of settled agriculture to the rise of city-states and world empires, human communities have been intricately designed, arranged, ordered, and mapped. Territoriality, then, can be thought of as an assemblage of material objects, cultural signifiers, and ideological constellations mediating the reproduction of society as a whole (Elden 2013). Indeed, rather than the mere spatial arrangement of objects, territoriality engenders a specific *body of knowledge* that gives meaning and rationality (a *rationale*) to a particular spatial ordering. The disciplinary control of human labor is therefore made possible through the intellectual means of organizing social production, whether in the field, factory, or state.

From this broader perspective, then, I view the edifice of sovereignty as the historically specific combination of *rights and territory*—or the right to exploit labor and the territorial organization of social production. My hope is that this interpretation helps to both reinstate the reality of sovereignty (against more sovereignty-skeptic interpretations), *and* to problematize the modernist myth of an indivisible and infallible sovereign power within the nation-state. More concretely, locating sovereignty within the framework of rights-territory/exploitation-discipline allows us to demystify the basis of sovereign power under capitalism, so often assumed as the sole preserve of the state. To elaborate this perspective, I draw upon Jacques Bidet's (2016) synthesis of Marx and Foucault in order to reveal the transformation of rights and territory under capitalism into *property-power* and *knowledge-power*. As the two sides of "modern" sovereignty, both capital and the state combine property-power and knowledge-power to achieve their own rationales of governance: one based on the production of surplus value, and the other on the production of political order.

The ultimate purpose of this class-relational reading of sovereignty is to clarify the terms of struggle within contemporary food sovereignty politics. While the articulation of FS is highly context-specific—engendering a diverse and expansive number of practices, discourses, and strategies—I suggest that, in seeking to challenge and reappropriate sovereign power from the state-capital nexus, the immanent political content of FS struggles implies the transformation of property-power and knowledge-power toward a regime of *self-directed labor and cooperative territorial organization*. These strategic pathways thus seek to overcome the "ontologies of separation" intrinsic to Western modernity (Escobar 2020, xxi), through the reconnection of people to the land, building communal forms of food system management, and expanding sustainable agricultural development.

The Capitalist State: A Poulantzian Approach

While the terrain of sovereignty may be more fluid and fragmented than we are used to thinking, the very question of the *state* continues to be the elephant in the room. As noted above, the prevailing common sense of "modern" politics rests on the notion that political rights are uniquely bestowed by, and territory a principal concern of, the nation-state. And yet, as with the concept of sovereignty, "many have been bamboozled by the blinding familiarity of the state" (Bratsis 2006, 2). Unsettling this familiarity is especially important in light of Latin America's so-called Pink Tide. As Grugel and Riggirozzi (2012) argue, left-progressive governments across the region embarked on a project of "rebuilding and reclaiming" the state from its neoliberal slumber through greater public intervention into the economic sphere and expanding spaces of inclusion within the public sphere. However, this anti-neoliberal turn was not simply bestowed from above but actively crafted from below by a variety of social forces, such as "Indigenous peoples' movements, unemployed workers, neighborhood organizations, shantytown dwellers, and landless peasants" (Rossi and Silva 2018, 9). These popular movements increasingly sought to *create* rights through de facto forms of territorial governance. Similarly, the struggle for food sovereignty across the ALBA was fundamentally shaped by the constituent power of grassroots movements seeking to embed the ideals of *popular sovereignty* into the constituted power of the state (Betances and Figueroa Ibarra 2016).

Unsurprisingly, contemporary Latin American scholarship has increasingly sought to grasp the meaning and significance of state power during the progressive wave (Rey 2010, 2012; Dargatz and Zuazo 2012; Tzeiman 2013; Ouviña and Rey 2018). The most fertile branch of this scholarship has been heavily influenced by the work of Italian Marxist philosopher Antonio Gramsci, whose principal concepts—particularly "hegemony" and "passive revolution"—have been widely adapted to the analysis of Latin America's left turn (e.g., Rey 2004; Tapia 2011; Roio 2012; Modenessi 2013, 2019; Oliver 2013, 2017; Modenessi and Svampa 2016; Quevedo 2019). Gramsci's concept of hegemony has played a significant role in helping to dissolve our blinding familiarity with the state by challenging the traditional image of a discrete/unified entity sealed off from the rest of society. Rather, the hegemony of the "integral state" is dependent on the production of "common sense," or a series of discursive practices permeating the terrain of civil society that normalizes hierarchies of race, gender, and social class (Gramsci 1971, 57–58, 333–34). With the idea of "passive revolution," meanwhile, Gramsci sought to describe a series of "revolutions from above" across late nineteenth-century Europe. These elite-led projects aimed above all to reconfigure society's social relations in order to mollify subaltern struggles, but without fundamentally altering the socioeconomic basis of society in general (109). As Massimo Modenessi contends (2019, 152), the concept of passive revolution helps to account for the Latin American Left's contradictory hegemonic project of *redistributing* wealth and power to the popular classes through the *deepening* of extractive capitalism and the demobilization of radical social forces. From within this framework, Gramscian scholars have traced the complex social relations between states and social movements—each being integral to the success of the other, yet existing within a tense and often contradictory relationship of cooperation, incorporation, or domination (Tapia 2011; Bringel and Falero 2016; Oliver 2017, 33–35).

However, as insightful as this Gramscian framework may be, it tends to remain limited to the state/social movement relationship at the expense of a more class-relational reading of socioeconomic production (cf. Webber 2017a, 167–68). Seen from the central problematic of this book, which aims to uncover the social sources of sovereignty and the necessary strategic breaks for reclaiming sovereign power among rural/working class movements, I offer a complementary yet alternative interpretation based on the work of Nicos Poulantzas, particularly his final book, *State, Power, Socialism* ([1978] 2014). While certainly inspired by Gramsci's work, Poulantzas makes more explicit the *politics of production* intrinsic to capitalist society. Analogous to my reading of sovereignty as the combination of property-power and knowledge-power, Poulantzas underscores the "despotic" exploitation of labor within the production process mediated by the division between manual and intellectual labor. And just as the power of sovereignty is divided between the state and capital, the monopolization of intellectual labor is fundamental to the reproduction of class power within spaces of production and the state apparatus itself (Poulantzas 2015, 56). Though conceptually commensurate with Gramsci's notion of the "integral state," Poulantzas goes one step further by revealing the "presence" of the state within relations of production, constituted by systems of property rights, forms of abstract/universal knowledge, and the class struggles that emerge from them. All of this suggests a closer examination of "the political and ideological as well as the purely economic moment of production" (Burawoy 1985, 8).[4] Seen from the framework of this book, the formally "economic" moment of property-power—to privatize the means of production and to exclude others from them—is always already implicated within the "political and ideological" moment of knowledge-power—the intellectual labor mobilized for social production.

Poulantzas's reading of Gramsci and latterly Michel Foucault led him to characterize the state as a "strategic field of struggle" extending across the entire social formation. This network of power relations, spanning from government institutions right down to the relations of production, eschews the false binary of struggling "within" the state, or simply "outside" it. Rather, the principal task of radical movements is to affect the entire strategic terrain—from centers of communal self-management to electoral institutions (Poulantzas 2014, 260). Poulantzas described this multiplied terrain of struggle as the "democratic road to socialism," which posed an alternative to both the Leninist strategy of smashing the bourgeois state and the liberal predilection to working within the confines of parliamentary democracy. Many have noted the striking convergence between this view of socialist strategy and the concrete politics of food sovereignty in Latin America (as well as the Pink Tide in general), which to variable degrees was affected through a dual strategy of building popular spaces of participatory democracy in parallel with liberal democratic institutions (see Muhr 2011; McKay, Nehring, and Walsh-Dilley 2014; Schiavoni 2015; Ellner 2017; Nelson 2019; Lubbock 2020a). Despite significant changes in economic policies and political institutions, radical social forces across the ALBA have struggled to shift the logic of state power away from its liberal-bourgeois mold. Even in the case of Venezuela—arguably the most radical experiment in socialist politics within ALBA—the complexity and contradictions of the Bolivarian state, and the attendant class struggles transecting its strategic terrain, have rendered the goal of attaining food sovereignty more distant than ever. And yet, the challenges faced by food sovereignty protagonists emerge from a series of dynamics and pressures far beyond the borders of the state.

The ALBA as a Regional "Strategic Terrain"

While Poulantzas did not directly address the formation of international regions, neo-Poulantzian scholarship has helped to extend this framework toward multiscalar spaces and processes, particularly in the case of Latin American regionalism (see Nelson 2015, 2022; Berringer and Kowalczky 2017; Berringer and Davi Ferreira 2022; Botão 2022). Bob Jessop's "strategic relational" approach provides a useful optic for unpacking the complex relations between different political scales (local/national/regional) and the social forces that (re)produce the always-changing configurations of space and scale (Herrod 2011). This framework is particularly important to the study of "food regimes" that operate across a variety of scales and a multitude of actors (cf. Otero 2016). As Jakobsen (2021) rightly notes, understanding the international relations of food and agriculture prompts an integrative approach to the coeval dynamics of global governance institutions, world regions, national states, and classes of agrarian labor. In this vein, Jessop's methodological focus centers on the dynamic and contingent aspects of *political agency* and the manner in which socially situated agents relate to each other in unexpected ways through the process of "strategic and spatial selectivity," as the contextually driven agent-strategies that attempt to grapple with the complexity of sociospatial transformation.

In bringing this theoretical framework into dialogue with the politics of food sovereignty in the ALBA, chapter 3 unravels the relationship between scales, spaces, and actors transecting the regional strategic terrain. Through this multiscalar perspective, I aim to shed light on whether ALBA's approach to food sovereignty was doomed from the start, as ill-conceived policies that were poorly implemented; or, whether the unprecedented socioeconomic crisis in Venezuela—characterized by hyperinflation and acute food shortages—was the ultimate cause of ALBA's virtual collapse. As with all social questions, the answer is not either/or, but both/and. As we will see throughout this book, it was largely the pace and ambition of regional projects compared to ALBA's limited organizational capacity that rendered many food sovereignty initiatives stuck at the negotiating table, or barely operational once established. Many of these obstacles emerged (paradoxically) from the central role of Venezuela to the creation, and subsidization, of the ALBA; despite the fact that Venezuela's extraordinary oil wealth provided a unique opportunity to regionalize food sovereignty and socialism in the twenty-first century, this centrality also pegged the existence of the ALBA space to the health of the Venezuelan economy.

For all these reasons, the book's focus is largely centered on the history, politics, and economic development of Venezuela. This is not only due to the overwhelming presence of the Venezuelan state in the function of ALBA. Rather, as I noted above, the only tangible outcome of ALBA's food policies is in a string of Empresas Mixtas Socialistas del ALBA (Mixed Socialist Enterprises of ALBA), all located within Venezuela. Thus, unraveling the politics of food sovereignty in ALBA begins with the emergence of the Bolivarian state.

The Crisis of "Exceptional Democracy" and the "Bolivarian Revolution"

For most of the twentieth century, Venezuela has been known as the "exceptional democracy" (Ellner and Tinker Salas 2007). Having established a stable and relatively well-functioning democratic regime since 1958, Venezuela stood in marked contrast to its regional neighbors, many of whom entered a protracted period of authoritarian rule during the 1970s. The stability of Venezuela's democracy was based on the Pacto de Punto Fijo, established between the three main political parties—Acción Democrática (AD), Comité de Organización Política Electoral Independiente (COPEI), and Unión Republicana Democrática (UPD)—which vowed to work together to guard against the return of dictatorship and to exclude more radical currents.

While the country's vast oil wealth would provide the material foundation for national unity—through the rentier-based distribution of public goods, employment opportunities, and political clientelism—it also obscured the deeper contradictions of Venezuela's "exceptional democracy." A sudden windfall in oil wealth in the 1970s, buoyed by the rise of global commodity prices, saw a raft of grand development projects spearheaded under the administration of Carlos Andrés Pérez. With the rapid drop in oil prices in the 1980s, Pérez's grand vision quickly collapsed. The neoliberal reforms enacted by Pérez (now in his second stint as president in 1989) led to intense social crisis, precipitated by a string of liberalization policies that cut back public spending, wage freezes, financial deregulation, and privatization of the social security system, all in return for an IMF loan (Lampa 2017, 200; Bistoletti 2019, 57–58). The final straw came with the raising of gasoline prices, which sparked a number of intense and violent protests across the country (the *caracazo*). Throughout the 1990s, Venezuela underwent enormous political upheaval, with two unsuccessful military coups against the increasingly unpopular Pérez administration in 1992 (the first of which was directed by a young military officer, Hugo Chávez), the impeachment and removal of Pérez from office on charges of embezzlement in 1993, and a year later, the unprecedented election of a presidential candidate outside of the traditional Punto Fijo bloc (Kingsbury 2016, 501).

These contradictions of Venezuela's "exceptional democracy" help to contextualize the remarkable rise and electoral victory of Hugo Chávez in 1999, who was seen by many to be the man to restore a sense of national pride among the people (Derham 2010). Central to this restoration was a metamorphosis of *el pueblo* as a political subject no longer seen as a passive mass without agency—as Venezuelan elites were accustomed to believing (Bonilla 1970, 267–80)—but as a key protagonist in the transformation of Venezuelan society. Underwritten by a new popular constitution, the "Bolivarian Republic" of Venezuela embodied a shift from an exceptionally elitist democracy to a *sociedad democrática, participativo y protagónico* (democratic, participatory, and protagonistic society).[5] Yet Chávez's relatively modest pace of reform was enough to send the traditional ruling classes into a sense of existential dread. Launching a series of counteroffensives against the Bolivarian state, from nationwide general strikes to a short-lived coup d'état in 2002, divisions between the old ruling class and the new political force of *chavismo* reached a crisis point, the solution to which lay in a truly radical break with the status quo. As part of Chávez's turn toward "socialism in the twenty-first century," the state began to actively promote the policies of "endogenous development" geared toward economic diversification and social welfare, the elimination of large-scale private agricultural holdings (*latifundia*), and the expansion of communal councils, communes, and agricultural cooperatives.[6] In the end, the turn to twenty-first-century socialism ultimately produced a series of unintended consequences and political conflicts that limited the capacity of the state to deal with the precipitous drop in oil revenue. Much like the fate of Pérez in the late 1970s, the collapse in oil rent in 2014 led to a disastrous economic crisis, registering a 40 percent drop in GDP between 2014 and 2017 (worse than the U.S. Great Depression), acute food shortages, hyperinflation, and an average real wage of around $1 a month (Schincariol 2020; Hanke 2019). Moreover, the economic sanctions imposed by the Trump administration from 2017 saw the Venezuelan economy go from crisis to catastrophe (Weisbrot and Sachs 2019).

As I argue in the following chapters, ALBA's fate was always intimately tied to Venezuelan state. But the structural crisis afflicting the Bolivarian Republic, and ALBA itself, goes much deeper. Whereas previously, during the early 2000s, the commodities boom had given rise to an "irresistible character of extractivist inflection," a social consensus (either implicit or explicit) that the exploitation of natural resources could square the circle of a "progressive capitalism," this "commodities consensus" quickly unraveled with the subsequent collapse in world prices (Svampa 2013). In seeking to redress dwindling fiscal reserves through austerity policies and intensified resource extraction, the political base of leftist governments has undergone severe fragmentation and declining electoral fortunes. As a result, ALBA began to lose some of its biggest members. With the election of Lenin Moreno in 2018, replacing the more left-wing Rafael Correa, Ecuador announced the end of its nine-year relationship with the ALBA (Telesur 2018). A year later, the Bolivian president, Evo Morales, would be forced out of office by the military and replaced by a far-Right interim government that suspended its membership from the ALBA bloc. The current terrain of Latin American politics is therefore radically in flux.[7] And while ALBA, and the Latin American Left in general, are certainly not out, the fundamental social questions that led to its precipitous decline have yet to find an answer.

A Note on Method

Despite Poulantzas's close relationship with the legacy of Althussarian "structuralism," his final book evinced a more nuanced methodological approach to the Marxian problematic of the state and class agency. As he put it, "one cannot ask any theory, however scientific it may be, to give more than it possesses—not even Marxism, which remains a genuine theory of action. There is always a structural distance between theory and practice, between theory and the real" (Poulantzas 2014, 22). Taking a cue from this cautionary statement, my focus on "capitalist site[s]" of power and contestation does not assume a universal logic determining the thought and action of socially situated agents (Gibson-Graham 2006, xxx). In recognizing the inherent complexity of sociopolitical crisis and transformation, my analysis of food sovereignty politics aims to frontload the radically contingent outcomes of class struggle, in which structural contexts become extraordinarily malleable as political actors attempt to manage, co-opt, or transform their institutional context. This is not simply a rehash of "structuration theory" (Giddens 1984), in which structures shape agents and agents change structures; rather, in line with Poulantzas's sentiment above, I follow Samuel Knafo's methodological wager to abandon overly structuralist readings of sociopolitical dynamics in favor of a radically empiricist analysis of agency in order to problematize the very assumptions we carry when faced with "structural" contexts (Knafo 2017, 250). In other words, a grounded empiricism into the concrete strategies and relations between actors helps to better understand how structural contexts are *used* in unanticipated ways by agents attempting to relate to, or gain leverage over, other actors or groups (Konings 2018).

As encompassing as this study aims to be, it also has significant limitations. The literature on food sovereignty is as diverse and complex as the movements and peoples it seeks to describe. Over the past decade or so, critical scholarship on rural movements, land struggles, and alternative food ways have incorporated a wide range of sociological determinants in the making of food politics, including gender, race, indigeneity, and class (see, e.g., Razavi 2009; Alkon and Agyeman 2011; Daigle 2019; Figueroa-Helland, Thomas, and Aguilera 2018; Parraguez-Vergara et al. 2018; Huambachano 2018). This broader understanding of food sovereignty politics helps to bring into focus both the historical legacies of colonialism's "great land rush" that systematically dispossessed Indigenous peoples while simultaneously devaluing traditional modes of alimentary life (Weaver 2003; Ma Rhea 2017; Chao 2022; Colás 2022). Though we live in a very different world from that of the eighteenth century, the historical sediments of colonial hierarchies in knowledge, resources, and power continue to overdetermine the global politics of food (Canfield 2022). Contemporary food sovereignty movements thus situate their struggles across a variety of power structures and discursive frameworks, including regimes of commodification, "productivism," gendered conceptions of rights and property, and "raced markets" (Alkon 2012; Agarwal 2016; cf. Tilley and Shilliam 2018).

In shedding light on this wider field of food sovereignty studies, I hope to bring more clarity and transparency into the specific theoretical and methodological choices underpinning this book. In the first instance, this project was intended as a critical analysis of the state and its relationship to rural/working class movements from the vantage point of Marxian political economy, and the ways in which specific forms of class struggle and property-relations reconfigure wider political institutions across multiple scales. In the specific context of the subject matter of this book, Thomas Legler once noted that

> scholars of Latin American and South American regionalism need to get out of the office and into the field to conduct interviews with key informants, from national leaders and diplomats to transnational and regional activists, as well as ordinary citizens. (Legler 2013, 342–43)

This injunction speaks to the overtly state-centric aspects of regionalism, which takes the commanding heights of political power as the only relevant vantage point. However, my approach to fieldwork data-gathering was chosen not as a means of *disproving* the power of states but rather *to sociologically untangle* why it is that the sovereign state continues to sit front and center of a political project that claims to be a revolutionary exemplar of popular power. Again, posing this problem does not suggest that grassroots power within the Bolivarian project is ineffectual or simply nonexistent; rather, it suggests *problematizing the state form* through a critical class analysis that hopes to lay bare the specific modalities of power that give rise to particular social agencies.

This theoretical and methodological orientation does not, however, necessarily close down convergent analyses into the nature of racial/gendered hierarchies in socioeconomic systems. Perhaps with more time, and less anxiety over the fieldwork, these avenues may have been more fully explored. Yet this also brings to light a less-frequently discussed aspect of fieldwork that can have unanticipated consequences for the eventual direction of one's writing. As Can Mutlu (2015) points out, the question of *failure* looms large in any fieldwork-based project, whether due to an inability to meet a desired objective or the failure to access necessary information or data. In my case, it was the latter that continuously hampered any sense of progress (as I explain subsequently). Though hardly a satisfactory answer, part of the reason for my somewhat narrow choice of theoretical concern is due to the ways in which my time and emotional energy were fixated on achieving something relatively modest in scope. Had I been able to achieve these goals within the first few months, I may have had the opportunity to think more deeply about the place and the people I had encountered. All of this constitutes a small step toward reflecting on my journey to this point in time. Indeed, "to know where we are going next, we need to know where we have been before. To know that, we need to know how we got there" (Mutlu 2015, 940). In this sense, I have benefited enormously from thinking about how I arrived at this point and what my future research aims to achieve in light of both past successes *and* failures. As such, my recent encounter with the broader scholarship on colonial history and the racial/gendered hierarchies that are integrated into the history of the global food system constitutes the beginnings of a new research project on agriculture and international (dis)order, and the ways in which the historical legacies of alimentary domination continue to shape ongoing struggles over the rights to nature, food, and life.

Much of this book draws upon my fieldwork research in Venezuela over a twelve-month period between 2015 and 2016. During that time, I was fortunate enough to speak with a variety of individuals and groups undertaking very different types of work within the ambit of the ALBA and food sovereignty, including several peasant movement activists within the Coordinadora Agraria Nacional Ezequiel Zamora (CANEZ), Correinte Revolucionaria Bolívar y Zamora (CRBZ), Frente Nacional Campesino Eziquiel Zamora (FNCEZ), and the peasant educational collective Universidad Campesina Argimiro Gabaldón.[8] I also had the opportunity to speak with a number of people from local communes, alternative media platforms, ALBA officials, and workers within the ALBA-Arroz rice producing factories in Portuguesa, Venezuela.[9]

Outside of Venezuela, I spoke to two regional representatives of the Ecuadorian peasant movement La Confederación Nacional de Organizaciones Campesinas, Indígenas y Negras (FENOCIN), accomplished by virtue of my partner's uncanny foresight that it may have been time for a much needed (if brief) vacation. We met in Guayaquil and moved on to Quito, the capitol city in which FENOCIN's offices are based—I couldn't resist the opportunity to learn more about their experiences, and I am grateful to both my interlocutors for their generosity in taking the time to speak with me.[10]

The workers' occupation of the ALBA-Arroz network of factories is the main pivot of the book, but the story of how I ended up there is, in many ways, the cipher to understanding the contradictory process of food sovereignty in the ALBA. As we will see in chapter 3, the result of ALBA's many declarations and agreements in agrarian development crystallized in a series of factories within the Venezuelan territory, producing a range of goods for the national market, including rice, legumes, pork, chicken, fish, and dairy. Having encountered enormous difficulties accessing personnel at these factories (which I quickly learned after attempting to access the ALBA-Lacteos [dairy] and ALBA-Leguminosas [legumes] sites in the states of Barinas and Portuguesa), it was only by chance that I stumbled across an article in a local newspaper reporting on the workers' occupation at ALBA-Arroz in response to the dire state of the enterprise. Sensing a rare opportunity, and in a somewhat desperate gambit, I called the newspaper to see if they could put me in touch with ALBA's union representative (*vocero*). After obtaining a phone number for the ALBA-Arroz vocero, I was relieved to hear him enthusiastically invite me down to the factories to speak with the workforce about their situation. For all these reasons, the ALBA-Arroz factories are the only ALBA production sites presented in this book. And it is thanks to the workers' willingness to talk to an outsider about their experiences, struggles, and hopes for the future that my research, and this book, was made possible.

Taking stock of the difficulties faced during my fieldwork provides much insight into the sociopolitical crisis afflicting the Bolivarian state. As I will show further in chapters 3 through 5, the contradictions of the Bolivarian revolution led to a series of developmental bottlenecks, which neared collapse with the fall in oil prices around 2014. At the geopolitical level, U.S. imperial strategy saw relentless pressure against Venezuelan society in order to affect a more acceptable government to Washington (see Lubbock 2020a; Weisbrot and Sachs 2019). Furthermore, as Alan Macleod notes, U.S. geopolitical strategy was always wedded to a "propaganda model" in which seemingly objective Western media coverage faithfully echoed the official U.S. government portrayal of Venezuela as an "extraordinary threat" (Macleod 2018). In light of these challenges faced by the Venezuelan state, it should hardly be surprising why I found the ALBA factories to be largely inaccessible.

Indeed, apart from the centrality of the Bolivarian state within the ALBA, much of the reason for my central focus on Venezuela was due to the endless time spent navigating the labyrinthian maze of state bureaucracies. Sitting down with one official in a given ministry would result in clarifications as to which institutions held authority over a specific factory (and this chain of command often altered depending on who I talked to). There were also frequent promises to sign letters of authorization allowing me to access certain production sites. But these promises rarely, if ever, materialized. The very fact that ALBA's production sites reside entirely within Venezuela meant I had little choice but to continue my seemingly never-ending quest to gain access to the ALBA factories, at the expense of a more far-reaching fieldwork in other ALBA countries. My hope is that the broader comparative analysis of Venezuela's struggle for agrarian reform with other national cases within the ALBA (chapter 4) will widen our perspective on the prospects and limits of constructing a food sovereignty regime, both nationally and internationally.

Book Outline

Chapter 1 aims to unravel the central parameters of "food sovereignty" (FS), via three interrelated lenses: rights, territory, and sovereignty. As intimately connected elements of the sociological edifice of sovereignty, I trace their variable combinations through a variety of historical epochs and modes of production—from the Roman empire to capitalist "modernity." In offering an historical materialist reading of sovereignty, I hope to enhance our understanding *who or what is sovereign* within food sovereignty struggles.

Chapter 2 provides a historical sketch of Latin America's long road to regionalism during the postwar period, and the broader historical context to the creation of the ALBA regional space. The history of international regionalism can be traced to the political revolutions across the Western hemisphere, from the early United States to the proto-republics in South America. Forging continental-sized spaces of accumulation, settler-colonial states contained the potential to dislodge their much smaller European counterparts from the heights of world power. Yet only one of these spaces, the United States, would turn this potential into a reality. In forging the first truly "continent-sized island," the United States ushered in the era of "continental history" and the geographical realities of world power based on regionwide political complexes. By and large, Latin America's early experimentation with regionalism was entirely refracted through the U.S. hegemonic project, embodied primarily through regional security communities. Each development drive, from postwar modernization to neoliberalism, continually produced a series of social ruptures and cycles of struggle that laid the groundwork for the emergence of Latin America's "left turn." Yet even this geopolitical realignment possessed its own internal divisions, from the relative divergence of development projects between the Southern Common Market (MERCOSUR) and ALBA to the contradictions inside the ALBA bloc itself.

Chapter 3 unravels the social history and contemporary politics of Venezuela, as a means of grasping the specific contradictions of the ALBA regional space. The history of Venezuela is inextricable from the discovery of oil, which quickly became an elixir in the making of the "magical state" (Coronil 1997). With seemingly limitless wealth buried beneath its subsoil, the Venezuelan state conjured into existence grand narratives of national development and even grander development projects that sought to bring the country to the forefront of technological dynamism. Yet Venezuela's "exceptional" democratic stability was always guaranteed by the concentration of power within the state apparatus and the elite compact among the Venezuelan political class.

Chávez's Bolivarian Republic was the direct result of Venezuela's democratic breakdown in the face of economic crisis and popular struggles. Yet Chávez had to contend not only with hostile opposition forces but with the legacies of Venezuelan state formation, marked by the magical powers of extraordinary oil wealth and the inefficiencies of a bureaucratic state machine that more often worked against the realization of state-led development projects.

It is within this context that the nature and operation of the ALBA is situated. I examine ALBA's articles of agreement relating to the role of social movements throughout the regional institution and to the specific political economy embedded within ALBA's "Grandnational Concept." The chapter will show how the role of the sovereign state—in both its relationship to transnationally organized social movements and its approach to economic development—maintains an overarching presence. The underlying politics of food sovereignty in the ALBA space therefore appear in a radical discourse and philosophy converging around issues of the "social economy," yet *overdetermined by the strategic and spatial selectivity of sovereign state power in Venezuela*. The subsequent empirical chapters reflect this contradictory "nationalization" of ALBA's most radical features, in terms of how agrarian social movements are largely focused on political transformation within their national territories and how ALBA's "regional" production materialized into a network of *national* production companies oriented to the Venezuelan home market.

Chapter 4 turns to the first of these dimensions by analyzing the emergence and dynamics of food sovereignty politics in several ALBA states. The examination of the cases of Bolivia, Ecuador, Nicaragua, and Venezuela provides a rich portrait of food sovereignty projects across ALBA's members. While the rise of these radical state/society complexes offered a unique opportunity for the scaling up of food sovereignty principles, peasant struggles within ALBA states have had limited impact on the structures of agricultural production across the regional space. Guided by the parameters laid out in chapter 1, in chapter 4 I chart the terrain of food sovereignty through the lens of property-power and knowledge-power, as a means of navigating the complex process of struggle seeking to transform the regime of property rights and the dominant forms of knowledge and organization that shape the state-capital nexus.

Chapter 5 situates the struggle for food sovereignty at the other end of the production chain, in the form of industrial processing. As I show through a variety of conversations with workers at the ALBA factories, the shadow of statism dominated the production of food. ALBA workers possess both a strong level of intragroup solidarity, as well as a number of divergences of outlook. For the former, the values of *bolivarianismo*, deep commitments to the "social economy," and a shared hostility to bureaucratic structures all shine through. For the latter, most low-level workers had little faith in the current government to extricate itself out of its current morass. And while workers expressed a keen interest in establishing a regime of worker self-management in the factory, and hence transforming the elements of property-power (worker ownership) and knowledge-power (democratic decision making over factory organization), the power of state sovereignty and the contingencies of a national economic crisis proved to be insurmountable obstacles. As such, their strategic horizon remained limited, oriented toward merely the relaunching of factory operations under the old status quo.

The chapter also provides a vignette on the ALBA factory/commune relations in the parish of Payara. The troubled relationships between the factory, commune, and local government reveal the systematic breakdown in one of Chávez's key strategies for socialist transformation (the "Point and Circle" initiative). The eventual disempowerment of the Payara commune, previously self-managing the distribution of food among its members, ultimately fractured the foundation of the "communal state" and the wider terrain of food sovereignty as a system of democratization throughout the entire food chain.

CHAPTER 1

The Hidden Edifice of (Food) Sovereignty

A Marxian Approach

This chapter will lay out a theoretical framework for analyzing what I call the "sovereignty problem" in food sovereignty studies. As Antonio Roman-Alcalá notes, "'who is the sovereign within FS?' has emerged as one of the most crucial of the unanswered questions" within FS politics (2016, 1). Despite the centrality of sovereignty to the FS movement and scholarship, it is only in recent years that scholars have begun to put the sovereignty problem front and center. Echoing earlier debates in critical anthropology (e.g., Das and Poole 2004; Krupa and Nugent 2014), FS scholars have unsettled the traditional image of the unified sovereign state in favor of a more fluid and contested assemblage of sovereign powers across a variety of sites and actors.

Beyond this common grounding, each approach offers a variety of angles from which we can appreciate the multidimensional character of sovereignty. Amy Trauger suggests that sovereignty can be read as (1) spatial and social strategies of the state to claim territory; (2) management of life (*biopolitics*); and (3) the production of "imaginaries" concerning sovereignty's power and extent (2014, 1143). For Alastair Iles and Maywa Montenegro de Wit, sovereignty consists of (1) the capacity to act authoritatively; (2) the ability to influence political and economic processes; and (3) rights to participate and to be consulted (2015, 485). Antonio Roman-Alcalá argues that sovereignty extends across various scales—the "local" through "relations within civil society," households, villages, communities; the "national," with "state governments," administrations, agencies, legislative bodies; and "supranational," such as the Food and Agriculture Organization (FAO)'s Committee on Food Sovereignty, TNCs, "state-based" FTAs, and La Vía Campesina (LVC) (2016, 1391). Christina Schiavoni, meanwhile, speaks of different "scales" of production; the "geography" of the urban-rural divide; and "institutions" as both formal and informal modes of political organization (2015, 468–69).

Undoubtedly, the question of authority, institutions, and scales is central to unraveling the operation of political power. But how can we reconcile these diverse conditions to the supposedly common referent of sovereignty itself? As a possible answer to this question, I offer an alternative Marxian approach that aims to reveal the hidden edifice of sovereign power, though one that manifests in historically specific ways in different times and places. As Marx underscores, relations of exploitation—or the "rightful" appropriation of surplus labor by a nonproducing minority—have always signalled the locus of political power. Conjoined with the exploitation of labor is the means through which land, tools, and human bodies are put to work in order to achieve a certain social end (*rationale*). Drawing on Stuart Elden's notion of "political technology" (2013), this spatial order expresses the *territorial* basis of society and the organizing principles governing social (re)production.

From this perspective, I trace the common roots of sovereignty to the *right to exploit labor and the territorial organization of social production*. The first part of this chapter outlines the ways in which sovereignty was shaped under precapitalist modes of production. Despite their particular characteristics, precapitalist societies did not have a strict separation between the "political" and "economic." Rather, "economic" power was essentially fused with the prerogatives of political authority. In this sense, sovereign power had a striking clarity, with the locus of exploitation and political authority explicitly intertwined.

With the transition to capitalism, rights and territory take on a very different form. In the second part of the chapter, I argue that the advent of "modernity" radically obscured the edifice of sovereign power. With the emergence of capitalist private property and the commodification of everyday life, a seemingly pristine division between the political state and civil society marked the compartmentalisation between the sovereign and nonsovereign, or the political from the economic. However, read through the lens of rights-territory/exploitation-discipline, the pristine image of economic exchange and civil society dissolves into a more menacing assemblage of power and domination. From within the hidden abode of production, the power of capital quickly resembles the sovereign powers of the state—a "rationalized," scientific organization of production mediated through the disciplinary control of human bodies. To articulate the particular form of sovereignty under capitalism, I borrow from Jacques Bidet's (2016) reading of Foucault with Marx, which sees the "modern class relationship" as grounded in the combination of property-power and knowledge-power. While the "class factor" of property-power corresponds more heavily to those who own capital, knowledge-power is never absent from the realm of capitalist production (Bidet 2016, 7–8). Conversely, the moment of knowledge-power is consummated at the height of political power, within the state apparatus itself. And yet, I suggest that the moment of property-power is not entirely absent from the state either. Rather, like private property, the logic of the "modern" state rests upon its exclusive ownership of the nation, a permissive condition facilitating its powers of control. Thus, both capital and the state combine these two elements for their own ends, one to produce surplus value and the other to produce political order. In decentering the locus of sovereignty away from the state and toward multiple sites of exploitation/territorialization, Poulantzas's theory of the capitalist state provides a useful supplement to this class-relational reading of sovereignty, in which the state/capital nexus springs from a common source of monopolizing the intellectual labor required for the organization of society.

Finally, I mobilize Bob Jessop's "strategic-relational approach" in order to extend Poulantzas's insights to institutional scales beyond the state level. In linking the class dynamics of capitalist production and accumulation with modes of regulation and forms of hegemony, Jessop expands the analytical frame from the strategic field of the state to the *strategic field of the region*. A multiscalar approach to the ALBA helps to shed light on the ways in which space, scale, and institutions are not merely static frames of reference but fundamentally produced by the complex combination of social production, class struggles, and institutional resolutions.

The Sovereign Clarity of Politics:
Rights and Territory Before Capitalism

Though we may often forget, "modernity" is a relatively recent invention. The history of human communities spans far longer than the mere five hundred or so years since the so-called Enlightenment. While this "premodern" era forms a radically diverse roster of tribes, chieftaincies, city-states, and empires, they were all united by a relatively common characteristic. This was, as Henri Lefebvre put it, a world governed by *absolute space*, in which people, places, sites, and land were organically fused around a sense of sacred order: "This was a society which, if not utterly transparent, certainly had a great limpidity. The economic sphere was subordinate to relationships of dependence; violence itself had a sovereign clarity" (Lefebvre 1991, 267). Though written in the context of medieval Europe, Lefebvre's argument takes on a broader relevance to the nature of political power during the precapitalist era. What united these diverse forms of political community was the fusion of the political with the economic. There was no "economy" to speak of, at least understood in the traditional sense. Before capitalism, social production and its distribution was decidedly *political*, from top to bottom. The condition of property, the mechanisms through which surplus labor was appropriated (*exploitation*), and the conventions regulating the distribution of social wealth were all mediated by political status and prestige. In recognizing this pattern across the precapitalist world, Marx suggested that it was within the relations of exploitation that "we find the innermost secret, the hidden basis of the entire social edifice, and hence also the political form of the *relationship of sovereignty and dependence*, in short, the specific form of the state in each case" (Marx 1981, 927, emphasis added; cf. Anderson 1974a, 402–3).[1]

The Roman Empire, for instance, maintained a marked distinction between public and private, and between civic law and private property law. So powerful was the Roman conception of private property that it constituted a "sharply delineated private sphere in which the individual enjoyed his own exclusive dominion" (Wood 2008, 124; see also Tuck 1979, 10–12). But this did not signal an "economic" realm all to its own; the space of private property was not separated from the civic political domain in an abstract sense. Rather, it was an "amateur government by members of the propertied elite" (Wood 2008, 125). Thus, the dominant class straddled the private/public realms (*dominium* and *imperium*), ruling in "its two different aspects" (126), which led to "a substantial degree of [elite] local self-government [which] had created a tendency to fragmentation of sovereign power" (Wood 2012, 5–6; cf. Kehoe 2007, 135).

The political technology of the Roman Empire reflected this fragmentation of sovereignty, marked primarily through militarized territorial expansion. As a corollary to its land-based economic growth, mediated by the conquest of land among the solider-citizen-farmer, the Roman imperium was shaped by concentric circles encompassing the "limits" (*limes*) of empire, rather than hardened borders. As Poulantzas put it, "This morphographical ordering coincides with the sites of exploitation and the forms of political command: space is homogenous and undifferentiated because the space of the slave is the same as that of the master; and the points at which power is exercised are replicas of the sovereign's body [in the imperial center]" (2014, 101). Within these "replicas" of the sovereign's body—the great *latifundia* of the Roman elite—there existed variably sophisticated patterns of labour organisation and supervision over slave and tenant producers (Kehoe 2006; cf. Elden 2013, 54). Indeed, the forms of exploitation and labor regimes found on the landed estates were heavily shaped by the commercialized agriculture prevalent in late Roman period: Mediterranean polyculture and its organization for sale on the market placed a premium on capital investment, to a degree that was unsuited to the devolution of labor characteristic of landlord-tenant relations. Thus, the tight control of estate management by the landlord and other supervisory layers tended toward the use of slave labor, as well as seasonal wage workers (Harper 2011, chap. 4).

The collapse of the Roman Empire and its dissolution into Europe's "feudal revolution" merely entrenched this fragmented landscape of sovereignty even further. The complete fusion of political authority with economic appropriation under feudalism led to the proliferation of lordly territorial power centers, interlocked into a complex hierarchy of ever-more powerful lords and their subordinate vassals, which Perry Anderson famously dubbed the "parcellization of sovereignty" (Anderson 1974b, 148). Yet unlike the Roman Empire, private property was unknown in the feudal world. As Benno Teschke puts it, feudal lords "held their land in tenure as a fief that carried, along with specific rights to exploit the peasantry, military and administrative duties to the land-granting overlord" (2003, 58). In this way, land was not "owned" as such but simply held through differential juridical rights—conditional property (*dominium utile*) by the local lord, and nominal ownership (*dominium directum*) by the overlord (Teschke 2003, 58; see also Bethell 1998, 77). However, one could argue that this is merely a difference between de jure and de facto property ownership; for while feudal kings did not explicitly (or legally) proclaim their ownership over the land, "they didn't need to; it went without saying" (Bethell 1998, 77), precisely because land itself was the wellspring of political power.

Similar to the situation of the late Roman period, feudal lords were not completely absent from the process of organizing production. But unlike the direct management of production within the Roman *latifundia*, socioterritorial organization was more fractured and diffuse under feudalism. While tenant laborers were largely in control of their tools, land, and production techniques, macrolevel organization of field management was shared between lord and serf, as in the case of irrigation and watercourse management (Comninel 2012, 134). Even at a more minute level, with the subdivision of field strips for crop rotation, "the court of the lord was essential in regulating this system.... The more productive the soil, and the greater its maximum potential population, the more important was the court's role in coordination and regulation... With open-field agriculture, virtually every aspect of production is directly subject to legal regulation" (135).

As a reflection of this fluid political technology, feudal frontiers were not absolute but constantly in flux, albeit homogenized by the image of a united Christian "world." Thus, "delimitations are constantly intersecting and overlapping in a series of twists and turns; and subjects, while remaining on the spot, move about in accordance with the changes of the lords and sovereigns to whom they are personally tied" (Poulantzas 2014, 103).

The eventual decline of feudalism and the coeval expansion of European colonialism kick-started a profound transformation in the social and spatial register of sovereignty. This was less a sudden rupture than it was a long process of change in which the old carried within it the seeds of the new. Parcellized sovereignty soon gave way to "absolutist sovereignty," with political authority centralised in the body of the king or queen, and the state over which they presided—*L'état, c'est moi!* (Anderson 1974a). And yet, "while the king monopolized the rights of sovereignty, he never actually controlled the means for its exercise" (Teschke 2003, 172). The absolutist state thus rested on a precarious balance between centralized de jure sovereign state power and decentralized de facto sovereign control of land, labor, and property among nobles at home and colonists abroad (cf. Benton 2010).

Central to this transitional moment in the making of "modern" sovereignty was the phenomenon of "primitive accumulation." For many historians both within and beyond the Marxist tradition, the key pivot of primitive accumulation took place in the English countryside, as peasants became forced off their customary lands and landlords transformed into agrarian capitalists as the unintended results of class struggle (Dobb 1946; Thompson 1975; Yelling 1977; Neeson 1993). The rise of private property on the land has often led to a convenient portrait of separation between the economic power of capitalist landlords and the political power of the sovereign state (e.g., Wood 2012, 13). This new social arrangement was famously captured in Jean Bodin's sixteenth-century treatise on sovereign statehood: "It is most expedient for the preservation of the state that the rights of sovereignty should never be granted out to a subject, still less a foreigner, for to do so is to provide a stepping stone where the grantee himself becomes the sovereign" (cited in Jackson 2007, 47). While Bodin's notion of sovereign power—as the absolute preserve of the state—reflects the standard narrative of modern sovereignty, it also overlooks the degree to which the state did, in fact, grant a set of extensive de facto sovereign powers among certain individuals and groups.

This alternative reading can be most clearly seen in the other side of primitive accumulation, which as Marx noted was closely bound up with the discovery of gold and silver, the enslavement of American Indigenous and African peoples, and the plunder of India, "all things which characterize the dawn of the era of capitalist production" (Marx 1982, 915). The Iberian empire in South America was pioneered by individuals, like Hernán Cortés, whose independence and de facto sovereign authority was matched only by their naked brutality and systematic violence against Indigenous communities. It was both these qualities that the Spanish Crown sought to tame, lest the Hapsburgs lose their claim to new lands and access to new labor (Bakewell 2002, 299–300). In response, the Crown established a vast, bureaucratic machinery encompassing complex layers of territorial authority and economic exploitation that formally represented the absolute sovereignty of the Spanish Crown. Such an endeavor was built not only in order to keep local sovereigns at bay but to meet the challenges of mining the mountain of silver at Potosí, which in turn required an expansive regime of "enfranchised" forced labor service (*mita*), integrated regional markets, and armed commercial transport routes (Johnson and Socolow 2002). The demographic collapse of Indigenous populations led ineluctably to greater investments in agriculture and manufactures on behalf of colonists themselves, leading to a variable pattern of labor exploitation—from African slaves to seasonal wage labor. Yet, in the process, "absolute" royal sovereignty was inevitably beset by the "contradictions between imperial reason and private powers" (Serulnikov 2003, 42), particularly with respect to the development of "customary sovereignty" among local colonial authorities (Adelman 2009, 52) and the propensity for independence and self-government at the peripheries and frontiers of empire (Lubbock 2020b, 250–51; Bushnell 2002, 23). Thus, while the question of, and struggle over, rights and territory raged on at the close of the eighteenth century, this question would eventually be settled in favor of independence at the beginning of the nineteenth, even if the terrain of "national" sovereignty in Latin America remained implacably fractured until the end of the nineteenth century (Barton 1997, 49).

The colonization of North America, on the other hand, took a markedly different course. Unlike the Hapsburgs, the British Crown did not require the formation of a transcontinental bureaucracy. Royal authority extended outward via the actions of "free" subjects seeking new lands, even if they were formally beholden to the crown as the purveyor of rights (Muller 2017). Facing neither an Indigenous empire nor an expansive mining prospect, English settler-colonialism in North America pivoted on a more circumscribed, yet more revolutionary, notion of rights and territory. The English colonial episteme of private property was effortlessly self-referential, one that justified conflict and dispossession not through a presence but an absence (Epstein 2021). For the English philosopher John Locke, if a person mixes their labor with the land and "improves" it, their agency is validated and the land becomes theirs by natural right; if their labor fails to improve the land, they forfeit their right to possession as well as personhood. Despite occupying the land and producing through it, the "Indians" did not exercise true dominium, in light of the "wild woods and uncultivated waste of America" (Locke 2003 [1689], 116). "The kings of the Indians in America," Locke wrote in his *Two Treatises of Government*, "are little more than generals of their armies... though they command absolutely in war... at home and in time of peace they exercise very little dominion, and have but a very moderate sovereignty" (147). Indigenous modes of political organization—communal ownership of land and consensual sovereignty (McNeil 2013; Townsend 2019, 106)—disqualified their claim to property and personhood, precisely because they lacked the Lockean index of the *individual body* as the essential referent to rights and territory (Chaplin 2001; Epstein 2021). The "colonial lives" of private property, as Brenna Bhandar puts it (2018), were thus rooted in a mode of violence against those in possession of customary lands and communal organization. As a consequence of this "eliminatory" mode of colonial conquest, new sources of labor had to be brought in, firstly through indentured European laborers and latterly through the rapid expansion of African slaves during the eighteenth century, feeding the labor demand for tobacco and rice plantations (Bergad 2007, 24).

The figure of the industrious individual stood in opposition to all collective and corporative arrangements—from the absolutist state to aboriginal peoples—in its unending war against "waste" (Neocleous 2011). Locke's theory of individualism would go on to furnish the settler colonial West (particularly in North America) with the ideological resources shaping the course of territorial expansion and land settlement among property-owning farmers. In relative contrast to the Spanish and Portuguese conquests, in North America both family farmer and plantation owner worked through "political institutions that gave extraordinary decision-making powers to local populations through town councils and representative assemblies, chosen through elections in which only males were permitted a vote" (Bergad 2007, 23). Thus, while radically overdetermined by racial and gendered hierarchies, North America developed a political technology in which "state or national sovereignty would be exercised in conjunction (and sometimes in tension) with the 'self government' of individuals and households occupying their own land" (Clark 2020, 179; cf. Grandin 2019).

While the colonial projects across North and South American contain several distinctive characteristics, particularly the predominant activities of production (mining/export-agriculture) and the relative contrast between Indigenous labor regimes (franchised/eliminatory), they were both rooted in a shared epistemic grammar in which racial or ethnic difference became the foundation upon which the entire bundle of rights, territory, and sovereignty would hinge (Smallwood 2019). From the frontier "homesteader" to the owner of the slave plantation, property and sovereignty became radically fused within "settler sovereign landscapes," as territory became steadily marked by precise geometric division between commodity owners (Palmer 2020).

The dissolution of parcellized sovereignty under feudalism thus gave way to a protracted transition toward a new combination of rights and territory that was both more centralized yet ultimately fragmented. If these colonial projects had anything in common, it was the shared belief that other peoples had no right to the lands they occupied and no system of governance worthy of recognition. In place of an established, recognized order over which to rule, European colonizers viewed these lands as terra nullius, which required new methods for claiming legitimate rights to rule, namely, "linearly defined territoriality, expressed abstractly in maps... cartographic language... [and] abstract mathematical and geometric methods for understanding and claiming space" (Branch 2010, 285). "Modern" territory, in other words, was born in the colonies, only to be reimported to Europe thereafter.

But it was the radical transformation of rights, territory, and sovereignty grounded in the figure of the "possessive individual" that proved decisive both for the North American colonies and for capitalism as a mode of production (Macpherson 1962). As Greg Grandin writes, the prevailing wisdom in the early United States led to "restraint when it comes to property rights, lack of restraint when it comes to territory" (2019, 42). The expanding frontier, and the violence it entailed, nurtured individual liberty as well as frontier sovereignty. Yet as the age of colonialism and commerce morphed into the era of industrialism and corporations, the fragmentation of colonial sovereignty began to fade from view. In both the "Old" and "New" worlds, a *formal* separation between economic and political power, among enterprising individuals and the sovereign state, began to emerge. Under this arrangement, rights were bestowed by the state and enjoyed by free individuals within civil society commanding nothing but the commodities in their possession. Territory itself became increasingly shaped by geometry, calculation, cartography, and surveillance. Yet this novel social form also became cloaked in a shroud of abstraction. If precapitalist societies maintained a sovereign clarity, capitalism obscured the very nature of sovereign power.

Violent Abstractions: Property-Power and Knowledge-Power

How can something abstract—a theoretical postulate, a sign, or a property title—entail a form of violence? In and of themselves, they cannot. As Henri Lefebvre warned, however, it would be a categorical mistake to view these entities as forms in themselves. "Nothing could be more false" than to take abstraction "for an 'absence'—as distinct from the concrete 'presence' of objects" (Lefebvre 1991, 289). Rather, "*there is a violence intrinsic to abstraction . . . by virtue of the forced introduction of abstraction onto nature*" (emphasis in original). For Lefebvre, the precapitalist world was organized around "absolute space," centered on the sacred, natural, and site-specific, which cements "the bonds of consanguinity, soil and language" (48). Capitalism, in contrast, engenders an *abstract space*, in which the relentless drive toward commodification, homogeneity, and alienation represents the "devastating conquest of the lived by the conceived" (Lefebvre [1980] 2006, 10).

This is why, as Aida Hozić puts it, "The history of modern capitalism could be easily summed up in just two words: *violent charade*" (2021, 174, emphasis in original). Classical political economy substituted an historical account of capitalism's emergence for a biblical allegory—a tale of "original sin," with the "frugal élite" rising up on the back of their ingenuity against the "lazy rascals" content to wallow in their profligacy (Marx 1982, 873; cf. Perelman 2000). Yet this biblical charade merely eclipsed the violent dispossession of "lazy rascals" from their customary lands and means of life. Once accomplished, the regime of private property transformed the basis of rights to the individual owner of whatever commodities they possessed and enjoying the freedom to dispose of their possessions as they see fit. One person may own a factory, a farm, machines, and fertilizer, the other nothing but their own body and capacity to work (labor-power). But in the eyes of the law, they are equally possessors of commodities and enjoy the same freedom of exchange and rights to economic liberty.

It was this idyllic, abstract image of market exchange and political equality that Marx laid bare as an illusory freedom: "The sphere of circulation or commodity exchange, within whose legal boundaries the sale and purchase of labour-power goes on, is in fact a very Eden of the innate rights of man. It is the exclusive realm of Freedom, Equality, Property and Bentham" (Marx 1982, 280). What, then, happens to the moment of exploitation as the historical register of political power? To answer this question, Marx leads us into "the hidden abode of production," behind whose walls the world of Bentham and "innate rights" ceases to exist and the sovereign power of capital emerges from the shadows.

In a rare insight from the liberal tradition, the American philosopher and legal scholar Morris R. Cohen once identified the principle of *exclusion* as the wellspring of capital's sovereign power: "To the extent that these things [certain objects] are necessary to the life of my neighbor, the law thus confers on me a power, limited but real, to make him do what I want" (1927, 12). Yet, as Cohen observed, the exclusionary power of property had been largely effaced from bourgeois law:

> The character of property as sovereign power compelling service and obedience may be obscured for us in a commercial economy by the fiction of the so-called labor contract as a free bargain and by the frequency with which service is rendered indirectly through a money payment. But not only is there actually little freedom to bargain on the part of the steel worker or miner who needs a job, but in some cases the medieval subject had as much power to bargain when he accepted the sovereignty of his lord. (Cohen 1927, 12–13)

On the one hand, Cohen's keen insight merely articulated what Marx had already apprehended fifty years earlier. While the juridical form prescribes the equal exchange between commodity owners—the capitalist as owner of the means of production, and the worker as the owner of their corporeal capacity to work—it is only after this exchange has taken place, within the production process itself, that capital exerts its power to extract as much surplus-value from the worker as possible (Marx 1982, 730).[2] On the other hand, Marx did not fully recognize, as did Cohen, that the conditions of capitalist exploitation rested on the re-incarnation of the relationship of sovereignty and dependence, even while the "new potentates" of industry (875) carried on in their violent charade of frugality, ingenuity, and civility.[3]

Following Jacques Bidet (2016), the right to exploit labor under capitalism emerges as "property-power," as one half of the edifice of capitalist sovereignty. While property-power is presupposed by "the market," this abstract (market) structure is also "instrumentalized" by a dominant social group, transforming the juridical basis of economic exchange into a series of relations "which are by no means juridical, such as, for instance, those designed to intensify work" (33). The very nature of property-power thus appears to straddle the legal and extralegal domains, in which "the hiving off of 'surplus value' [exploitation] is both formally consistent with law [wage-contract] and at the same time a reversal of law into an 'asymmetrical' disposition" (29). In this way, the sovereign power of capital reveals itself through a surplus of action beyond the juridical form, as a de facto (extralegal) power.

The second half of capital's sovereign power is, like all other historical forms of sovereignty, grounded in a specific mode of territorialization, or a series of "ideas, practices and technologies" that mark out "a particular field of political interaction" (Branch 2017, 133). While the modern concept of territory is most often associated with the nation-state and defined by the limits of a state's borders, the political technology of capitalism engendered a much wider transformation of spatial ordering, forms of knowledge, and means of organization. This was, as Alfred Crosby (1997) argued, a shift in mentalité that embraced an entirely new measure of reality reducible to discreet, abstract quanta. Such a shift in subjectivity was itself a reflection of the objective conditions of a society in transition. With the (violent) expansion of private property rights and commodification came a new territorial logic premised in equal parts on homogeneity and calculation.

It is precisely at the intersection of property-power and knowledge-power that the violent charade of capital becomes most apparent. Thus, while property-power emerges from the right to own, the *corresponding right to exclude* furnishes capital with sovereign control over human bodies in its drive to maximize surplus-value (Marx 1981, 477; Poulantzas 1975, 180). Industrial capital emerged through the gathering together, organization, and surveillance of workers as a "single productive body," over which the power of capital appears as "purely despotic" (Marx 1982, 449, 450). Beyond the mere arrangement of materials used in production, the organization of collective labor had to consider "the activity of the men [sic], their skill, the way they set about their tasks, their promptness, their zeal, their behaviour" (Foucault 1977, 174). Thus, the "rational," scientific organization of production became inseparable from the disciplinary powers of surveillance and punishment. By the turn of the twentieth century, the despotism of capital had become barely distinguishable from traditional forms of political authority. As Mike Davis notes:

> In 1933 the typical American factory was a miniature feudal state where streamlined technologies were combined with a naked brutality that was the envy of fascist labor ministries. In Ford's immense citadels at Dearborn and River Rouge, for example, security chief Harry Bennett's "servicemen" openly terrorized and beat assembly workers for such transgressions of plant rules as talking to one another on the line. (Davis 1999, 55–56; see also Noble 2011, 23)

The "terror" inflicted by capital over labor should be read alongside the etymology of the word itself, which shares a common root with "territory," pertaining to "land," but also to "frighten" and "deter" (Neocleous 2003, 102). Yet the terror of capital (and the territorialization of labor) was never passively accepted by workers. Rather, class conflict was built into the relations of exploitation from the start, with strikes, occupations or sit-ins representing the periodic burst of this struggle into plain sight (Harvey 2006, 32).

If peoples' resistance against corporeal discipline presented a certain challenge to industrial capital, it was "nature itself" that was seen "as an obstacle" to capital on the land (Fitzgerald 2003, 104; cf. Mann 1990). In taking inspiration from Henry Ford's conquering of human bodies, agrarian capital (particularly in the United States) sought to bring the techniques of "rational" industrial management onto the land, and to "make every farm a factory" (Fitzgerald 2003, 5). However, as we will see in chapter 2, the incessant conquest of the lived by the conceived merely undermined "the original sources of all wealth—the soil and the worker" (Marx 1982, 638).

While the naked despotism of early industrial capital may appear to be a thing of the past, the congealed violence of exploitation is far more visible than is often thought (see Anderson 2017). Within the world's largest company, Amazon, its warehouse workers are facing the same pressures as those who once worked at Ford's factories. As one community member commented on one of Amazon's UK-based warehouses in Rugerley, "The feedback we're getting [from workers] is it's like being in a slave camp" (cited in O'Connor 2013). On the other end of the global commodity chain, particularly the apparel industry, the prevalence of "sweatshop labor" represents a segment of workers who are (often) paid below their value (i.e., not even enough to cover subsistence costs), a form of superexploitation facilitated through highly coercive and punitive workplace practices (Ross 2004; Kumar 2020). More broadly, in the neoliberal era increased rates of migration to countries in the Global North have given more leverage to capital over a highly vulnerable sector of workers, whether in the form of foreign worker programs to outright slavery or debt bondage (Gordon 2018; cf. Mezzadri 2017; Rioux, LeBaron, and Verovsek 2019).

In stitching these historical and conceptual threads together, we begin to see how the "economic" moment of capitalist production becomes shot through with the "political" moment of power and domination (cf. Wood 1981). In this sense, capitalist property does not simply sit *in* a territory; rather, property *is a territory*, by virtue of how it is governed politically (Blomley 2015). As a complement to property-power, capitalist territory is expressed as "knowledge-power," through which the organization of production is mediated by "the privileges of... 'competency', in the twofold sense of a *supposed knowledge that is doubled with a conferred authority*" (Bidet 2016, 68, emphasis in original; see also Poulantzas 2014, 55). This privilege of competency marks the relative separation between "manual and intellectual labor," in which "competent elites" (whether in the factory or state bureaucracy), monopolize the intellectual labor bound up with organization (Bidet 2016, 70; cf. Poulantzas 1974, 180). As Poulantzas warned, this does not mean that there is an "empirical or natural split between those who work with their hands and those who work with their head" (Poulantzas 2014, 55); rather, workers possess relative amounts of knowledge concerning their specific roles and, through the course of social production, become ever-more conscious of their fellow workers and their combined labor. But their position within the relations of production constantly works against their attempts to take hold of this knowledge and put it into use for their own ends.

If my critical analysis thus far has helped to reveal the hidden abode of capitalist sovereignty, what, then, of the traditional "container" of sovereign power? While the nation-state would appear to be an entirely different genus to the creature of capital, they both share a common root in the edifice of sovereignty. As with the historical constitution of capital, the state consecrates its territorial "enclosures implicit in the constitution of the modern people-nation" (Poulantzas 2014, 114). Like the regime of private property, the "property-power" of the capitalist state is premised on its rightful ownership territory, and to exclude others from it, expressing its "existential sovereignty" based on the principle of noninterference (Simpson 2004, 29; cf. Burch 1998, 143–44). And as with the factory's hidden abode, the interior of modern state space is ordered along a range of techniques and disciplines that emerge from the monopolization of "intellectual labor" geared toward "the controlled insertion of bodies into the machinery of production" (Foucault 1978, 141; cf. Poulantzas 2014; Foucault 1977, 223). The hegemony of "centrist liberalism" during the nineteenth century had consolidated a series of qualifications—based on class, gender, and race/ethnicity—that radically curtailed the *formal* equality of all citizens (Wallerstein 2011, 146; see also Glenn 2002; Epstein 2021). Just as each capital transects the realms of *juridical equality* and *political discipline*—i.e., from *commodity exchange* to the *production of surplus value*—so too does the state embody the figure of neutral arbiter that simultaneously marks out, classifies, controls, and excludes, which encompasses the production of "political surplus-value" (Teschke 2011, 73), a surplus of action beyond the legal domain and toward the domain of "disciplines" that extend outward into the extralegal realm (Poulantzas 2014, 84–85; cf. Foucault 1977, 222).

Like the ordering of factory production, the political technology of the capitalist state engenders an *abstraction of social space* and the production of a territorial "grid," "one that includes not only the factory but also the modern family, the school, the army, the prison system, the city and the national territory" (Poulantzas 2014, 105; cf. Foucault, 1982). In parallel to the organization of production, the organization of the nation-state was, is in the last instance, "exercised in the name of the *norm*, which is irreducible to the truth of science" (Bidet 2016, 79, emphasis added). And yet, the norms that underpin such techniques, and their territorial articulations, could not be legitimated indefinitely. The new matrix of abstract, juridically constituted rights, imbued with a distinctive class content, brought forth their own challenge from the popular classes. Thus, the rise and consolidation of parliamentary sovereignty, later referred to as "representative democracy," was the result of a series of class struggles around the questions of rights and territory, primarily led by worker struggles but also significantly by the early women's movement (see Przeworski 1985; Eley 2002).

How, then, does the dispersed network of sovereign power across individual spaces of capitalist exploitation, as well as concentrated sovereignty within the nation-state, resolve into a common framework? Or to put it differently, how can we square the circle of the sovereign state and sovereign capitalist? A potential solution to this problem can be found in Poulantzas's relational theory of the capitalist state. As opposed to traditional approaches that see the state as simply a discrete object, or an autonomous subject, for Poulantzas the capitalist state is a "material condensation" of class forces, spread throughout the fabric of society—from bureaucratic loci to the extended field of the relations of production (Poulantzas 2014, 73; cf. Bidet 2016, 142). The idea of the state as "material condensation" refers to two interrelated dimensions. Firstly, the "materiality" of the state is underwritten by the relations of production, expressed by the state's "presence" in the constitution of these relations (Poulantzas 2014, 39). This presence can be detected through the shared monopolization of knowledge-power, or the separation between manual/intellectual labor, among both capital and the state. However, as Poulantzas warns, the relationship between the state and the relations of production are not simply reducible to this division per se. Rather, the state enters into, and reproduces, these social relations through a variety of apparatuses that qualify and train labor-power—the school, family, occupational training, as well as through political parties, cultural apparatuses and the media (60). The materiality of the capitalist state therefore leads toward the predisposition, the "selectivity," of policymaking, which *by and large* tends to reproduce the political power of capital (Gallas 2017, 266).[4]

Secondly, the notion of "condensation" expresses the state's organization of class relations throughout society. While the capitalist state primarily organizes the dominant classes into a relatively coherent "power bloc," dominated classes are also "present" within the state, albeit through different mechanisms and "distances" from the core of the state apparatus. The notion of "distance" points toward the *relational* nature of the state, and the ways in which the state extends outward from its administrative centers right through to the relations of production across society. As I argued earlier, the principal mechanism that maintains this distance between the state's decision-making centers and the popular classes is the monopolization of knowledge-power within the state apparatus, expressed through the division between manual and intellectual labor (Poulantzas 2014, 56; cf. Bidet 2016, 68).

From this reading, the state itself becomes a "*strategic field and process* of intersecting power networks," rather than simply a walled citadel separated from "civil society" (Poulantzas 2014, 18–19, emphasis in original). The upshot is that class struggle traverses the entire "strategic terrain" of the state (74), albeit at differential "distances" from its institutional embodiment; that is, struggles for electoral power in parliament are more "proximate" than class struggles within a factory or field (cf. Demirović 2019). Yet every social struggle necessarily implicates the power and legitimacy of the state, insofar as they are ultimately *political struggles*, whether around the point of production or through the ballot box (see Wood 1981, 92; Wood 1995, 20). It is, in the end, the balance of class forces that shape the orientation of the state and its policies (Poulantzas 2014, 53).

Beyond Capital and the State: Multiple Sovereignties of Democratic Socialism

My historicization of sovereignty thus far has attempted to clear the way for a better understanding of the strategic pathways necessary for the construction of a food sovereignty regime. If, as Edelman (2014, 959) contends, "food sovereignty theory has usually failed to indicate whether the 'sovereign' is the nation, region or locality, or 'the people,'" the above analysis suggests that modern sovereignty transects all of these sites and scales, though in a very particular way. While capital maintains sovereign power over a multitude of locales *within spaces of exploitation/discipline*, it is the capitalist state that renders the "nation" legible, as an abstract space of belonging among "the people" who nevertheless remain ensnared by a complex grid of hierarchization, surveillance, and control.

In struggling in and through the interstices of the state-capital nexus, food sovereignty movements have also traversed the moments of rights and territory in order to construct their own claims to sovereignty. During its initial engagement with international fora—particularly the various food-related organs of the United Nations—LVC placed particular emphasis on the rights of national self-determination against the power of states and firms in the Global North. This initial engagement with the "sovereignty" discourse thus formed a type of "strategic essentialism" in which the rights of nations became a means of reclaiming certain rights (e.g., land) in the short term, while providing space for reconfiguring the nation of sovereignty more substantially in the long term (McMichael 2014).

Within this context, LVC slowly transformed its discursive frame from the rights of nations to the rights of "peoples" to produce and manage food systems (LVC et al. 2001). LVC thus revalorized the protagonistic role of rural peoples "to make decisions about their material, natural and spiritual heritage" (LVC et al. 2007). The road to food sovereignty was now conceived as a more complex process in which "all peoples, nations and states are able to determine their own food producing systems."

However, by introducing the role of peoples *alongside* that of nation-states, an immanent tension emerged over the question of who carries the (sovereign) right to decide. On the one hand, LVC's values point toward the autonomous organization and control of food systems by those directly involved in socioeconomic production and distribution (LVC et al 2007; cf. Claeys 2012). On the other hand, these self-declared (de facto) rights to own and manage the land and means of production do not necessarily provide agrarian actors with the requisite power to maintain them indefinitely. In other words, place-specific (de facto) rights may not gain formal (de jure) validation or recognition (Fox 2007, 221). Peasant struggles thus navigate the unstable boundary between de facto and de jure rights, often engaging in land occupations and other forms of legal transgressions in order to make their voices heard and see their rights formally recognized (Brabazon 2017; cf. Patel 2009, 670). In negotiating the space between formal and informal rights, peasant movements offer a powerful example of Poulantzas's notion of the "democratic road to socialism," a political project based on the autonomous construction of popular spaces of inclusion that challenges/conjoins onto the formal institutions of the liberal democratic state, as we will see further. These insights are central to the foregoing arguments throughout this book, in light of the formal and informal political procedures that radically permeate the ALBA, the Venezuelan state, and the dynamics of agrarian change within them.

As well as carving out new forms of sociopolitical rights through autonomous struggle, agrarian actors within FS movements construct different territorial practices embedded within popular political technologies (see Halvorsen 2018; Clare, Habermehl, and Mason-Deese 2017). As part of their struggle against the commodification of land (Alonso-Fradejas et al. 2015), FS protagonists seek to overturn the predominant Anglo-Saxon worldview that "treats land as the passive object of human activity and ignores all forms of value that are not easily priced on the market" (Kolers 2009, 64). In 2006, during the (FAO)-sponsored "International Conference on Agrarian Reform and Rural Development," a parallel paper was drawn up by various civil society groups that set out a new vision of territory that recenters life and communal identity (see LVC et al. 2006). In this way, LVC conceives of territory as a bundle of spatial signifiers that engenders alternative ways of knowing that fuse the idea of land rights with territorially specific values (Grajales 2010).

However, given that notions of territory are place- and culturally specific, the practices of territoriality and identity formation are equally diverse across LVC's members. One example of this diversity emerged from the First Continental Encounter of Agroecology Trainers of LVC in the Americas, organized in 2009 on the campus of the Instituto Universitario Latinoamericano de Agroecología-Paulo Freire (IALA) in Venezuela. This "dialogue of knowledges"—(*diálogo de saberes*), as it is more commonly known among Latin American LVC protagonists—facilitated a debate among the participants over issues of identity and within the broader struggle for food sovereignty across the region. As Martínez-Torres and Rosset (2014) note, this debate principally revolved around three relatively general categorizations of peasant life and the differences between them: "peasants," "Indigenous," and "rural proletarians." As shown in table 1, each identity roughly corresponds to a different set of relations held between individuals or groups to their unit of territorial organization, whether a community, family unit, or collective. While this categorization is by no means static, it highlights the difference ideas, strategies, and interests make in the production of territory.

Despite the diversity of territorial practices within FS politics, the relative transformation of the Latin American state in the twenty-first century has provided a new space of participation for agrarian actors. In contrast to modern state territoriality, which is produced "horizontally . . . as a two-dimensional bounded space or mosaic of 'like' spaces, such as those constituting the international system of states or patterns of local real-estate holdings" (Delaney 2005, 31; cf. Burch 1998), Latin America's "postliberal" state crystallizes around a regime of "vertical territoriality" (Delaney 2005, 32–33; cf. Arditi 2008), as a

TABLE 1. Peasant, Indigenous, and proletarian organizations and agroecology

Identity Frame	Unit of Organization	Transmission of Knowledge	Emblematic Struggles	Sources of Affinity with Agroecology
Indigenous	Community	Coded in Cultural Traditions	Defense of Territory and Construction of Autonomy	Indigenous Cosmovision and care for the Mother Earth
Peasant	Family	Experiential, Farmer-to-Farmer	Access to land, prices, subsidies, and credit	Low production costs, self-provisioning combined with marketing
Proletarian	Collective	Classrooms and Technical Assistance	Land occupations, strikes, transformation of the economic model	Socialist ideology, dispute with Capital

SOURCE: Martinez-Torres and Rosset (2014, 11)

multiplicity of territorial scales constitutive of a national territory. While "verticality" is not unknown to Western states, the postliberal turn places much greater emphasis on the decentralization of powers toward more local levels of governance and participation. The political technology of Latin America's left turn thus brings to the foreground different sets of values, discourses, and practices that "secure individual rights but also accommodate more diverse identities, units of representation, and state structure" (Yashar 1999, 88). As we will see further in chapter 4, this transition in the political technology of the Latin American state represented a significant opportunity for FS movements to embed their rights claims and territorial practices into a broader institutional context.

In light of the preceding analysis of sovereignty under capitalism, and the forms of rights and territory constitutive of FS politics, the immediate question remains: *what might sovereignty look like under food sovereignty?* As a possible answer to this question, Philip McMichael once captured the basic social content of FS politics and its specific articulation of sovereignty, in which peasant movements assert "the right to alternative forms of democratic organization and the securing of material well-being through multiple sovereignties based in cultural, environmental, and economic sustainability" (2009, 39). Indeed, these alternative forms of organization contain "*substantive* conceptions of rights, economies and ecological relations" that transgress the liberal conception of rights with "a politics of (collective rights)" (33). These collective property rights ultimately point toward the decommodification of land, democratization and socialization of production relations, ecological resilience (agroecology), and the establishment of protagonistic governance practices (see Tilzey 2018).

The transformed nature of rights under food sovereignty therefore represents a concerted effort to break the biopolitical dependence on capital and the state through the (re)assertion of the "sovereignty of labour" (Mészáros 1995, 711–12). However, it is not simply the taking back of the labor process that will guarantee "sovereignty" for food sovereignty protagonists. Even the analogous concept of "land sovereignty," understood as "the right of working peoples to have effective access to, use of, and control over land and the benefits of its use and occupation" (Borras, Franco, and Suárez 2015, 6), may not go far enough either. The famed "small farmer" at the center of food sovereignty discourse is often at the mercy of wider market forces, whether commodity or credit markets, over which they have little control and thus potentially face a more diffuse (territorial) structure of domination. Even if small producers are not necessarily dependent on commodity exchange and market competition (i.e., engaged in "self-sufficient" farming) and thus in control of their land and labor, they may well remain isolated among the wider sea of capitalist-state "rationality" and territoriality. In other words, peasant producers (in alliance with other subaltern actors) require a much wider set of organizational forms that reterritorialize a given community, city, or nation in line with popular political technologies that challenge the division between manual/intellectual labor and nurtures the democratization of society's "general intellect" (Marx 1973, 706). All of this, I argue, is the real social content implicit within McMichael's notion of "multiple sovereignties," in which the multiplication of sovereign powers adequate to a food sovereignty regime converges toward spaces of *democratically self-directed labor and cooperative territorial governance*. Or as Bidet puts it, multiple sovereignties "aim at the control of the market through organisation... and control of organisation through immediate discourse, equally shared by all" (2016, 250).[5]

As I noted previously, the diverse struggles among FS movements, particularly those in Latin America, share a striking resonance with Poulantzas's writing on the "democratic road to socialism." Poulantzas recognized that merely engaging with liberal democratic institutions (i.e., elections, civic freedoms) was not enough to fundamentally transform the capitalist state; likewise, the Leninist strategy of building a "dual state" through the formation of self-governing workers' councils that eventually conquers the state from the outside poses the risk that, in place of representative democratic institutions, a bureaucratic dictatorship fills the political vacuum (Poulantzas, 2014, 251). Both of these strategic errors were, Poulantzas contends, the result of a misreading of the capitalist state. While liberalism views the state as a neutral arbiter, standing above society's competing claims, Lenin saw the bourgeois state as merely an instrument to be wielded by the bourgeoisie. Yet neither of these conceptions acknowledges the complexity and contradictory content of the capitalist state.

Poulantzas argued that the struggle for socialism would have to traverse a *democratic road*, in which popular struggles would alter the representative institutions within the state, but without undermining those institutions' role in elaborating national-popular hegemony. On this latter point, Jessop suggests that "given the difficulties of coordinating dispersed and fragmented democratic organs at the base without relating them organically to representative democracy, they may become strong enough to short-circuit the initiatives of a left government without ever acquiring the strength and cohesion to rule alone" (Jessop 1985, 300).

As we will see further in chapter 4, the left turn in Latin America, particularly among ALBA's three largest members (Bolivia, Ecuador, and Venezuela), offers a striking example of this compromise between decentralized spaces of participatory democracy that work with, rather than against, liberal/representative democratic institutions (see Lalander 2011). These postliberal political technologies strongly converge with McMichael's notion of multiple sovereignties, with the concrete practices of FS protagonists seeking to construct spaces of cooperation among "communities, peoples, states and international bodies" (LVC et al. 2007). The multiplication of sovereignties within FS politics is more than just the horizontal scaling of "autonomous" spaces of production. Rather, multiple sovereignties also scale vertically, through "nested hierarchal arrangements" (Harvey 2012, 69), with each scale shaped by their specific material and organizational qualities and the level of experience/competency contained within those domains (see Duncan 1996, 41–42; Sassen 2006, 422; Quastel 2016). In the context of food sovereignty, the vitality of community decision making is directly linked to the site-specific nature of agricultural production that cannot take place at a high level of abstract problem solving (unlike, for example, macrolevel fiscal policymaking). The vision of multiple sovereignties within FS politics thus ineluctably grounds itself within the multiplication of property-power/knowledge-power, establishing democratic control and decision making among producers, distributors, and consumers that is functionally linked to higher scalar levels of organization.

Strategic Selectivity and the Politics of Scale in the ALBA

Getting to grips with how FS protagonists engage with regional institutions like the ALBA requires a broader macrosociological perspective that links the microfoundations of agency and class struggle with the wider institutional contexts in which they unfold. Critical political geography has greatly contributed to our understanding of the politics of scale in the context of capital's continual search for "spatial fixes" (Harvey 2006) that seeks to overcome labor resistance and accumulation crises (Silver 2003; Gough 2004; Macartney and Shields 2011). Yet much of this work tends to overemphasize the *global scale* as the ultimate expression of capitalist power and working-class resistance (e.g., Swyngedouw 1997; Robinson 2004). As Gibson-Graham suggest (2002), "the market" (and indeed "capital") is not simply an abstract global entity that inevitably bends others to its will. Rather, global political economy contains a multitude of market transactions, local economies, and political institutions that defy the predominant logic of commodity production at a variety of scales. This therefore prompts a different methodological register that places agency and contestation at the heart of potentially abstract notions like the market and capital in order to shed light on the always incomplete and contingent nature of power and authority (cf. Knafo 2017; Hesketh 2016).

In this vein, Bob Jessop's "strategic-relational" approach offers a conceptual bridge between the iron law of capital accumulation on the one hand and a purely empiricist examination of class struggles on the other (1985, 343–44). In extending Poulantzas's relational theory of the state, Jessop distinguishes between *accumulation strategies*, *modes of regulation*, and *hegemonic projects*. The first refers to specific growth strategies under the hegemony of a particular fraction of capital (productive, commercial, financial), laying the material basis of political life. The second indicates how and on what basis the production and circulation of material wealth takes place via institutionalized rules and codes demarcating the distributional channels among various classes and class fractions. Finally, hegemonic projects denote a complex articulation of discourses and practices that unite various classes—both dominant and dominated—that seeks to reproduce the foundation of capitalist class rule and thus the relations of production as a whole (Jessop 1991; Jessop 2002).

As a result of this chaotic social process, state institutions produce not simply coherent policy but a contested and microfoundational iteration of "strategic selectivity" in policymaking, which ultimately "involves examining how a given structure may privilege some actors, some identities, some strategies, some spatial and temporal horizons, [and] some actions over others" (Jessop 1999, 51). As noted earlier, the combination of accumulation crises and class struggles involve not merely "social fixes" but also spatiotemporal fixes that establish spatial and temporal boundaries adequate to a given conjuncture (Ngai-Ling and Jessop 2006, 317). Strategic selectivity is thus always accompanied by a *spatial selectivity*, wherein subnational regions, urban centers, or even higher scalar levels of governance assume greater centrality to a given pattern of accumulation and its corresponding bloc of hierarchically organized capitalist fractions (Jones 1997).

The rise of international regional spaces and institutions can be similarly read through the lens of strategic and spatial selectivity. The constant revolutionizing of the productive forces and continually expanded scales of production engenders enormous concentrations of physical infrastructure that manifest in regional or continental-sized agglomerations. As Arrighi (2006) has shown, each major crisis afflicting the capitalist world economy tends toward not merely the geographical shift in the organization of production but also a parallel shift toward cumulatively larger political territories in which new rounds of accumulation take place. As we will see in chapter 2, the rise of the continent-sized US regime at the turn of the century added an extra degree of pressure on other parts of the world to adapt to new regional-scales of accumulation (cf. Harvey 2006, 444).

Read in this way, every international regional institution contains its own mix of strategic and spatial selectivity—the EU as a "multilevel region," the North America Free Trade Agreement (NAFTA) and Japan's "flying geese" regime as a "hub and spoke model," and today's Asia-Pacific as a market-led system of regional cooperation (Larner and Walters 2002, 393). Seen through a neo-Poulantzian lens, regional formations thus may be understood as *second-order condensations* of social relations of power, representing both a denationalization of state power and the *reproduction* (not "dilution") of state power via differentially constituted scales, spaces, and classes (Brand, Görg, and Wisson 2011; Jessop 2002; Demirović 2011).

Bringing this framework to the case of the ALBA, the strategic and spatial selectivity of this regional institution primarily emerges from the legacy of past social and geopolitical struggles characterizing Latin America's resistance to neoliberal discipline (Angosto-Ferrández 2014). Consequently, ALBA's counterhegemonic project emphasizes discursive and material practices that are adequate to resisting such discipline, such as the nurturing of popular forms of socioeconomic participation, the expansion of social welfare policies, and the strengthening of regional cooperation and complementarity. However, these practices are shaped by a number of contradictions. As we will see in chapter 3, the material basis of ALBA's existence radically overdetermines the limits of regional food sovereignty. From the institution's inception, the mobilization of Venezuela's oil wealth became the decisive driver in the first two ALBA initiatives (created even before ALBA's inauguration in 2004 but forged in its spirit of intent): the Caribbean Energy Cooperation Agreement providing low-cost, low-interest oil to Caribbean states, and latterly the Comprehensive Cooperation Agreement between Venezuela and Cuba. The subsequent rise in oil prices, and thus resources rents, would go onto underwrite the creation of ALBA's socioeconomic policies, particularly within the realm of food production. As such, the socioecological foundation of food sovereignty in ALBA comes not primarily from the soil but what lies beneath. Yet this does not simply mean that oil wealth undermines food sovereignty per se; indeed, the material resources needed to support peasant production and agrarian infrastructure placed Venezuela (and ALBA more generally) in an advantageous position. Rather, the institutional complex of the Bolivarian state itself imprinted a specific mode of policymaking on the regional scale that was ad hoc and relatively disorganized. As we will see in chapter 3, the specific character of the Venezuelan state has always been crucially shaped by the flow of oil and the power it bestows. As Fernando Coronil famously put it, Venezuela's oil wealth produced a "magical state," in which "state representatives, the visible embodiments of the invisible powers of oil money, appear on the state's stage as powerful magicians who pull social reality, from public institutions to cosmologies, out of a hat" (1997, 2). Thus, the centrality of the Bolivarian state has arguably created a *magical region*, a term that is perhaps most appropriate in relation to the politics of food sovereignty in the ALBA.

Thus, ALBA's mode of regulation conforms to a kind of interpresidentialism, with numerous summits, agreements, and initiatives seemingly pulled out of a hat but with very few actually brought to life. Of course, the input into, and implementation of, ALBA's policies do not simply come from presidents. Numerous working groups, interministerial commissions, and civil society actors all come together to form principles and practices of regional development policy. Yet the institutional materiality of the ALBA, comprising as it does a contradictory constellation of class forces, has kept the popular classes at a relative distance from the organs of decision making at the regional level. By and large, the nested hierarchies connecting local agrarian communities to the summits of regional politics become increasingly frayed as we move up the ladder of institutional scales. While the precise reasons for this will be examined in chapters 3 and 4, the end result leads to a somewhat fetishized notion of popular/food sovereignty that ultimately resolves back into the sovereignty of the bureaucratic state.

Conclusion

This chapter aimed to bring some clarity to the nature of sovereign power, both theoretically and historically. As I argued in the introduction, previous scholarship tended to assume the temporal circumscription of sovereignty, as a principal characteristic of "modernity." I further suggest that this stunted view of sovereignty has led to a series of dilemmas within the FS literature on how and on what basis rural actors may begin to assume sovereign power as their own. Thus, while my own theoretical approach to sovereignty shares a number of convergences with the contemporary FS scholarship, I aim to make more explicit the historical connections between previous modes of production and forms of sovereignty on the one hand, and the immanent social content of food sovereignty on the other.

The guiding thread of sovereign power across different times and places can be seen within the variable forms of *rights and territory*, or the right to exploit labor and the territorial organization of production. Precapitalist modes of production engendered a relative fusion of the political and the economic, insofar as the moment of exploitation tended to coincide with the locus of political power, and the relationship of sovereignty and dependence. Territorial organization of production and society was also the preserve of the dominant strata, even if manifested in a variety of ways (particularly the more diffuse practices of territorial organization under feudalism).

The advent of capitalism, however, radically altered the grammar of sovereignty. In recognizing the power of property as one grounded in the power to dispossess and exclude, the violent abstraction of "equal rights" among owners of commodities becomes radically unsettled. The power to exclude simultaneously confers upon capital the power to territorialize the production process (including human bodies) in the drive for surplus value, ranging from the most despotic use of force to the subtlest form of technical organization. The modern state, in turn, derives its power of sovereignty through its power to exclude its territory from others, as well as the techniques and disciplines employed to bring order to the body politic. Thus, modern sovereignty, shared between capital and the state, emerges through the fusion of property-power and knowledge-power, as the right to own and exclude as well as the ability and conferred authority to organize and territorialize. Poulantzas's relational theory of the capitalist state provided a broader critical framework through which to apprehend the parallel yet interrelated dimensions of capitalist/state power, and the institutional materiality of the state that organizes the basis of class domination throughout society.

From this conceptual/historicist reading of sovereignty, it becomes apparent that the politics of food sovereignty, as practiced by contemporary peasant movements, is already inscribed within the multiple sovereignties structuring capitalist territoriality—among a variety of spaces of production and political institutions. In attempting to democratize property rights and produce popular forms of territorial control, *both in and against the state*, food sovereignty protagonists converge with the broader notion of "the democratic road to socialism"—the discourse that colored many of the political projects among several ALBA states, and Venezuela in particular.

Finally, Jessop's strategic-relational approach makes more explicit what is only implicit in Poulantzas's formulations. The concept of strategic selectivity helps connect the materially grounded accumulation strategies of dominant classes with the general production of consent and compromise forged through modes of regulation and hegemonic projects. A given set of parameters for accumulation strategies, modes of regulation, and hegemonic projects thus shapes the selectivities of policymaking, themselves reflective of the contradictions inherent within capital accumulation and political domination. Practices of power are as much spatially selective as they are strategically selective. Accordingly, unpacking the dynamics that go into the making of the ALBA regional space requires a multidimensional framework that meanders through the sociorelational edifice of sovereign power, the meso level of the state's institutional materiality, and the macro level of regional formation and fragmentation. The remaining chapters of the book bring this framework to bear on the politics of food sovereignty in Venezuela and the ALBA.

CHAPTER 2

Capitalist Geopolitics and the Rise of "Continental History"

Latin America's Long Road to Regionalism

This chapter traces the interconnections between the historical development of capitalist geopolitics and the formation of world regions during the long twentieth century. Contemporary scholarship on international regional institutions tends to begin its historical narrative at the dawn of the post-World War II era and the emergence of Europe's first moves toward regional integration (e.g., Paul 2012). As well as artificially bounding the historical scope of region building, such scholarship also adopts a problematic separation between the disembodied *economic force* of "globalization" and the *political reaction* of regional orders (Postel-Vinay 2007, 564). In contrast, I aim to make more explicit the socioeconomic and ecological forces that derive from historically situated agents and their attendant strategies that both shape and are shaped by the dynamics of global capital accumulation.

As a result of the rapid expansion of the productive forces across the emergent world market, the nineteenth century was witness to the emergence of "continental history," in which the size and scope of political communities would reach truly regional proportions. The Western hemisphere was home to several such instances of continental-sized polities, which all (for a time) attempted to bring order to expansive frontiers, both political and ecological. Through a series of geographical determinants, historical contingencies, and class conflicts, the consolidation of the "continent-sized island" of the United States would go on to exert enormous geopolitical pressures across the international system, placing a heightened premium on political organization on a regional scale.

It is this historical context from which we can draw a deeper understanding of Latin America's long road to regionalism. Though initially ensnared by the dictates of Cold War geopolitics, Latin American leaders had always sought to carve out a new, modern version of Simón Bolívar's nineteenth-century dream of uniting the continent, specifically with regards to maintaining a competitive edge within the era of continental history. Patterns of uneven development across the region, in conjunction with the contradictions of import substitution industrialization, the "Green Revolution," and the overriding dominance of U.S. power, continually thwarted the many attempts at a comprehensive regionwide arrangement, resulting instead in a proliferation of regionalization schemes. The transformation in the international division of labor in the 1970s, which was crucially shaped by the politics of Cold War imperialism, significantly affected patterns of agrarian development, state forms, and sovereign regimes, engendering unique sets of rights, territorial politics, and sovereign power. Yet the neoliberal onslaught would foster a new sense of rebellion throughout the region, which in turn laid the groundwork for the rise of the new Latin American Left and their reassertion of "Our America" (Nuestra América). The so-called Pink Tide of the early twenty-first century marked the latest phase of region building. And yet, this new push for a posthegemonic regionalism was not without its own tensions and contradictions.

U.S. Hegemony and the Problem of Regional Order

The shift of global power from British to U.S. hegemony was, as with all such historical transitions, the manifestation of deeper socioecological contradictions of the capitalist state-system. The British Empire's "extensive" regime of accumulation engendered a huge expansion in the productive forces across the globe—primarily transport infrastructures—as a response to the imperial center's voracious appetite for food and raw materials (Moore 2010a, 394; Collingham 2018). In consequence, Britain's integration of peripheral spaces into the circuits of global capitalism inadvertently elevated these new areas of production within the overall world hierarchy of grain production and supply. With the consolidation of settler colonial state-spaces, European agriculture was soon displaced by a sixfold increase in imports from these areas (Friedmann 1990, 14; Mazoyer and Roudart 2006, 368–69). The ever-more intensive exploitation of the ecological base by these emergent centers of world agriculture—seen throughout the great plains of the United States, Canada, and Argentina (to name but a few)—contributed to the systemic crisis of the capitalist world economy through a commodities glut and the consequent Great Depression of the 1870s.

What truly distinguished these spaces of accumulation was their sheer size, creating new colonial state-spaces that were far larger than anything seen in Europe. However, due to a series of ecological determinants and contingent class conflicts (see Lubbock 2022), the United States would eventually go on to become a veritable "continent-sized island" (Goldstein and Rapkin 1991, 946), whose expansive industrialization was ultimately underwritten by enormous resource frontiers capable of creating forward and backward linkages with industry, thus leading to a truly diversified national economy and sizeable home market (Arrighi 2006, 300; Moore 2002). It was precisely during this historical moment, in fact, that the two sides of capitalist sovereign power were beginning to readjust, insofar as the elevation of knowledge-power became ever more decisive in the fight against market competition. The proliferation of "specialized hierarchies of top and middle managers" throughout U.S. corporations facilitated the development of vertically integrated organizational structures internalizing "the sequential sub-processes of production that linked specific primary inputs to specific final outputs" (Arrighi 2006, 302). These organizational transformations had thus reterritorialized corporate accumulation regimes that were now embedded within truly continental-sized agglomerations, providing considerable power over labor, as well as other national (and international) competitors (Moore 2002, 188; cf. Barkan 2013, 44).

In many ways, the entire World War II conflagration could be seen as a global instance of geopolitical strategy attempting to adapt to the extensity and intensity of accumulation within the U.S. continent-sized island. German and Japanese expansionism, and the regional spheres the two powers attempted to carve out (in the shape of *Großraum* and the Great East-Asian Co-Prosperity Sphere) were fundamentally premised upon solving the first great "agrarian question," in terms of adequate ecological space for the feeding of both national-imperial projects and the concomitant expansion of urban populations (Tooze 2008, chap. 6; Collingham 2015; Matsumura 2016).

Friedrich Ratzel, considered by some the father of geopolitical thought in Germany during the late nineteenth century, established a specifically agrarian outlook in his system of regional political geography. For Ratzel, a nation-state was akin to living organisms whose Lebensraum ("living space") became a specific material context of action in the form of an ecological ensemble—the relation between people and the earth. Partly inspired by Darwinian notions of the struggle for survival, Ratzel emphasized the importance of carving out ever-larger living spaces for a given people (*Volk*) (Heffernan 2003, 45). More fundamentally for Ratzel, the Lebensraum concept was inherently agrarian in nature. Partly due to his personal background (steeped in agrarian romanticism), and to the changes in tariff policies carried out by the German state in favor of industry, Ratzel urged the formation of a greater living space for the purpose of revitalising the agricultural basis of the German *Volk*. Though he was not resistant to commercial trade expansion, Ratzel believed that "only with a secure agricultural foundation and an adequate Lebensraum could permanent commercial expansion take place" (Smith 1980, 61).

The German political theorist and legal scholar Carl Schmitt would translate the notion of living space into a political program of absolute strategic necessity—from Lebensraum to *Großraum* (pan-region)—that "challenge[d] Lockean governance in the name of sovereign equality" (van der Pijl 2014, 84). What took place during this transformation in political geography, therefore, was the reproduction of sovereign equality (the hardening of borders between insiders and outsiders, or in Schmitt's terms, "friends" and "enemies") but on a much larger scale (legal recognition between *regional* sovereigns). Thus, for Schmitt, "the age of (nation-)states and the post Versailles *Kleinstaaterei* (mini-state proliferation) was irretrievably over. The future, he argued, belonged to a different type of political unit, for which the Monroe Doctrine provided the historical and legal precedent" (Teschke 2011, 76).

On the other side of the Eurasian continent, Japanese intellectuals were also beginning to experiment with the idea of regional spheres of influence. In response to the post-WWI context of overproduction across the capitalist world economy, Japanese leaders sought to avert postwar recession (and the rise of socialism) through the creation of an autarkic regional economic space (Matsumura 2016, 153). Masamichi Royama, a leading figure in the Showa Kenkyukai Study Group working on the new geopolitics of the East Asian region, argued that the establishment of Japan's "national living sphere" was in fact "not imperialism but regionalism for the purpose of defence or development" (cited in Keuchi 2003, 84). The imperative of national development, which always has a symbiotic relationship with the development of industry-led defence outlays, fundamentally hinged on the number one staple crop of Japanese society: rice. With a general migration of capital from the countryside and into the urban-industrial sectors, the creation of an imperial space centered around Asia would help to ease the burden of raw material constraints in a geographically small and resource poor nation such as Japan (Brandt 1993; Macpherson 1995, 53). In effect, the pattern of Japan's capitalist transformation was reflective of precisely what Ratzel railed against, insofar as the making of the greater co-prosperity sphere "benefited imperial workers to the detriment of farmers... [and] thus served as a device for redistributing income from farmers to workers" (Kimura 1995, 568).

The evolution of regional spaces among fascist states should not be taken as simply the territorial expression of dictatorship, standing in supposed contrast to the regime of liberal democracy. Indeed, the geopolitical imaginaries constructed among German and Japanese intellectuals found fertile ground within the epistemic networks of U.S. power. In the early 1940s, the publisher of *Life* magazine, Henry Luce, proclaimed that "tyrannies may require a large amount of living space... [but] freedom requires and will require far greater living space than Tyranny" (cited in Smith 2003, 319). The American geographer Isaiah Bowman took to Ratzel's concept of Lebensraum as the cornerstone of U.S. primacy within a world of regions: "*Lebensraum* for all is the answer to *Lebensraum* for one" (cited in Smith 2003, 319). And yet, for Bowman and U.S. planners, the question of Lebensraum was not based on territorial expansion; rather, American Lebensraum was "an economic question" (Smith 2003, 319).

Even after the defeat of these regional challengers to the West's "Wilsonian universalism" (van der Pijl 2014), the emerging institutional architecture of global governance eventually ended up consolidating the regionalization of world politics, rather than undermine it. Roosevelt's notion of the regional "Four Policeman" (United States, USSR, Britain, China) eventually lost out to the State Department's preference for universal multilateralism in the shape of the UN General Assembly (the Security Council, wielding the monopoly of legitimate force, was the basic compromise between these two extremes). Yet the rapidly escalating antagonism between the United States and USSR—including the victory of communist forces in China that required the entrance of Japan as the regional ally of Asia (Katzenstein 2005, 48)—simply increased the necessity of regional forms of governance. The emergence of "integration theory" was not only premised on seeking adequate spatial complexes for the continental scale of capital accumulation (Cocks 1980, 27; McCormick 1989, 79–80), it was also a fundamental tool in the Atlantic heartland's quest for hegemony throughout the international system. As Murphy observes, for the early postwar theorists, "functional integration could be ... an alternative solution to the problems that generated late nineteenth-century imperialism" (Murphy 2005, 92). This latter strategy was in no small part aimed at checking the expanding influence of the Soviet Union, as well as the highly significant and combative communist parties across Europe, particularly France, Italy, and Greece (Krige 2008).

Thus, the postwar project of regional integration was, like the interwar period, premised on the exigencies of specific accumulation strategies and their spatial-agglomeration effects, yet this time refracted through the making of an Atlanticist hegemonic project underwritten by the U.S. "imperium" (van der Pijl 2014, 123–28; Katzenstein 2005). The Soviet "containment" strategy that came to dominate U.S. foreign policy during the postwar period formed the underlying logic for various regional security communities throughout Asia and Latin America (Katzenstein 2005, 45). U.S.-Latin American relations became the principal laboratory from which emerged many of the ideas and practices undergirding this (regionalized) mode of global governance (cf. van der Pijl 2014, 126–27). The signing of Latin America's regional security Rio Pact in 1947 would set the trend for other regional security regimes, from the North Atlantic Treaty Organization to the Southeast Asia Treaty Organization (Grandin 2007, 39).[1] From this geopolitical arrangement, "the US delightfully had the best of both worlds: the global organization it had sought since Wilson's era, but also the freedom of action under the Monroe Doctrine" (LeFeber 1993, 93). Yet the very fact that U.S. policy makers favored regional security regimes so early on (headed by the preeminent U.S. position within them) revealed the underlying role that the Global South was supposed to play within the postwar order: as pliant spaces of raw material supplies or open markets to the three regional nodes of global capitalism (United States, Western Europe, and Japan). Economic integration among weaker states, by definition, dilutes this subordinate position in the international division of labor through the establishment of collective tariffs and common markets. This was the central premise of postwar integration initiatives throughout Latin America, which fundamentally aimed to challenge the continued dependency of national economies on the dynamics of accumulation within the Global North. And as we will see, it continues to inform contemporary region-building, from MERCOSUR to the ALBA.

However, it was soon realized that the limited role assigned to the Global South would be the undoing of U.S. influence throughout the non-Western world. As the prominent policy advisor Walt Rostow remarked at the time, "Even if Marx and Lenin did not exist, we would still have a problem" (cited in Peck 2010, 36). For all the intensity of Washington's bid to portray the communist "menace" as some international conspiracy, the fact remained that the continuation of U.S. imperialism throughout the Global South would simply do the USSR's bidding, by fostering continual subaltern rebellions that typically took the form of *independent* radical socialist or communist social forces. It is against this wider geopolitical backdrop that must be kept in mind when we consider the postwar trajectory of Latin American states and regional initiatives, as they attempted to exploit, through ever more intensive means, the ecological bases of their own territories in the struggle to survive the tempest of the capitalist world market.

Creating (and Containing) Class Struggle:
Between Imperium and Regional Autonomy

The post–World War II order, spearheaded by the United States' "economic" Lebensraum (cf. Rupert 1995), witnessed the establishment of a worldwide productivist paradigm of import substitution industrialization (ISI) that applied directly to those states in the Global South which for so long depended on foreign markets for their primary commodity exports and imported manufactures. Together with the adverse hemispheric impact from the American recession of 1957–58, protests and urban riots against Vice President Nixon's tour of the region and the openly communist revolution in Cuba had all brought home Rostow's earlier message to U.S. foreign policy makers: that even without the existence of Moscow, Latin American states would be prone to genuinely popular revolutions. In many ways, they vindicated Brazil's intense desire to further Latin American developmentalism for the sake of achieving regional order. Nevertheless, and precisely because of the Cuban debacle, the Brazilian dream of a new Pan-Americanism soon gave way to John F. Kennedy's Alliance for Progress, launched in 1961, which sought to implement more fully the "generous" side of U.S. foreign relations in the Latin American countryside, albeit coupled with an imperialistic "fist of steel" (Smith 1991, 76; cf. Weis 2001, 327).

Kennedy was carrying forth an earlier instantiation of U.S. development discourse, as a major component in its foreign relations. The immediate impact of the Cuban revolution led Eisenhower's ambassador to the UN, Henry Cabot Lodge, to argue that "we should focus on the Declaration of Independence rather than on the Communist Manifesto where [the focus] has been... and in doing so we should not endeavour to sell the specific word 'Capitalism' which is beyond rehabilitation in the minds of the non-white world" (cited in LeFeber 1993, 14). In turn, Kennedy proclaimed to be building "a hemisphere where all men can hope for a suitable standard of living and all can live out their lives in dignity and in freedom.... Let us once again transform the American Continent into a vast crucible of revolutionary ideas and efforts" (cited in Grandin 2007, 47). The discursive appropriation of the trope "revolution" helped infuse a popular idiom with the hidden undertone of the *capitalist revolution*.

The socioeconomic content of the Alliance for Progress, particularly with the consolidation of the "Green Revolution," aimed to fully implant the neoimperialist discourse of Kennedy's capitalist revolution throughout Latin

America. "The first and necessary stage of [the Alliance's push for] modernization," notes McCormick (1989, 143), "was the commercialization of agriculture on a more large-scale, mechanised basis. Land reform was to be geared more to that goal than to any break-up of the haciendas and redistribution of land to the peasantry." In this way, property-power in the countryside, principally reflected in the maintenance of large-scale *latifundios*, was the permissive condition for the transformation of knowledge-power condensed within the Green Revolution (Patel 2013). This phase of agrarian transition was crucially marked by energy- and chemical-intensive production methods (Petras and LaPorte 1970). As a continuation of capitalism's general extension and intensification of the Earth's nitrogen cycle (Perkins 1997, 211–18), and largely pioneered in the United States, the Green Revolution of the 1960s and beyond comprised a gargantuan increase in yields per hectare by combining more capital- and energy-intensive technologies with synthetic chemical compounds and genetically enhanced seed varieties (see tables 2 and 3). Yet successful chemical input-use was premised on acquisition not simply of the product but also of the knowledge and technical expertise needed to execute them in the right proportions. Again, the sheer weight of capital-intensive production, and the productivity differentials they opened up, meant that despite the hesitance of small farmers, "the question for growers became not whether to use the materials but when, how much, how applied, and for how much money" (Perkins 1997, 216). Advantages of increased scale and scope meant that larger units of production could capture both larger capital inputs per unit of land and labor as well as the needed technical upgrading in knowledge and management; rarely did foreign advisers trek to the remote villages to help small farmers become more accustomed to what they had just purchased in the new chemical input markets. As a consequence, both the land and people working on it were often at extreme risk from chemical exposure and toxification.

Despite these efforts at revolutionizing Latin American agriculture, productivity per agricultural worker was only one-fourth of industrial workers, while agriculture grew at around 3.5 percent (1950–67), compared to industry's 6.3 percent growth rate. In comparison to average growth in the overall regional economy (5.2 percent), agriculture was underperforming while industry was moving in the opposite direction (Stavenhagen 1974, 126, 129). In light of these difficulties, it was recognized that the time was at hand to move away from simple security communities and toward more robust forms of regional cooperation and development. These regional initiatives were signifi-

TABLE 2. Fertilizer (nitrogen, phosphorus, and potassium) consumption in selected countries (annual averages in thousands of tons of plant nutrients)

Country	1957–59	1964	1971
Argentina	15.9	48.5	86.9
Brazil	227.8	255.5	957.9
Colombia	61.0	94.8	177.0
Chile	55.4	120.1	158.5
Mexico	131.4	300.5	594.4
Peru	62.6	91.9	119.0
Venezuela	11.6	32.0	69.4

SOURCE: Furtado (1976, 146)

TABLE 3. Tractors used in farming in selected countries (thousands of units)

Country	1957	1961–65	1971
Argentina	70.0	139.0	180.0
Brazil	57.9	70.1	99.4
Colombia	—	23.4	27.9
Chile	15.0	—	30.5
Peru	—	—	12.3
Mexico	—	64.8	92.0
Venezuela	—	13.1	19.2

SOURCE: Furtado (1976, 146)

cantly shaped by the geopolitical imaginaries among Latin American figures that recognized the reality of continental history as an expression of industrial power (Puntigliano 2011). In his *Foreign Affairs* article of 1959, then expresident of Ecuador Galo Plaza argued for the establishment of a "regional market" in order to further stimulate Latin America's push into the producer goods and consumer durables sectors. In Plaza's view, the territories of the United States, USSR, China, and India were already "regional markets of enormous magnitude. Only Latin America remains divided into 20 separate economic units" (Plaza 1959, 609–10). Some years later, at a conference held in 1966 at Georgetown University, Gustavo Lagos, a Chilean intellectual and later minister of justice under the Frei administration, noted the structural necessity of moving toward a larger politicoeconomic space for the South American nations. Like Plaza, he noted that the sheer scale of capital accumulation during the second half of the twentieth century (marked primarily by the "continental federations" of the United States and USSR) necessitated a concerted push toward tighter political and economic cooperation between the smaller South American states (Milenky 1973, 10–11).

Soon after Richard Nixon's inauguration in 1969, Plaza (then secretary of the OAS) was contacted by Nixon to gain some insight into how U.S.-Latin American relations could be placed on a stronger footing. Plaza recommended the formation of a fact-finding mission, with Nelson A. Rockefeller as the mission's head. Yet Rockefeller's grand tour of the region was, like Nixon's a decade earlier, met with intense bouts of protests and civic unrest from the continent's subaltern classes. It became immediately apparent where the region would have to go in order to quell social unrest. Thus, alongside Plaza, Lagos, and other Latin American leaders, Rockefeller saw regional integration as the surest path to prosperity and stability. Despite Rockefeller's recommendation, the United States had little interest in seeing a South American regional formation potentially dilute U.S. economic dominance. Nevertheless (and perhaps because of this) the Tratado de Montevideo (Treaty of Montevideo) was signed in 1960 by Argentina, Brazil, Uruguay, and Chile, and later joined by Paraguay, Peru, and Mexico, thus creating the Latin American Free Trade Association (LAFTA). By 1968 the number of member states reached eleven. The idea behind LAFTA was to institute a negotiated and gradual elimination of trade barriers (buffeted with countless clauses and concessions for particular countries on particular commodities) and the eventual formation of the Latin American Common Market (LACM) within twelve years (Phillips 2004, 48). The association produced some notable results, but perhaps not those envisaged by Latin American developmentalist thinkers: agriculture and primary products accounted for 70 percent of intra-LAFTA trade, rather than manufactures. By 1967 the push for the LACM was all but abandoned, due to the diversity in size, structure, and socioecological basis of its member states, the low levels of physical and communicative integration between them, and the concomitant concentration of trade between the biggest players, Argentina, Brazil, and Chile (Phillips 2004, 49–50; cf. Haas and Schmitter 1964, 721).

Yet these developmental bottlenecks did not put a break on the geopolitical imaginary of integration. The spatial divisions that expressed the continent's differential development patterns reemerged in subsequent integration initiatives, which brought together groups of states that were closer in both geography and levels of development, such as the Central American Common Market, the Andean Pact, and the Caribbean Community (Fawcett 2005, 39). The overall strategic and spatial selectivity of early Latin American integration was therefore overdetermined by the relative dominance of agriculture at the expense of industrial goods, thus leading to a further geographical fragmentation of the Latin American continent. Meanwhile, the global economy was undergoing a seismic shift. The worldwide turn to neoliberal discipline engendered a new mode of social regulation and economic organization that led to entirely new discursive conceptions and patterns of mobilization among political elites and peasant movements across the entire region.

The Lost Decade: Economic Liberalization and Neoliberal Discipline

The severe readjustments experienced by Latin American states during the 1980s were due to the conjunctural shift in the organization of international capitalism. The general crisis of the capitalist world system, with falling rates of profit within the core states (United States, West Germany, and Japan), forced the most sluggish of these three competitors, the United States, to drastically change the rules of the global game in order to stave off unbearable competition and ensure its continued dominance (Kiely 2005, 56–64). Having severed the U.S. dollar's link to gold, the floating exchange rate mechanism freed the United States from traditional balance of payment constraints, in which internal devaluation and external expansion into foreign markets were buttressed by the international system's continued reliance on the dollar as measure of value and (for many commodities) the de facto medium of exchange. More significantly, the oil crisis of 1973 saw OAPEC states (the Arab states within OPEC), led by Saudi Arabia, instigate an oil embargo, precipitating a major shockwave throughout the world economy in the form of skyrocketing oil prices. Cash-flushed oil states became new sources of credit to Latin American governments via U.S. banks operating within the less-regulated Eurodollar markets (Selva 2017). For many Latin American states, new credit lines were essential for covering their balance of payments, which had been traditionally financed through increasing volumes of ground rent appropriated from the countryside (Grinberg and Starosta 2009). Yet the "Volcker shock" of 1980, which hiked U.S. interest rates in the battle against inflation and domestic class conflict, put enormous pressure on states in the Global South with respect to their dollar-denominated debt repayments.

The neoliberal turn in Latin America did not simply originate through debt crises and balance of payment constraints, even if this became the general trend by the 1980s. Rather, the imposition of neoliberal discipline was from the start a class project seeking to break the power of organized labor in the cities and countryside. In other words, it was a radical and violent reassertion of capitalist sovereignty and the consolidation of property-power and knowledge-power among (Western) transnational capitals and their local comprador classes (see T. Clark 2017). Hence the early arrival of neoliberal experimentation in Chile—which was squarely aimed at combatting the administration of Salvador Allende and his well-organized worker and peasant social base—was also mediated through intense modes of violence and coercion. The Chilean case was but one of several examples of U.S. imperial power in the region, exemplified by the Operation Condor network of "anti-Marxist" terror campaigns coordinated and funded by the U.S. military (McSherry 2005). This military wing of U.S. imperialism was complemented by the introduction of a novel political technology spearheaded by a new generation of American "monetarists," who had been given an entire Latin American nation as a laboratory for untested economic ideas.

Beyond these overtly violent transitions to neoliberal discipline, it was Mexico's default on its sovereign debt in 1982, and the regionwide collapse that resulted from it, that would open up a policy space for the "New Economic Model" across the entire region. The Mexican debacle was taken to be a sign of things to come, with a huge exodus of finance capital across the region; even more prudent states with relatively stable and manageable debt levels, like Colombia, were severely affected by regionwide capital flight (Bulmer-Thomas 2003, 353). It seemed at first as if the neoliberal transition might work under favorable circumstances. With world interest rates (and oil prices) falling and a stronger U.S. economy, Latin American states rapidly expanded their exports. Yet the IMF and World Bank's debt restructuring deals were adversely affected by two interrelated factors: firstly, the rise in export volumes did not compensate for the drop in commodity prices on the world market, which ultimately led to a net loss of earnings (Kay 1995, 22); secondly, negotiations over renewed lending were not well-received by private investors (wary of Latin America's structural balance of payments problems), leaving the lion's share of international lending to the IFIs. Repayment on these loans became an ironclad condition for lending, so much so that by 1987 the IFIs were net recipients of capital from the region (Bulmer-Thomas 2003, 358).

In the agricultural sector, this new accumulation regime, based less and less on the introduction of new sources of wealth (land and labor productivity) entailed highly contradictory effects on the composition of Latin America's agrarian spaces: "The frontiers that could yield a cornucopia of nature's free gifts were fewer than ever before, and the scientific-technological revolution in labor productivity, greatly anticipated in the 1970s, never materialized" (Moore 2010b, 229).² In the face of falling prices and productivity, it was ultimately the rural poor that suffered lower levels of consumption. In consequence, the rural population of Latin America declined by more than half of total population to a quarter between 1960 and 1990. During this time, the value of agricultural exports also fell by one-half to one-fifth, and as a share of GDP from 17 percent to less than 10 percent (Kay 1995, 21; see also Long and Roberts 2005, 63).

Contrary to economic orthodoxy, neoliberal economic reforms led to low growth in the agricultural sector, around 2 percent in the 1980s and 2.6 in the 1990s, compared to 3.5 percent between 1950 and 1980 (Kay 2004, 234). Lower domestic output was compensated for through increased food imports during the 1970s, with the food import-export ratio reaching 40 percent in the 1980s and 60 percent in the 1990s (235). As a result, rural production became skewed in favor of remunerative products favoring urban tastes and foreign consumers (e.g., fruits, livestock, and sorghum) (Ortiz 2014). These "Nontraditional Agricultural Exports" (NTAE) were increasingly organized through foreign multinationals, or through the internationalization of domestic firms. As this sector further developed in the 1990s, value flows from agricultural production were increasingly integrated into the finance and service sectors, as key components in the organization of capital/knowledge-intensive systems of production within the NTAE sectors (Robinson 2008, 58–64).

Under these conditions, rural populations underwent a "semiproletarianization" in which peasants devoted more of their time to off-farm activities, either in urban centers or in seasonal wage labor on larger farms (Kay 2004, 241). In sum, the consolidation of neoliberal discipline resulted in the generalization of weak growth, rising under- or unemployment, poverty, and inequality, as well as a decrease in total population (Hermann 2016, 529). Latin America had thus entered what would soon be known as "the lost decade."

As a corollary to this novel accumulation regime based less on new sources of wealth and more on higher rates of exploitation, the neoliberal mode of regulation tended to relegate the role of the state in the process of economic development, even if the state as such did not necessarily see a decline in its overall power (Lahiff et al. 2007). Rather, "neoliberal enclosures required, in the first instance, fundamental alterations by the state in the structure of rights to property in the juridical and legal sphere that it monopolised" (Akram-Lodhi 2007, 1446). This distinctive sovereign regime consequently led to the relative fragmentation of the state apparatus itself, in which various competencies become externalized toward private groups: "Governments in the region enlisted the support of non-governmental organizations (NGOs) to encourage peasant organizations and communities to make greater use of the 'market mechanism'... and, in their politics, to eschew direct action and utilize instead 'the electoral mechanism'—in other words, to adopt peaceful/legalistic forms of struggle in pursuit of their interests" (Petras and Veltmeyer 2002, 52–53).

This marked a substantial transformation in the strategic selectivity of the neoliberal state, in which various competencies traditionally integrated into the state itself were "outsourced" to more agile, formally independent organizations. Yet these groups were not simply boosters of the neoliberal project. For many NGOs, there was a dilemma as to whether or not participation in agrarian reform and social fund implementation under conditions of neoliberal adjustment conveyed a passive acceptance of these social dislocations, "which nearly all NGOs have criticized as socially regressive and unacceptable" (Bebbington and Thiele 1993, 51). On the other hand, it was the very nature of NGOs—as institutions that were more efficient and effective with limited funds—that condemned such groups to rules of reproduction that continuously pushed them into the arms of neoliberal hegemony; unlike the seemingly unlimited funds of a state budget, NGOs are effectively dependent on external sources of funding obtained through neoliberal institutions (55). The effects of structural adjustment enhanced the propensity for state personnel to abandon an atrophied public sector for the NGO sector, carrying with them their university educated knowledge of classical sociology and biological science (Bebbington and Thiele 1993, 54; see also Silva 2009, 25).

Thus, the emergence of a near-universal turn to "neoliberal sovereignty" in Latin America affected a series of shifts in rights and territory. By transforming state functions to a night-watchman mode and away from the postwar *gran patron*, as well as ceding key industries and social service provision to domestic and foreign capitals that correspondingly shifted the terrain of rights away from the popular classes back toward property owners, Latin American states took on a new set of political technologies. Firstly, the regime of disciplinary neoliberalism elevated the hegemonic discourse of liberal (rather than *social*) democracy and thus engendered a switch from a positive rights guarantor to a negative rights guardian (Silva 2009, 24–25). Secondly, the territorial manifestation of neoliberal sovereignty emerged through a radical reorganization of social space, via the intensification of transnational flows and organizational forms of production. Changes in the productive forces and strategies of accumulation thus led to variable degrees of "flexible accumulation," creating an ever-more malleable labor market and increased precarity within the ranks of the working class in both the factory and field (Spronk 2013, 81; Kay 2008, 924–25).

Thirdly, the hegemonic project of neoliberal discipline was equally supported through the "deradicalization" of educational institutions (catered more toward business/industry-oriented curricula), the establishment of enormous media latifundios (Dello Buono 2010), and the transformation of a once-radical cadre of intellectuals into a loyal choir singing the praises of neoliberal "rationality." Strategic and spatial selectivities thus unfolded along a type of "denationalization" (Jessop 2002; Roncallo 2014), transposing socioeconomic power above and below, typically through subnational decentralization forging "economies of agglomeration" within urban centers (though wracked with informal work in barrio peripheries), as well as through foreignization of space mediated by increased foreign direct investment and profit expatriation (de la Cruz 2011; Robinson 2008; cf. Hesketh 2017, 61–63).

As with the challenges faced by Latin American states during the closure of the ISI boom, the systemic pressures of neoliberalism were met with a wider push toward regionalization. Gustavo Lagos's prophetic remarks concerning the continent-sized confederations of the United States and USSR were now borne out by the increasing regionalization of the global trade regime, in the interests of economizing on geographical distance and transaction costs. From a regional perspective, this transformation in the rights/territory complex (in the form of neoliberal sovereignty) congealed into a regime of "open regionalism," broadly characterized by enhanced regional demand for FDI, the deepening of intraregional trade, and increased social polarization and precarity of labor (Devlin and Estevadeordal 2001, 22–25).

Nevertheless, there remained important differences across Latin America's multiplex regional landscape, which corresponded to the underlying accumulation regime, mode of regulation, and hegemonic project of each regional space. NAFTA and MERCOSUR, for instance, are perhaps the most significant as well as qualitatively different cases. NAFTA's accumulation strategy was premised on a specific economic division of labor between its three members (with Canada and Mexico as low-cost raw material/semi-assembled supply "spokes" to the U.S. manufacturing "hub") facilitated through ironclad freed-trade legal commitments and ideological appeals to "market rationality" (Ciccantell 2001; Kühnhardt 2010, 28–29). The U.S.-led construction of NAFTA ultimately stemmed from concerns for increased regional competitiveness over rival regional poles, namely the German-led European Community and Japan's regional "flying geese" model. NAFTA's obsession with regional competitiveness led to a dismissal of concerns over the negative effects on labor or ecology (Fairbrother 2009, 148; Ciccantell 2011). This trilateral economic space was also based on a contradictory discourse, which "allowed the simultaneous existence of both the possibility of economic integration with Mexico as an equal partner and the established image of Mexico as a dependent other" (Skonieczny 2001, 451). Discursive constructions of this kind were internally related to the politicoeconomic reality of the NAFTA space, which quickly yielded a "peso crisis" in Mexico and meagre economic performance in both Mexico and Canada (seen through high rates of unemployment, declining real hourly wages, and ecological degradation), leading ultimately to the delegitimization of NAFTA's hegemonic project (Pastor 2001, 120).

Yet U.S. designs for the Western hemisphere went far beyond the mere trilateralization of cross-border flows—they fundamentally harked back to the Monroe Doctrine's vision of an entire hemisphere dominated by U.S. hegemony. The Miami Summit in 1994 thus presented the diplomatic platform for the United States's proposed Free Trade Area of the Americas, which would stretch from Alaska to Tierra del Fuego (with projected completion by 2004). For Latin America's biggest economy, Brazil, the FTAA threatened to subsume the region under an expanded NAFTA-like regime, which would have threatened the possibility for diversification. The solution to this challenge lay in promoting a different, more autonomous regional market in South America.

The origins of Latin America's most developed regional project, the MERCOSUR, goes back to the earlier round of regional integration agreements in 1986 between the two largest players, Argentina, and Brazil (Gardini 2010). It finally came to fruition as the "Southern Cone Common Market" in 1991, signed by Brazil, Argentina, Paraguay, and Uruguay. The economic content of the MERCOSUR space was not radically different from the neoliberal pattern, yet its sociopolitical effects certainly deviated from the norm of subservience to Atlantic capital, becoming an institutional ensemble "located somewhere between NAFTA and a common market" (Katzenstein 2005, 231). MERCOSUR has always positioned itself as an inherently *integrationist* project, aiming toward a common external position as a protection against the wider world market. MERCOSUR could offer a more stable platform for trade and production given the much lower levels of unevenness across its member states than would be the case if they had joined the proposed FTAA (or even bilateral agreements with the United States). Trade levels among member states grew significantly, from 4.1 to 20.3 billion USD (1990–97), with the percentage of intra-MERCOSUR trade relative to members' global trade at 14 to 25 percent (1992–97) (Muñoz 2001, 83).

Nevertheless, MERCOSUR is hobbled by a number of intervening factors. Firstly, it is entirely premised on intergovernmentalism, which leaves interstate relations at the level of diplomacy rather than regionwide legislation (Phillips 2003, 220; Katzenstein 2005, 231). Secondly, this pattern of relations between members leads inevitably to a democratic deficit with respect to the citizenry of the bloc, who may have formal channels of consultation (Consultative Social and Economic Forum), yet in practice have little influence on policy (Lubbock 2022, 545). Thirdly, and despite the more level playing field within MERCOSUR as opposed to what would have happened in case of integration with the United States, the levels of development, and the specificities of each member's economy, creates asymmetries of opportunity and cost, leading either to unequal benefits or to treaty agreements that remain too vague and indeterminate to have any regionwide effect (Malamud 2005, 427–29). Put in strategic-relational terms, the predominant accumulation strategy of all MERCOSUR states relies overwhelmingly on an "extractivist" model (whether mineral or agro-industrial), which severely skewers trade patters toward countries in the Global North, or the BRICs (Petras and Veltmeyer 2014, 124–25). As a result, regional integration within the MERCOSUR space has been limited to either "resource seeking" or "market seeking" behavior by the largest continental firms, which precludes any regionwide integration of value-added production chains whose final products may compete within the wider world market (Burges 2005). The material substratum of the region's economies, focused largely on a renewed impetus toward mineral or agro-industrial expansion, therefore produces an accumulation regime premised on the national capture of value-added processing activities coupled with uneven demand for energy resources (particularly the enormous demands pursued by Petrobras, the Brazilian energy giant). What appears as a rational hegemonic project for each *national* space in fact adds up to an *irrational* result of depressed regional integration. Thus, the enormous levels of product exemptions written into MERCOSUR's articles of agreement reflect a mode of regulation overdetermined by executive elites seeking to protect and accommodate nationally constituted sectoral interests (Carranza 2006, 817–18; Pezzola 2018).

Given the turbulence MERCOSUR had to endure—with Brazil's devaluation of the real in 1999 and the Argentine economic collapse of 2001—it became increasingly clear that member states' cooperation had to ensure the stability of its social fabric. With the ascension of Lula da Silva to the Brazilian presidency in 2002 from a "developmentalist front" coalition within the Workers' Party, a new social compact between the "grand bourgeoisie" and the subaltern classes would enable Brazil to endure the strains of region building and insertion into the world market on a potentially more solid (and popular) footing via an altered alignment of the state toward the promotion of social production and real accumulation, rather than allowing finance capital free reign (van der Pijl 2006, 198; Boito and Berringer 2014). As such, Brazil's approach to regional integration was far more substantial during this time in comparison with the high watermark of neoliberalism in the 1990s, which emerged from Lula's strategic aim to forge its regional leadership in opposition to the Northern colossus (Phillip 2003). Yet the Lula "enigma" was merely reflective of a much deeper fissure that began to emerge between the Latin American region and the Atlantic core.

Reclaiming *Nuestra América*:
Contradictions of the New Latin American Left

The analysis of neoliberalism in the previous section was relatively muted on the nature and impact of popular movements and antisystemic mobilizations during Latin America's lost decade. The disintegration of the traditional Left, as a consequence of authoritarian repression and neoliberal discipline, produced a social vacuum throughout the region, as well as new modes of social organization. In contrast to the early twentieth century, in which peasants often preferred the more manageable (and less risky) exploitative relations with their *patrones* to the precarious form of wage labor in urban centers, the late twentieth century saw an entirely opposite dynamic—with capitalism in full-blown (yet inherently uneven) form, the evisceration of the campesino pattern of everyday life changed the calculus of survival: "People moved to the cities because urban conditions, for all their horrors, were better than those in the rural areas" (Gilbert 2004, 99). Coupled with the already numerically small working classes, the incidence of rural-urban migration and the consequent squeeze on those already employed created a burgeoning underclass characterized by informal work, microentrepreneurialism, violent crime, underemployment, or outright unemployment (Portes 1985; Portes and Hoffman 2003).[3] Across the entire region, from the Caribbean to the Southern Cone, these stress fractures unleashed waves of "austerity protests" and "food riots" (Walton and Seddon 1994, chap. 4). These sociostructural tendencies help explain the rise of "new social movements" throughout the region, who no longer had recourse, or even good reason, to pursue class struggle of the classical sort. Disenchanted with political parties and the capture of state power, these movements tended to be defensive in their forms of resistance while bringing issues of justice, dignity, identity, solidarity, and traditional cultures into the center frame of their struggles, even if they found common cause in resisting neoliberal reform (Silva 2009).

Perhaps the most prominent example to capture the attention of academics and activists was the Zapatista uprising in 1994 (Hesketh 2017). Starting out as an armed revolt by the EZLN (Ejército Zapatista de Liberación Nacional) in rejection of the NAFTA accords and taking heavy casualties from the Mexican army's counteroffensive, the Zapatista resistance repertoire quickly transformed into a more symbolic struggle for the world's attention toward the plight of agrarian communities in Chiapas. The Zapatistas' demands strongly resonated with the aspirations of other advocacy networks, in and beyond Mexico, by constructing a "master frame" of democratic participation, emphasizing diversity and horizontalism in decision making, linking injustice to neoliberalism, and utilizing the internet to disseminate their message (Olsen 2006). Such transnational linkages helped put external pressure against the Mexican government on issues of human rights and the militarization of the Chiapas region. The nature and evolution of the EZLN struggles carried various commonalities with other agrarian movements during this time. Probably due to increasing rural-urban migrations and the relatively stronger presence of Indigenous communities remaining in the countryside, it was during this time that "the struggle for land [was] accompanied by a distrust of the state in rural areas," a pattern that can be seen with CONAIE in Ecuador, the Consejo Regional Indigena del Cauca in Colombia, and the many Indigenous movements that make up the social base of the Movimiento al Socialismo party in Bolivia (Teubal 2009, 15–16).

If these rebellious currents were no longer enamored of the traditional methods of class struggle and compromise, they were, at least nominally, also much less beholden to the nation-state as the exclusive space of struggle. In addition to the "new social movement" discourse, Latin American social movements tended to mobilize through forms of "transnational activism" (Tarrow 2005). Prominent examples include the Foro Mesoamericano network, which formed in 2001 in response to the neoliberal integration projects of Plan Puebla-Panama and later expanded its target of resistance to the Central American Free Trade Agreement (CAFTA) (Spalding 2008). At a region-wide scale, the Hemispheric Social Alliance emerged in 1997 in order to challenge the FTAA (Saguir 2010). From struggles for labor rights in *maquiladoras* (sweatshops) and Indigenous rights (Carty 2006; Mato 2000) to the resurgence of regionwide networks of rural social movements (Deere and Royce 2009), contentious politics in Latin America appeared to take on an ever-greater transnational form (Silva 2013).

Highlighting this new spatialization strategy among the region's social movements is particularly important when tracking the trajectory and changing character of agrarian struggle. What emerged during the 1990s was not simply a newfound militancy among those in the countryside but an entirely new field of discourse and practice adequate to the changing contours of world (dis)order. No doubt the most prominent of these transnational movements has been LVCs. Though preceded by various international meetings among peasants (Edelman 2014), the movement officially emerged from the Mons conference in 1993, where numerous peasant organizations from around the world banded together under the name La Vía Campesina (LVC—"the peasant way"). A few months after this inauguration, dozens of peasant movements marched under the LVC banner against the GATT meetings in Geneva. Later in 1996, LVC was a prominent actor at the World Food Summit held in Rome, challenging the FAO to include farmers' movements as legitimate participants within negotiations on global food governance. Since then, LVC-affiliated groups have participated in a score of anti-neoliberal protests against the WTO (particularly with regards to the issue of trade dumping) in Geneva (1998), Seattle (1999), Cancun (2003), and Hong Kong (2005) (Desmarais 2007, 8). These diverse struggles paralleled and in many ways were nurtured by the first World Social Forum (WSF) held in the city of Porto Alegre, Brazil (January 2001), which (in addition to thousands of participants across the world) saw over eighty peasant movements represented under LVC, hosting an enormous plenary session on peasant struggles across the world. At the second WSF, held the following year, LVC delegates hosted a large seminar on "Socialism, the Hopeful Alternative," which centered on such themes as market protections, agrarian cooperatives, and food sovereignty more broadly (Leite 2005, 81, 108, 115).

For Latin American peasant movements, these types of transnationally organized counterspaces emerged from the much longer lineage of the Campesino-a-Campesino movements that began in the 1970s and '80s. As we saw at the beginning of this chapter, the Green Revolution tended to favor landed capital over small farmers, even if the latter had access to new technological packets. In the face of falling yields and ecological degradation, mainstream development agencies slowly shifted toward the idea of "sustainable development." Yet global governance institutions lacked the means or the wherewithal to gain the place-based knowledge necessary for the realization of sustainable agrarian development (Holt-Giménez 2006, 151–58). In contrast, local agrarian networks, working in cooperation with development NGOs, were much better placed to implement sustainable agroecological techniques as a response to the failures of the Green Revolution. Beginning with small exchanges of knowledge and techniques among Mexican and Nicaraguan peasants, the campesino-a-campesino method slowly expanded its network across the entire region (Holt-Giménez 2006, 14–16; see also Val et al. 2019).

However, the central contradiction of LVC's discourse—crystallized in the slogan "Our resistance will be as transnational as capital"—was that its greatest ally would come in the form of a new state apparatus. At the most immediate level, this renewed cycle of resistance among rural social forces pointed toward a bottom-up form of strategic and spatial selectivity, though an inherently complex one. On the one hand, the increasing transnationalization of capital, and its institutional expression in the WTO and elite global summits, encouraged an equally transnational form of resistance among social movements. On the other hand, resistance to neoliberal sovereignty—which had partially displaced the classical locus of sovereignty away from the nation-state and hence the citizenry as such—brought with it a renewed emphasis on sovereign independence (Silva 2009). In bringing the state back in, antineoliberal social movements, which for so long had eschewed traditional institutions as vehicles for popular demands, found themselves in close partnership with political parties and state institutions (Rossi 2018).

The strategic marriage between states and social movements formed the fundamental source of the ALBA, as well as the foundational potential for the regionalization of food sovereignty. And yet, as we will see more closely in chapter 3, ALBA's accumulation regime and mode of regulation is traversed by a series of contradictions that radically unsettles the regional hegemonic project. At the most fundamental level, ALBA states rely to a predominant degree on the continued exploitation of natural resources, whether agricultural or mineral. Too often development projects, whether in the form of new commercial or transport infrastructures or through extending (both vertical and horizontal) resource frontiers, constitute major threats to Indigenous and other subaltern communities, as well as the ecological sustainability of their ways of life and claims to sovereignty over ancestral lands (Bebbington 2009).

The class character of these frictions emerges from the continued struggle over the capture of ground rent between rentier classes comprising state managers and national/foreign owned capitals. However, it is important to note that within this politicoeconomic terrain, it is the social content of a particular state's mode of regulation and hegemonic project, rather than the material character of accumulation as such, that determines its relative developmental direction. As Higginbottom (2013, 200) notes, struggles over *the domestic capture* of ground rent has been far more successful within ALBA states as compared to non-ALBA states. Yet "success" in these terms cannot simply be read off from the domestic acquisition of foreign exchange. Rather, material wealth merely constitutes the limits of the possible whose extension and direction of change will be determined by the outcome of social struggle (Poulantzas 2014, 26), which we will see further in the following chapter.

Conclusion

This chapter offered an historical reconstruction of Latin America's long road to regionalism in the context of changing material and territorial configurations of global capitalism under U.S. hegemony. Capital's continued revolution in the productive forces, and the spatial complexes these engendered, congealed into a world-historical "regional" (or continental) sized space of accumulation in the North American "island." The forces of capitalist and geopolitical competition induced a powerful diffusion of this politico-territorial form among leading industrial states that were historically confined to territorially fractured regional realms. Despite Germany's and Japan's sizeable industrial rise, they could not compensate for America's seemingly endless resource frontier.

With the defeat of these regional contenders, the U.S.-led world order would eventually consecrate the regionalization of world politics, albeit under security-oriented managerialism. As with much else during the early Cold War years, U.S. geopolitical strategy was refracted through containing the communist "menace," which more often than not appeared in the active formation of regional "security communities." Yet neglect of development diplomacy would simply stoke the fires of subaltern resistance against the new global order. It was precisely this danger of subaltern insurgency that informed the economic and geopolitical strategies of the U.S. Fordist compact. In response to the Cuban rupture in the U.S. *corpus imperium*, the Green Revolution—as the ecological arrow in Kennedy's geopolitical quiver—unleashed the enormous power of Western agricultural science upon the Latin American region, with devastating effects on both human and ecological landscapes. The uneven balance of forces between nature on one side, and the state and capital on the other, had entered a particularly intense and destructive phase.

The systemic crisis of the capitalist world economy beginning in the late 1960s ushered in a transition away from discourses of national development and political inclusiveness (however fleeting these may have been in practice) toward a new form of rights, territory, and sovereignty that spoke to the invisible hand of (global) market discipline. The inter- and transnational class offensive against subaltern groups in Latin America launched by the United States and fractions of Latin American ruling classes led to a reorganization of the region's class structures, which reflected deeper transformations in the increasingly "globalized" world economy. The push toward regionalization, with MERCOSUR leading the way, sought a way out of this geopolitical subordination, without necessarily extricating itself from the same social contradictions of capitalist development.

Yet the severity of neoliberal discipline had merely ensured its own downfall. The myriad social struggles that wracked the Latin American continent laid the foundations for a renewed left-wing insurgency in both the streets and at the ballot box; thus, the dominant neoliberal discourse emphasizing the efficacy of electoral politics over direct action ultimately backfired. The outcomes of these struggles resulted in a notable rebalancing within many Latin American states toward a rights/territory/sovereignty regime, in which capital would, *in theory*, become far more subordinate to the state apparatus itself and the popular social forces comprising its social base. However, Latin America's new Left was caught within a contradictory bind of furthering the accumulation of ground rent for the sake of social development. Understanding the nature of these contradictions and struggles, and their bearing on the path to food sovereignty across ALBA's states, constitutes the central focus for the remaining chapters.

CHAPTER 3

From Magical State to Magical Region
The Social Origins of ALBA

As the Venezuelan anthropologist Fernando Coronil once argued, the abundant natural wealth beneath Venezuela's subsoil provided the state with the material basis for a seemingly limitless capacity to augment social and economic development: "As a 'magnanimous sorcerer,' the state seizes its subjects by inducing a condition or state of being receptive to its illusions—a magical state" (Coronil 1997, 5). Tracing the historical trajectory of Venezuelan development over the long twentieth century, Coronil's analysis of oil as the magical elixir of national unity brings into focus the specificity of Venezuelan capitalism, based on its subterranean "prize" rather than the labor of its citizens (29). One consequence of Coronil's focus on oil and the power of natural wealth, however, is the relative obscurity of labor and the broader layer of subaltern agency that plays an equally important role in the process of Venezuelan state formation (cf. Lubbock 2018). Indeed, in retelling the story of economic development from the "commanding heights" of political power (Coronil 1997, 13), much remains unanswered with respect to the concrete social classes that forged the contested terrain of the magical state and the strategies devised by the Venezuelan ruling class as a result.

In contrast to Coronil's top-down view of the Venezuelan oil state, Iselin Strønen presents a vibrant ethnographic study of individuals, communities, and classes through the "lens of oil," illustrating the myriad ways in which oil "enters social relations... [and] how its social dimensions are intertwined with its structural embeddedness in local and global political economies" (2017, 8). While her insights into the messy process of community-based participatory democracy are illuminating, Strønen does not seek "an analysis of the oil economy per se," while largely sidestepping the issue of "how exactly oil wealth entered and circulated in the political and social system during the Chávez era" (8).

The aim of this chapter is to chart a middle path between these approaches from above and below, via a grounded Marxian analysis of the political economy of state formation in Venezuela, the contending class forces that molded the state's institutional materiality, and the eventual (re)construction of the magical state via a new hegemonic project (chavismo) under the leadership of Hugo Chávez. To capture the complexity of this historical narrative, the chapter draws upon Nicos Poulantzas's theory of the capitalist state, as well as his concept of "authoritarian statism." As a "transformed form" of the capitalist state, authoritarian statism reflects an underlying crisis in the power bloc, which is "solved" through the enhanced power of the executive branch and the relative disorganization of the popular classes (Poulantzas 2014, 166). This concept thus helps to trace some of the particularities of the Venezuelan state during the Chávez era within the broader lineage of state transformation from the 1970s.

The chapter then traces the social and geopolitical context in which the ALBA was born. As we saw in chapter 2, ALBA was launched at the height of Latin America's opposition to the U.S.-sponsored FTAA. Reflecting the growth of anti-neoliberal movements spanning the region, ALBA sought to give institutional expression to the political climate of the time. However, as we will see throughout this chapter, Venezuela has always played the cardinal role in the development and function of ALBA. From ideological leadership to the material circulation of oil rents, the centrality of the Venezuelan state produced a series of consequences that would eventually undermine the very coherence of ALBA itself.

Class Struggle and the Making of a Magical State in Venezuela

Before the advent of oil, Venezuela was, like the rest of Latin America, economically dependent on the export of agricultural goods. For much of the nineteenth century, political power flowed through vast coffee plantations across the Andean highlands (Yarrington 1997). Yet the discovery of the first oil wells in the early twentieth century would become the death knell of Venezuelan agriculture. As new mining opportunities absorbed capital and labor away from an uncompetitive agricultural sector, petroleum's share of Gross National Product jumped from 9.5 to 34.7 percent (1925–36), with agriculture falling from 34.6 to 18.8 percent (McBeth 2002, 112, 114; see also Carlson 2017; Brown 1985, 375).[1] These transformations led to an accumulation regime and hegemonic project that singularly fused around the turning of the oil spigot:

"Although the land and its products were celebrated in poetry as well as in the visual arts, music, and popular songs, agriculture did not provide a common source of national identification in Venezuela" (Coronil 1997, 88).

Despite the emergence of democracy in 1945, with the ascension of Romulo Betancourt and the Acción Democrática party on the back of a previous cycle of class struggles throughout rural and urban spaces (Hein 1980, 231), the AD's more "pluralistic" political regime could not entirely solve the contradiction of administering an oil state in the face of a militant peasantry. Even with a shrinking agrarian population, peasants remained a political force that could not be ignored. A substantial fraction of the social base of the AD was centered in the countryside, representing a newly enfranchised segment of the population. And despite the interruption of Venezuelan democracy between 1948 and 1958 (with the Pérez Jiménez dictatorship), rural support for AD remained strong, which led to electoral victories in 1958 and 1963 (Powell 1971, 287–88). Indeed, as Powell notes, the agrarian classes' support was decisive, "since the urban electorate proved to be highly fragmented, diffusing its majority power through a large number of splinter groups, personalist parties, and vague coalitions of various ideological hues" (291).

With the overthrow of the Jiménez regime in 1958 and the inauguration of the "Fourth Republic," Venezuela became known as the "exceptional democracy" (Ellner and Tinker Salas 2007). Standing in marked contrast to its regional neighbors, many of whom entered a protracted period of "bureaucratic authoritarianism" during the 1970s (O'Donnell 1973), Venezuela enjoyed a stable democracy based on the Pacto de Punto Fijo (Fixed Point Pact), established between the three main political parties—AD, COPEI, and UPD. This pact was intended as a guarantee against the return of dictatorship and to exclude more radical currents like the Venezuelan Communist Party.

Such intra-elite cooperation could only take place through the circulation of oil rents, for "the organized sectors in Venezuela demanded their cut from the national purse in return for their 'support' of the [democratic] revolution" (Derham 2010, 167). In light of this electoral quid pro quo, agrarian reform was high on the list of priorities for AD leaders. Yet agricultural policy was increasingly oriented away from social support for peasants and toward the transformation of agriculture into a source of cheap food for expanding urban populations (Powell 1971, 292; Huizer 1973, 70–72; Derham 2010, 179). Continuous pursuit of agricultural modernization across the entire Punto Fijo era did little to halt the decline in agriculture's share of GDP, from 7 to 6.1 percent between 1961 and 1980. Despite an *increase* in total land area under cultivation, state support for the large landowning class failed to augment agricultural supply to the home market, given the raft of disincentives to agrarian investment in an oil-dominated economy. Instead, with access to new lines of state credit derived from the augmented volume of ground rent, the landed classes either paid down debt, redirected credit to nonagricultural investments, or simply moved their funds to overseas accounts. As a result, food imports increased by a factor of ten throughout the decade (Petras and Morley 1983, 12–13).

During the late 1960s and early '70s, under the administration of Rafael Caldera, the national economy entered a period of relative recovery, even while political unrest increased. Working class demands for a greater share in expanding national income led to an increased frequency of strikes between 1969 and 1973 (Ellner 1993, 42). With the election of Carlos Andrés Pérez in 1974, labor unrest declined as a result of the changing balance of class forces within the national power bloc. Riding the wave of high oil prices from 1973, Pérez invoked a presidential decree to nationalize Venezuela's oil operations in 1976, now subsumed under the newly christened Petróleos de Venezuela, S.A. (Petroleum of Venezuela, Joint Stock Company—PDVSA). With a new windfall of oil dollars (derived both from higher global market prices and nationalization), the state increasingly pushed into more strategic sectors, including iron and steel (Bye 1979, 58). Having been granted "emergency powers" by the National Assembly, Pérez was free to pursue his ambitious development policy (the Fifth National Plan) that sought to rapidly industrialize the Venezuelan economy, with state-led capital accumulation increasing from 34 to 55 percent of total capital formation between 1975 and 1980 (Rey 1998, 117–18; Coker 2001, 192).

While Pérez introduced a raft of measures designed to benefit labor, including minimum wage legislation and other employment rights, the working class was effectively marginalized from the formation of economic policy. Leaders within the country's largest trade union, Confederación de Trabajadores de Venezuela (CTV), warned against a hasty and largely uncoordinated development plan underwritten by a clientelist relationship with the biggest fractions of Venezuelan capital (the so-called Twelve Apostles) and an increasingly personalistic and unaccountable mode of regulation from within the executive branch (Ellner 1993, 50–56; Rey 1998, 118; Ortiz 2004, 79). As a consequence, workers became increasingly squeezed within this state-led accumulation regime, with labor's share of national income falling from 51 to 47 percent between 1970 and 1980 (Coker 2001, 192).

Oil, Class, and the Rise of Authoritarian Statism in the Fourth Republic

Cycles of class struggle that traversed the strategic terrain of the state significantly (re)shaped the Fourth Republic under Pérez and the subsequent crisis of the Punto Fijo regime. In many ways, the transformation of the Venezuelan state converged with Poulantzas's concept of "authoritarian statism." Originally applied to the case of Western Europe, the concept sought to reflect the "political crisis" and "crisis of the state" across the Atlantic core, engendered by a new neoliberal accumulation regime and hegemonic project, "the strong state and free economy" (Gamble 1988; cf. Poulantzas 2014, 113). For Poulantzas, the Global South (and Latin America in particular) was experiencing a somewhat different form of state transformation: "*a new form of dependent State...* [which] involves significant points of dissimilarity with the new form of [authoritarian statism]... in the dominant countries" (Poulantzas 2014, 204, emphasis in original). This dissimilarity was marked by a series of military coups across the Southern Cone, leading to the consolidation of "bureaucratic authoritarian" regimes (O'Donnell 1973).

Yet Venezuela was an exception to this rule. Indeed, its pacted democracy, immanent political crisis, and temporary solution through an increasingly interventionist state within the economy all converge with Poulantzas's notion of authoritarian statism. Taking over the leadership of a country beset by political crisis and class struggle during the Caldera years, Pérez set about reorganizing the balance of class forces within the state's power bloc, in the context of a *strong state and developmental economy* (Coronil and Skurski 1982). In other words, while both European states and the Venezuelan landlord state had decisively moved against labor in a bid to "normalize" the reproduction of political domination, in the latter case it was the state that took on the burden of accumulation (even with private capital in a subordinate "partnership" role). Pérez's ultimate goal was to radically deepen the entwined relationship between "bourgeois politicians" and "political capitalists" via the concentration of power within the executive branch (Coronil and Skurski 1982, 70; cf. Coronil 1997, 247).

Yet in doing so, Pérez recreated many of the contradictions inherent within this new state form. Characterized by an ever-deeper penetration of the state into the economic sectors, authoritarian statism "no longer acts as a stabilizing force; on the contrary, it is itself an important factor of destabilization" (Poulantzas 2014, 212). With Pérez's increasing accumulation of foreign loans for investment in industry and infrastructure, the Venezuelan state ceased to be a stabilizing force; as part of the state's increasingly insulated and bureaucratic form, new loans were managed through a series of "parastatal" institutions acting in a semiautonomous fashion that kept public debt off the national balance sheet (Derham 2010, 229). Despite the increase in per capita income, the benefits of Pérez's development plan did not reach the popular classes, who continued to suffer from inadequate social services, housing, and education (Velasco 2010, 671; Derham 2010, 220–26). Consequently, strike activity during the last years of Pérez's administration reached a level previously seen during the height of labor conflict in 1973 (Ellner 1993, 49).

All of this helped to propel Luis Herrera Campíns to the presidency in 1979. Running on a platform of political reform, Herrera Campíns proposed a program that stood out for its unique support for a more participatory form of politics as a means of "demystifying the image of the 'almighty state'" under the Pérez years (Velasco 2010, 679). And yet, a contradiction emerged between the state's mode of regulation and the hegemonic project. While the latter rested on the promotion and projected image of more "participation" and "state advocacy," the former shifted toward a regime of austerity as a means of rolling back bloated state spending and subsidies of the previous administration (679, 681). As a consequence, the economy underwent a severe credit crunch, high interest rates, a collapse in demand, and price inflation (Borgucci and Fuenmayor 2013, 184). With the onset of capital flight and the devaluation of the national currency, Herrera Campíns was forced to implement capital controls and distribute oil dollars at preferential rates to domestic producers. Despite these makeshift responses, the material foundation of the Punto Fijo era was nearing its breaking point.

The accretion of neoliberal reform in the 1980s merely completed the slow but steady transformation toward authoritarian statism begun under the Pérez administration. Indeed, by 1989 Pérez was back in the electoral spotlight. Having run his previous campaign under the banner "Democracy with Energy," Pérez now styled himself as the national savior—the "Man with Energy"— standing against the predations of the international financial institutions (Coronil 1997, 327, 372). No sooner was he elected, Pérez set about on a *Gran Viraje* (the Great U-Turn) by implementing a string of IMF-backed reforms that decimated most economic sectors, particularly agriculture (Lander and Fierro 1996; Di John 2005). With the evisceration of society's social and ecological fabric, in the form of both land and labor that could find no productive outlet except in the petroleum or construction sectors (Lander and Fierro 1996, 58), the sporadic fighting between subaltern actors and the state apparatus finally erupted into the widespread caracazo riots of 1989 (López

Maya 2003). All of these elements of political crisis fracturing the state apparatus revealed the intensification of authoritarian statism, which had amassed a "veritable arsenal, which is not simply of a legal-constitutional character, does not always come to the fore in the exercise of power: it is revealed to the mass of the population . . . above all through sudden jolts to its functioning" (Poulantzas 2014, 210). The sudden jolt of the caracazo uprising similarly prompted a whole series of "extra-institutional procedures" in the form of violent repression of popular grievances (López Maya 2003, 135).

The caracazo ultimately signaled an "organic crisis" fracturing Venezuelan society, which came to a head by the late 1990s (Romero 1997). As Gramsci argued, in the face of an organic crisis transecting the economic, political, and social terrain, "social classes become detached from their traditional parties," while "the immediate situation becomes delicate and dangerous, because the field is open for violent solutions, for the activities of unknown forces, represented by charismatic 'men of destiny'" (1971, 210). The decade of Venezuela's organic crisis closely parallels Gramsci's reading: while Hugo Chávez's attempted military coup in 1994 was ultimately unsuccessful, this charismatic man of destiny was able to reunite Venezuela's untethered social classes around a new hegemonic project that sought to finally oust the dysfunctional Punto Fijo bloc.

Electing Chávez: A Convergence of Class Interests

The election of Hugo Chávez in December 1998 represented a radical departure from the elitism of Venezuela's pacted democracy. The first step in transforming the old Punto Fijo regime involved the introduction of a new constitution rooted within popular demands. Having won a referendum on the drafting of a new national constitution in 1999, the newly elected constituent assembly set to work bringing the peoples' will into the legislative body of the state. Despite Chávez's anti-neoliberal message and radical populist discourse, a series of "elite-outliers" keenly participated in the project of *bolivarianismo*. Business elites who voted for Chávez did so precisely because of their subordinate position within the old power bloc; from their point of view, a government dominated by Chávez's Movimiento V (Fifth) República (MVR) party would provide better prospects for state access (Gates 2010; cf. Brading 2014, 54).

While the new constitution introduced in 1999 formally reflected the contours of this somewhat delicate balance within the new hegemonic bloc—particularly articles 112 and 115 guaranteeing economic freedom and private property as well as central bank independence—it also stipulated a more expansive role for the state in the national economy (Orhangazi 2014, 223). Yet the introduction of constitutional reforms during the first two years of Chávez's administration pushed the integrity of this new power bloc to breaking point. While the pace of reform was relatively modest—maintaining private property, fiscal conservatism, and central bank independence—Chávez also passed forty-nine new laws in 2001, including the Organic Hydrocarbons Law, the Land Law, and the Fisheries Law (Webber 2010, 23–25). Much like the first Pérez administration, Chávez passed these laws by presidential decree, yet the content was not discussed within the National Assembly, nor even Chávez's own party.[2] Thus, from a relatively neutral position in 1999, Venezuelan capital quickly shifted into a mode of confrontation, particularly around the land law and the prospects of land expropriations (Brading 2014, 56).

Class Conflict and the Struggle for *Bolivarianismo*

Confrontation between the Bolivarian state and the old power bloc came to a head in December 2001. By this time, Venezuela's traditional ruling classes, outraged by the modest assault on their privilege, organized a business strike involving PDVSA, FEDECAMARAS (the national business association), and the CTV (Venezuela's largest union organization, heavily dominated by AD loyalists). The following year, this tripartite group staged another national strike, which quickly turned into an all-out coup. With the Venezuelan media claiming Chávez had "resigned," the leader of FEDECAMARAS, Pedro Carmona, proclaimed himself the interim president and dissolved the National Assembly and judiciary as a means of reinstating neoliberal policies. However, mass mobilizations among the chavista base, as well as loyal factions within the military, quickly restored Chávez to power (Cannon 2004, 295; Brading 2013, 70–74).

Within this tense political climate, Chávez attempted a reconciliation with the opposition, particularly through the rehiring of PDVSA managers responsible for the strike in 2001. Yet this was a risky gamble, as the oil company once again possessed a managerial cadre dedicated to bringing Chávez's political program to a halt. Now grouped under the name Coordinadora Democrática, the opposition pursued a strategy of sabotage significantly assisted by U.S. capital, itself working in close partnership with the U.S. state (Golinger 2007, 102–3). As a result of the 2002–2003 "bosses strike," around 24 percent of GDP and $6 billion in revenues had been lost (Weisbrot and Sandoval 2007; Webber 2010, 26). Soon enough, cracks within the opposition bloc were steadily widening due to a coordinated effort between the Bolivarian state and various sectors of skilled and unskilled workers to regain control over the national oil industry. Various workers inside PDVSA began to seize control of operations and collectively choose their own supervisors. Indeed, this conjuncture helped to push Chávez into a more radical stance and to usher in the Bolivarian Revolution as we know it today: a political project based on the idea of "socialism in the 21st century" (Brading 2014). After the dust had settled, Chávez fired over nineteen thousand personnel from PDVSA's ranks of managers and engineers involved in the bosses' strike in an effort to gain strategic control over the most vital part of the Venezuelan economy. Yet it was precisely due to the centrality of PDVSA that company bosses veered away from any type of worker self-management within the firm. Despite early examples of spontaneous worker control and self-management, particularly during the bosses' strike, the PDVSA leaders decided that such moves toward worker participation were unwise within a sector upon which the entire economy hinged (Ellner 2008, 162).

This moment of confrontation between capital and the state presents a crucial conjuncture in the political economy of chavismo. As a result of these class struggles across the entire strategic terrain of the Venezuelan state—from a bosses' strike to a failed military coup—Chávez turned to a policy of exchange controls in order to stem capital flight, through the creation of a new institution, Comisión de Administración de Divisas, or CADIVI (the institution was renamed Centro Nacional de Comercio Exterior, in 2014). Implementation of exchange controls, in combination with a windfall of oil dollars, led to a conscious policy of currency overvaluation for the purpose of subsidizing capital and consumption-good imports (Purcell 2013; Hellinger 2017). Venezuelan capitals could apply for cheap dollars (exchanged for their local currency, the bolivar, Bs) to import goods that, in theory, would contribute to national development. At the same time, the state created a series of new institutions that would establish direct lines of financial support to its social base. Through a change in the Venezuelan Central Bank's charter in 2005, Chávez began to directly appropriate a larger share of oil-rent via the newly created National Development Fund (FONDEN) under the discretional management of the executive branch. Receiving around $29 billion between 2005 and 2010, FONDEN provided much-needed financing for social policy, including the ALBA (Labaqui 2014, 35; Cusack 2019, 105).

Yet as a result of the government's strategic selectivity in policymaking, national development plans rarely produced the desired results. Venezuelan capitals would often acquire cheap dollars in the promise of importing essential goods, while simply overinvoicing or importing empty containers, a type of fraud that amounted to around 20 percent of all imports and roughly $20 billion in 2012 alone (Lampa 2017, 210; cf. Kornblihtt 2015, 66–67; Sutherland 2016a). More significant, however, has been the prevalence of capital flight among Venezuelan elites (both in the private and public sectors), at around $295–341 billion between 2003 and 2014, as they circumvented capital controls through loopholes in regulation over international financial investments (Sutherland 2016b, 53; Lampa 2017, 208). Consumption could also be diverted through rentier arbitrage, in which Venezuelan goods (particularly gasoline) were sold across the border in Colombia at a sizeable profit (given the difference in real value between the Colombian peso and the Venezuelan bolivar). Finally, the widespread practice of *bachaqueo*, or the hoarding and reselling of goods for the sake of price speculation, radically reduced the normal availability of consumption goods. Despite the diversity of these contradictions, they all stemmed from the same sources: state policy over the (mis)management of oil wealth and weak or corrupt regulatory institutions. Thus, while many of these practices could be seen under previous administrations, particularly the oil-dependent nature of capital accumulation and the advantages enjoyed by commercial fractions of national capital, these tendencies became particularly acute during the Chávez era.

From a Poulantzian perspective, the institutional materiality of the Bolivarian state reflected the contradictions of the Venezuelan power bloc. The political content of Chávez's Bolivarian project (seen primarily in the plebiscitary redrafting of the constitution) and the hostility of the old ruling class bloc led to the concentration of power within the executive branch, at the expense of more hostile factions of the state apparatus. In order to construct a hegemonic project based on the material satisfaction of the popular classes, social expenditure in Venezuela rose from 8.2 to 13.6 percent of GDP (1998–2006), with social security comprising the largest share (at 28 percent of the total by 2009) (Nakatani and Herrera 2008, 295; Kornblihtt 2015, 71). The only way to achieve these goals was to bypass the more recalcitrant fractions of the state, by establishing a direct line of support to the people.

Building the Social Economy

As a result of these class struggles across the strategic terrain of the state, Chávez embarked on a more far-reaching program of economic reform. In a televised address in 2003, he laid out his vision of the *economía social* (social economy) with the goal of moving beyond the destructive character of capitalist development: "The social economy bases its logic on the human being, on work, that is to say, on the worker and the worker's family . . . in the human being" (Chávez; cited in Lebowitz 2006, 101). Underlying this socialist philosophy was the formation of a new system of production and consumption mediated through the democratization of the means of production, principles that were later integrated into two of Venezuela's six-year plans (rbv 2007; rbv 2013). Perhaps more than any other ALBA state, Venezuela became one of the region's principal examples of worker control and self-management (*autogestión*), organized through the establishment of cooperatives and "social production companies" (Empresas de Producción Social).

By the time of Chávez's inauguration, there were 813 cooperatives in existence, one of the lowest numbers in Latin America. With the creation of a special law for cooperative associations in 2001, in which the process of starting a cooperative was significantly streamlined (and the benefits derived from cooperative status greatly enhanced), the number of registered cooperatives expanded rapidly. The national cooperative supervisory department (Sunacoop) registered around 262,904 cooperatives by the end of 2008 (Azzellini 2009, 172). The flowering of the cooperative movement was accompanied by the expansion of "communal councils" (*consejos comunales*, CCs), a form of popular power outlined within Chávez's "five motors" of revolutionary change, one of which referred to a "new geometry of power" in which political rights and territorial decentralization would help to facilitate new spaces of participation (Azzellini 2016, 87; see also Massey 2009; Menéndez 2013). While the CCs ultimately consolidated their institutional status and rapid expansion via the state (Azzellini 2016, 94), they also emerged spontaneously. In line with the general thrust of the Bolivarian constitution of 1999, the CCs and cooperatives maintained a direct line of support and financing from the state and its immediate apparatuses, rather than from the less trustworthy local authorities at the municipal level (96). Thus, the flowering of a cooperative movement throughout Venezuela reflected the underlying social values of the Bolivarian constitution, emphasizing the importance of human-centered development based on self-management, co-management, and cooperative production (article 70, rbv 1999).

However, as Sunacoop later reported, only seventy thousand cooperatives (around 27 percent) were legally certified, the remainder registered merely for the purposes of accessing state credit or tax avoidance (Azzellini 2009, 173; Rojas 2006). Of these cooperatives, only 25 percent engaged in productive activities (agriculture, livestock farming, fishing, manufacturing, industry), while 49.38 percent were in the service sector (tourism, cleaning, industrial maintenance, hairdressing, etc.); 11.48 percent in transport; and 7.64 percent in communal banking (Azzellini 2009, 173). As we will see more closely in chapter 4, agrarian cooperatives had a high rate of failure due to a lack of prior training and insufficient levels of knowledge exchange with more experienced peasant groups, while cooperative participants were often unaccustomed to arduous work and more inclined to resell the cooperative's productive assets on the market in an attempt to move back to urban centers with cash in hand (Page 2010; Lavelle 2016; Purcell 2017). Yet even when cooperatives were well organized internally, their relationship with the state was often strained, with frequent complaints on behalf of individuals within their communal councils concerning bureaucratic inefficiencies, lack of information, broken promises, and insufficient coordination between complex layers of state institutions (Azzellini 2015, 145; cf. Enríquez and Newman, 2015).

The larger, mostly industrial-scale "Social Production Companies," on the other hand, were envisioned as strategic spaces of the social economy, embedded not merely within national contexts but also throughout the wider regional terrain of the ALBA. It was thought that these companies would become the "standard bearer" of regional integration "from below" (El Troudi and Monedero 2006, 161–62). While these companies have seen a number of successful cases of worker control, many others continue to operate along traditional hierarchal structures of power and decision making typical of capitalist firms, which reproduces the divide between manual and intellectual labor (Kappeler 2013; Larrabure 2013). As we will see later, ALBA's production centers within Venezuela operate along these traditional workplace hierarchies, in contradiction with the underlying philosophy of the social economy.

The preceding analysis of class dynamics in Venezuelan and their politicoeconomic consequences form the contextual background for the analysis in chapters 4 and 5. But they also present a systemic contradiction that severely affects the overall political economy of the ALBA. For while these tendencies amount to a series of unintended outcomes of Chávez's anti-neoliberal drive, they inadvertently reproduce a type of "authoritarian statism" comparable to the first Pérez administration, despite the fact that the Bolivarian state is more firmly grounded in the dynamics of popular power.

Oil Diplomacy and the Emergence of a "Bolivarian" Foreign Policy

The struggle against neoliberal capitalism in Venezuela emerged not only at the national scale but through a concerted geopolitical strategy aimed at uniting the Latin American region around the wider principles of *bolivarianismo*. For Chávez, the immediate priorities for his multiscalar strategy—between nation and region—focused on shoring up the state's capture of oil wealth and consolidating Venezuela's international position as a buffer against further imperial aggression. The Bolivarian vision for international affairs centered on the idea of geopolitical "multipolarity," reflecting Latin America's long-standing norms of sovereign equality (rbv 2001b). One of the primary means through which Venezuela sought to forge a new system of international relations was through the deployment of its extraordinary oil wealth (Burges 2007, 1345). What truly consolidated this stance, however, was the confrontation with the U.S.-sponsored regional project, the FTAA. After the various international summits convened for FTAA negotiations, the strategic and spatial selectivity of the Bolivarian state began to crystallize around foreign policy and regional concerns, which significantly informed Chávez's early opposition to the FTAA negotiations during the third Summit of the Americas in April 2001 (Nelson 2015). As we saw in chapter 2, the numerous social movements that emerged during the 1990s had finally consolidated into a series of transnational networks whose discourse and activism significantly boosted the rationale for Chávez's anti-neoliberal regionalism. And yet, there were early signs that Chávez's appeals to the region's popular classes—essential to the radicalization of the ALBA bloc—were couched within a contradictory discourse.

In a series of conversations with the Latin American left-wing intellectual Marta Harnecker, Chávez explained the thinking and strategic rationale behind the formation of ALBA. Drawing upon military strategy from the Venezuela independence leader, Simón Bolívar, he noted how the immediate problem facing the postcolonial independence movement was the pressing need for political unity within the entire region in order to fend off external threats. Translated to the contemporary era, and in the context of uniting the peoples of Latin American under the ALBA banner, Chávez stated, "[Venezuela] as a country and as a proponent of the idea, it is our responsibility to move the idea forward through contacts with all the alternative movements in the continent and throughout the world: the World Social Forum, for example; alternative social movements in each country. We should figure out how to move forward and further develop the idea of [regional] integration" (Chávez; in Harnecker 2005, 121). Yet the strategic priority of political unity among states and peoples was cast in a peculiar (military) light. The analogy chosen was that of the "artillery" in the rear and the "cavalry" at the front:

> What do I mean by that? You know that in war the cavalry is in the front. Who has ever seen the cavalry as the rear guard? It is always the artillery that is the rear guard: the big heavy cannons that shoot from long distance. I buy my ar-

tillery with the economy; the cavalry with politics. So, as a result of the neoliberal model, we have the equation backwards: the horses are in the rear and the big and small cannons in the front. We have to invert it. We have to retake politics. It requires that statesmen, politicians with a grand vision, begin making the decisions. (Chávez; in Harnecker 2005, 122)

The struggle against neoliberal hegemony was therefore premised on the repoliticization of the economy—of bringing the "cavalry" to the front—while the artillery of the state would be paid for through economic (oil) revenue. But the question remained as to where the actual locus of political power and decision making was to reside. This question, in turn, remained at the heart of the regionalization of popular power across the ALBA.

ALBA's Council of Social Movements

From the start, the ALBA space was infused with the norms of popular participation as a key driver of the region-building process. According to Ruben Pereira, coordinator of the Council of Social Movements in the Executive Secretariat of the ALBA headquarters in Caracas, "there is no international organization that has called out to the social movements and collectives to be incorporated into the organizational structure relating to the mechanisms of regional integration" (interview, RP Caracas, April 5, 2016). During the 2006 WSF in Caracas, Chávez extolled the strategic virtues of forging a stronger partnership among states and social movements: "We have to link up all our causes, unity, unity, unity, movements united respecting diversity, respecting the autonomy, no one is planning to impose anything on anyone, only coordination, unity, because if we don't work together we will never triumph." (Chávez; cited in Martinez 2013, 63). In the subsequent year, ALBA declared the formal creation of the Council of Social Movements (Movimientos Sociales del ALBA 2009; see figure 1). During a parallel session at the summit, a wide collection of social movements from across the continent affirmed their official alliance with the ALBA institution. As well as emphasizing the struggle for women's rights, environmental protection, and food sovereignty (to name just a few issues), the convened group of social movement representatives called for their concrete participation within ALBA, which would "permit the achievement of participatory and protagonistic democracy in accordance with socially organized popular interests" (Movimientos Sociales del ALBA 2007).

A year after the initial meeting in 2007, at the fourth summit of the ALBA,

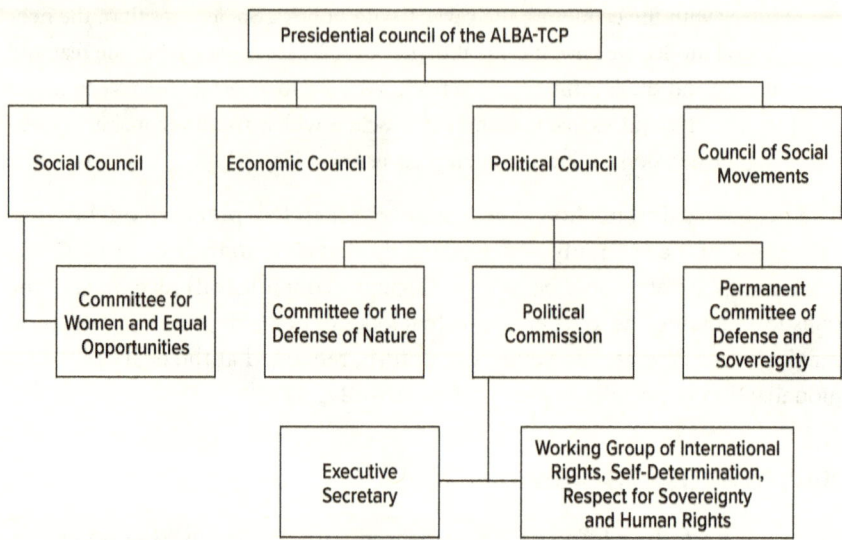

FIGURE 1. Institutional structure of the ALBA as of 2009.
SOURCE: ALBA-TCP (2010a, 127) (author's elaboration and translation).

social movements were given only a brief acknowledgement, without any sustained proposals for their further incorporation (ALBA-TCP 2008b). Due to the slow pace of institutional change, the Brazilian peasant movement Movimento dos Trabalhadores Rurais Sem Terra, LVCs, and other assorted groups proposed a parallel initiative in July 2008, embodied in "a hemispheric articulation of social movements and organizations around the principles of ALBA" (Movimientos Sociales del ALBA 2009). From this meeting came the final crafting of the Charter of Social Movements of the Americas, announced during the Third Social Forum of the Americas (October 2008), which was conceived as the struggle for "building the integration of peoples form below" (Movimientos Sociales del ALBA, 2008). At the first summit meeting of the Intercultural Plurinational Council of Social Movements of the Countries of the ALBA in October 2009, it was acknowledged that due to "realities and challenges that some member countries have experienced," as well as the influence of "other priorities and efforts within the ALBA-TCP," there had been a relative brake on the process of forging the CSM within the architecture of ALBA since 2008 (Movimientos Sociales del ALBA, 2009).

By the time of ALBA's tenth summit in 2010, the CSM was still framed as more of a proposal rather than an institutional reality. As noted in the Bicentenary Manifesto of Caracas, the time has come to install the Council of Social Movements. This entails establishing national Chapters in each country and that social movements assume, as propose, not only sector struggles of the working class, peasants, women, youth, etc., but that they also move forward and join the development of economic and social projects for the specific construction of alternatives to the predatory capitalism existing in our continent. (ALBA-TCP 2010b)

Three years later, during an ALBA social movement summit, the collective statement noted that "integration of peoples and for the peoples . . . requires the redesigning of the decision-making bodies. . . . We urge, therefore, to move forward with a full and organic incorporation of People's Power in the decision-making process of ALBA" (ALBA-TCP 2013).

The relatively slow and uneven progress in the formation of the CSM speaks to its complex spatial organization. Operating at multiple scales, the CSM is grounded in a series of national "chapters" (across ALBA and non-ALBA countries), through which various movements from different sectors (peasants, environmental groups, women's groups, etc.) put forward proposals to "spokespersons" (voceros) who channel these demands toward higher levels. In the case of Venezuela, the first steps toward the formation of the national chapter began in 2009, in partnership with ALBA's executive secretariat and officially established in 2011 (interview, RP Caracas, April 5, 2016; cf. Martinez 2013, 70). Social movements within the CSM thus embody a "double turn" in the construction of a new form of popular hegemony, which seeks to actively engage with (and eventually transform) traditional structures of state power, as well as to construct autonomous, transnational networks of social movement identity, consciousness, and strategy (Martinez 2013, 70; cf. Gürcan 2010; Emerson 2013).

The double turn of social movement hegemony strongly converges with Poulantzas's thoughts on the democratic road to socialism: "If they are to modify the relations of power, such struggles or movements cannot tend towards centralization in a second power; they must rather seek to shift the relationship of forces on the terrain of the state itself. This then is the real alternative, and not the simple opposition between 'internal' and 'external' struggle. In the democratic road to socialism, these two forms of struggle must be combined" (2014, 260). While the importance of, and proposal for, the CSM was understood early on, it would take many years, and as many summits, for this idea to take any kind of shape; as one member of a prominent Venezuelan peasant movement noted, the independent organization of social movements has achieved far more than any ministerial meeting (interview, FNCEZ Barinas, July 18, 2015). Despite formalizing the CSM's role during the ninth summit in 2009, direct relations between movements ALBA's core institutions (mainly at the political/ministerial level) remain quite ambiguous. As the Caracas-based activist Ambar García expressed to me, although the CSM occupies the second highest level within the hierarchy of ALBA, the idea that the CSM should wield substantial decision-making powers was never firmly entrenched at the elite level (interview, ALBA TV Caracas, June 20, 2016). This tension between the CSM and the Presidential Council within ALBA has been duly noted elsewhere (see Aguirre and Cooper 2010; Cutler and Brien 2013; Martinez 2013; Stevenson 2014; López and Lo Brutto 2016). Suffice to say, the deficit in decision-making powers among social movements speaks to the separation between manual and intellectual labor within the institutional materiality of the ALBA. To better understand how this takes place within the context of food sovereignty, the remainder of the chapter examines ALBA's development discourse and the institutional materiality through which it takes shape, particularly through the Grandnational Concept and Grandnational Enterprises.

The Grandnational Concept: Regionalizing the Social Economy

While Grandnational Projects (GNPs) and Grandnational Enterprises (GNEs) were first announced during the fifth ALBA summit in 2007 (ALBA-TCP 2007), it was in the subsequent year, during the sixth regional summit, held in Caracas, that a new productivist paradigm was declared under the label of "Conceptualization of Grandnational Projects and Enterprises in the Framework of ALBA" (ALBA-TCP 2008c). The new vision for regional development sought to give shape to its earliest aspirations to satisfying human need: "Trade and investment cannot be conceived as ends in themselves, but instruments to reach a just and sustainable development" (ALBA, 2004). As with previous regionalization projects during the postwar period, this regional development model aimed to pool the collective strength of its member countries in order to fend off geopolitical pressure from the "big industrialized powers and the hegemonic, economic [regional] blocs" (ALBA-TCP 2008c). By and large, the Grandnational Concept can be divided into two broad areas that correspond to the dimensions of *trade* ("cooperative advantage" and a regional "map of goods") and *production* ("endogenous development"). But the particularities of their implementation would lead to uneven and unanticipated results.

COOPERATIVE ADVANTAGE AND THE NEW MAP OF GOODS

The idea of "cooperative advantage" stands in marked contrast to the central trade theory of (neo)classical political economy (comparative advantage), in which free trade among nations will lead to an idealized equilibrium between all participants. Yet the reality of international trade, as clearly recognized by the ALBA institution, operates according to *competitive* advantage, in which the uneven development of capitalism forms geographically concentrated clusters of capital and technical advances that tend toward the reproduction of trade imbalances (Shaikh 2007). Thus, ALBA's trade philosophy focuses less on the accumulation of capital for its own sake and more on the enhancement of trade cooperation and socioeconomic well-being (Muhr 2010; Costoya 2011; Broadhead and Morrison 2012; Pearce 2013; Gürcan and Bakiner 2015). During the 2009 Cuba-Venezuela Mixed Commission meeting, Chávez laid out his vision for the operation of ALBA's cooperative advantage, with "the creation of the map of goods [*el mapa de las mercancías*] to advance toward new forms of production, complementarities and trade among nations" (Chávez; cited in Aponte-García 2011, 182). This "map of goods" is shaped by two strategic dimensions. Firstly, GNE's are structured by "sustainable value chains," which can be broadly understood through politically established regulatory structures, civil society involvement, local institutional factors, and societal values (Aponte-García 201, 186; see also FAO 2014). Secondly, the political economy of GNEs approximates a kind of "strategic regionalism" in which the map of goods promotes political harmony, cultural exchange, regional social policy, and the participation of a variety of social actors (Aponte-García 2011, 186).

The combination of sustainable value chains and strategic regionalism places ALBA somewhere "between capitalism and twenty-first century socialism," reflecting the underlying diversity of property rights, ranging from large private firms to nationalized industries and local cooperative enterprises (Aponte-García 2011, 187, 188; see also ALBA-TCP 2008c). Yet despite the range of property forms within any given Grandnational chain, it is the state itself that *organizes* both upstream and downstream components. The first decade of intra-ALBA trade was substantial, almost doubling from $5 billion (2000–2004) to $9bn (2005–2009). The biggest share of trade expansion was in the ALBA-Food Grandnational, rising from 12 to 32 percent of the total (Aponte-García 2011, 193). When we break down the Grandnational production chain (see table 4), intermediate processing was by far the most significant (89 per-

TABLE 4. Intra-ALBA trade in food, by economic category, to analyse regional production chain potentials. Subperiod 2005–2011, in U.S. dollars at constant prices (2005=100)

Member & Country of ALBA	Consumption	Intermediate Processing	Primary	Total
Antigua and Barbuda	16,786	494,647	57,266	568,698
Bolivia	37,240	1,192,735,298	13,507,433	1,206,279,971
Cuba	3,069,251	2,876,060	849,518	6,794,828
Dominica	272,784	1,245,315	15,865,299	17,383,398
Ecuador	3,396,363	1,048,117,340	127,189,030	1,178,702,733
Nicaragua	33,559	419,039,968	182,235,867	601,309,394
Saint Vincent/Grenadines	8,373	22,339,251	1,236,076	23,583,700
Venezuela	552,954	18,334,602	1,327,305	20,214,861
TOTAL	7,387,308	2,705,182,481	342,267,793	3,054,837,583

SOURCE: Aponte-García (2014, 243–4).

cent of total value), which contributed toward regional productive capacity and employment growth (Aponte-García 2014, 243). In line with ALBA states' differential needs and capacities—particularly Venezuela's high demand for food imports and predominant shares of agricultural exports among Nicaragua, Bolivia, and Ecuador—intra-ALBA trade tended toward the allocation of Venezuela's purchasing power to higher-value products of Nicaragua, Bolivia, and Ecuador (figure 2). Exports to Venezuela from its ALBA partners have seen a significant rise since the inauguration of the Food Grandnational, at least for Nicaragua and Ecuador (figure 3). Bolivia's much lower share is likely due to the overwhelming presence of soy and its derivative products in the country's export sector, primarily used for animal feed destined to Argentina and Brazil (Bolivia's two largest export markets) (cf. McKay 2018, 418). By 2014 Venezuela's imports from ALBA states entered a protracted decline as a result of the drop in oil revenues and the subsequent economic crisis.

This map of goods within the food sector thus corresponds to particular development drivers grounded within specific states (Hart-Landsberg 2013, 197), for example, medical services from Cuba, energy products from Venezuela, and food goods from Ecuador and Nicaragua. However, further expansion of intra-ALBA trade has been limited by a number of organizational problems. In 2009, when ALBA launched the second iteration of its Peoples' Trade Treaty (Tratado de Comercio de los Pueblos, TCP), a Working Group on Commercial Complementarity convened an initial meeting to hash out the details for trade negotiations to be held the following year. Yet these negotiations never materialized, due to lack of agreement over the parameters of the treaty (Cusack 2019, 102). A further complication emerged from the unique

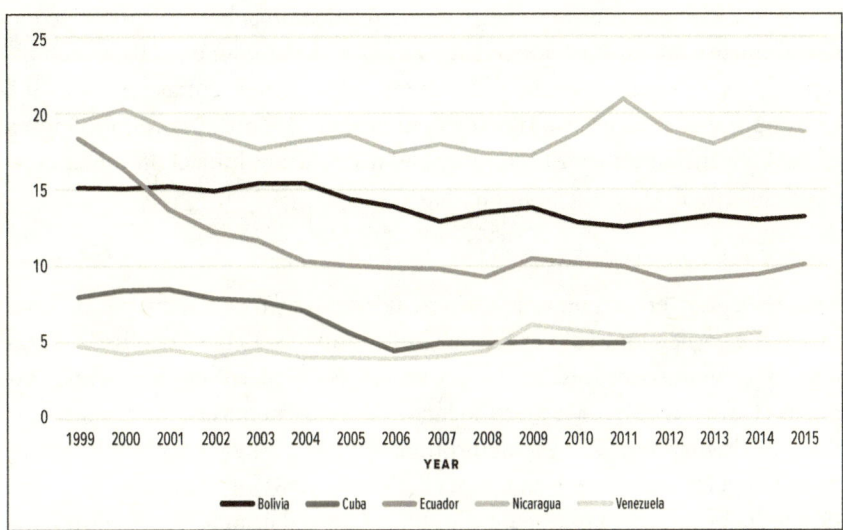

FIGURE 2. Agriculture, value added (percent of GDP), selected ALBA states.
SOURCE: World Bank

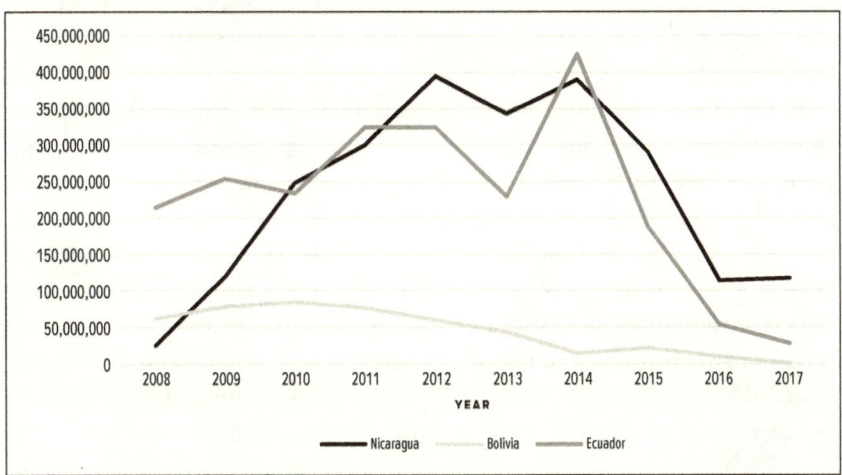

FIGURE 3. Selected ALBA food exporters to Venezuela (current US$).
SOURCE: UN Comtrade.

features of Venezuela's political economy, particularly the currency regime administered by CADIVI. The relative inefficiency in distributing hard currency to foreign export partners (e.g., Ecuador) resulted in a virtual nontariff barrier for exporters, insofar as Venezuelan producers maintained unencumbered access to Ecuadorian markets while Ecuadorian producers encountered long delays in their receipt of payment. These organizational bottlenecks served to delegitimize intra-ALBA trade in the minds of Ecuadorian officials, which ultimately informed their decision to renew the free-trade agreement with the Community of Andean Nations regional bloc (113). Thus, the contradictions of the Venezuelan state and economy had a significant impact on the uneven development of ALBA's regional trade.

ENDOGENOUS DEVELOPMENT

The concept of "endogenous development" (*desarrollo endógeno*) has become one of the cornerstones of Venezuela's Bolivarian development policy. Emerging from the postwar intellectual revolt against Western development paradigms (Gudynas 2013, 19–20), endogenous development was oriented around the holistic mapping of natural and human resources via collaborative relations between states and stakeholders (Perroux 1983). In breaking from the ISI model of "inward-looking development" geared around production/consumption patterns in the Global North, endogenous development established a type of "development from within" through cultivating strategic sectors (heavy industry, machinery/engineering, petrochemicals, and infrastructure), satisfying much broader domestic consumption, and focusing on regional and global exports (Sunkel 1993, 46–47).

While this development model significantly shaped Venezuela's wider economic policies, principally embodied within the first six-year plan (rbv 2001b), these ideas have come to encapsulate the underlying rationale for ALBA's regional development. The Eleventh ALBA Summit in Caracas, 2012, launched the "Economic Space of the ALBA-TCP (ECOALBA-TCP)," which outlined three strategic objectives of the GNEs. Firstly, ALBA aimed to insulate itself from the competitive pressures of the capitalist world market, via a "shared-development process under the perspective of a bloc and not as a mere aggregation of individual countries, which will also allow its international positioning" (article 1.1, ALBA-TCP 2012). Secondly, in order to undermine the "export or die premise," the development of productivity and economic diversification prioritizes the internal satisfaction of each state's development goals, based on diversification and the "integral growth of all sectors"—favoring domestic consumption and "exporting surpluses in a complementary fashion" (article 2.4). Finally, ALBA states will seek to support these goals through consolidation of their technological frontiers, through the cooperative exchange of research, innovation, and development (Article 2.3).

Within ALBA's vision of endogenous development emerges a complementary approach to *agroecology*, which strongly resonates with the central tenet of sustainable development within food sovereignty politics. In seeking to mend the "metabolic rift" generated by capitalist production (Foster 2000), food sovereignty actors nurture a form of "agrarian citizenship" as a "dialectical negotiation between nature, state, and society" (Wittman 2009, 820). These two components of the metabolic rift (ecology and labor) converge with ALBA's Grandnational Concept and its approach to endogenous development, with the aim of "executing environmentally sustainable projects, [and] promoting conditions for decent employment and equitable distribution of wealth" (ALBA-TCP 2008c). Additionally, the ECOALBA space aimed to foster "the equitable distribution of wealth and the *socialization of the means of production* [which] constitute two powerful tools to ensure social justice and the progress of our societies and economic systems" (ALBA-TCP 2012, emphasis added).

While ALBA's vision of regional development put forth an ambitious and radical approach to human-centered development, its concrete implementation has encountered a series of obstacles. Rather than fostering a regionwide shift toward agroecology, the prevailing accumulation regime within ALBA states has favored large-scale agro-extractivism. As we will see in the following chapter, while the politics of food sovereignty has been significantly *regionalized* over the past decade (particularly through the formation of regional networks of agroecological knowledge exchange and education), these initiatives face stiff barriers to a substantial "scaling up" of sustainable agrarian production. Indeed, the regionalization of food sovereignty largely takes place through autonomous peasant movements working across national borders, in relative separation from the institutional framework of the ALBA. Finally, as we will see further in chapter 5, the concrete social relations within the ALBA-Arroz factory network in Venezuela have not adhered to ALBA's goal of socializing the means of production for the purpose of fostering social equality and political empowerment. Rather, the ALBA factories remained trapped within traditional workplace hierarchies managed by chavista apparatchiks.

The Institutional Materiality of ALBA: A Strategic-Relational View

From their inception, Grandnational Enterprises were modeled on contemporary transnational firms. As Chávez noted with respect to the formation of the ALBA-Food GNE, "We are going to create a supranational company, like a transnational company, but in this case with the concept of a great nation, to produce food with the goal of guaranteeing food sovereignty to our people" (cited in Suggett, 2009a). Yet there is some ambiguity in exactly how GNEs function and the organizational form they assume (Califano 2015, 123). On the one hand, there is the Mixed Socialist Enterprise of ALBA (Empresa Mixta Socialista del ALBA-EMSA), established as a single production center (or factory system) confined to a single national territory. As a bilateral investment among ALBA states, the ownership structure is legally prescribed through majority ownership (51 percent) assumed by the host country, with the participating country holding the remainder (49 percent) (Solórzano Cavalieri, 2012, 146).

On the other hand, there is the transnational GNE, with production chains spanning across member states. And yet, to date, there is no transnational GNE within ALBA. The only multilateral investment project in the ALBA-Food Grandnational was the Soy Processing Plant "Eulalia Ramos" in Venezuela, established through an agreement between Venezuela, Cuba, and Bolivia (*El Universal* 2007). The plant was created to supply flavored soy milk to Venezuelan schools in the federated states of Anzoátegui, Monagas, Guárico, Sucre, and Bolívar (as well as through state-run distribution channels of Mercal and the Casas de Alimentación), with soy processing technology imported from Cuba and Argentina. However, by August 2012, several workers at the plant had chained themselves to the fence, demanding a response from the state-run Venezuelan Food Corporation (La Corporación Venezolana de Alimentos, CVAL) over the payment of owed wages in the context of the company's immanent liquidation. With banners showing the image of Chávez, the workers made clear that they were not antigovernment protesters but were strictly concerned with defending "labor rights" (Fernández 2012). Jesús Paraqueima, National Assembly candidate of the Venezuela Socialist Party in Anzoátegui, similarly denounced the sudden and "clandestine" dismantling and transferal of the plant from Anzoátegui to Guárico (*Noticias de Venezuela* 2012). Yet rather than moving operations to another state, ownership of the factory was simply transferred from CVAL to the state-run firm Empresa Integral Agrária José Inácio de Abreu e Lima SA and production was changed toward the processing of animal feed (MPPAT 2013, 804–5). As a result of this transfer, it is unclear whether Bolivia and Cuba still own a portion of the company or if they received any material benefit from their investment.

One of the few EMSAs located outside Venezuela is in Bolivia. The bilateral agreement to establish a Food Grandnational, signed into each state's respective national legislation in 2011, aimed to invest in a number of agricultural goods, including soy, corn, and rice, with the intention of constructing industrial processing centers for exporting soy-based oil products to Venezuela (*América Economica*, 2011; *Gaceta Oficial* 2011). By May 2013 the status of the company was still in the diplomatic stage, with official declarations but little evidence of its creation; the following October, it was announced that all necessary steps had been taken for the final realization of the firm (*El Mundo* 2013; *La Razón* 2013). Nevertheless, the initiative was never heard of again.

Perhaps the most curious ALBA food company is the ALBA de Nicaragua, S.A. (ALBANISA). More than simply an EMSA or even a regional Grandnational Enterprise, ALBANISA is a bilaterally owned corporate entity, held between Venezuela's PDVSA (51 percent share) and a Nicaraguan state-owned company, PETRONIC (49 percent). The firm mediates oil imports from PDVSA, which are then resold at a profit in Nicaragua at market prices. Rather than pay the entire import bill, Nicaragua redirects 50 percent of the bill toward the ALBA Caruna (Caja Rural Nacional), a privately owned financial cooperative that receives funds as a "loan" from PDVSA (payable over twenty-five years, with a two-year grace period, 2 percent interest, and 30 percent grant element) (IMF 2013, 15). The remainder of this loan is then split again, between direct cash repayment to PDVSA, or repayment in kind. The latter must be directed through the ALBA Alimentos de Nicaragua, a joint venture between ALBANISA and PDVSA, which purchases goods from Nicaraguan farmers and resells them within the Venezuelan market (IMF 2013, 15). According to one Nicaraguan government paper, Venezuela became Nicaragua's second largest import partner for food goods in 2010 (only behind the United States), to the tune of $248.8 million. ALBA Caruna has also financed 47,530 small and medium-sized farmers amounting to around $1.4 billion (DRIP 2012).

Yet, ALBANISA's institutional operation is remarkably opaque. Perhaps the most notable aspect of ALBANISA is its freedom from oversight or external regulation. Somewhat mimicking the institutional structure of the Bolivarian state, ALBANISA's proceeds do not go to the national treasury but remain within its own private account controlled directly by President Daniel Ortega and his close inner circle. As with Venezuelan institutions such FONDEN, the relative separation of this account from other branches of the Nicaraguan state apparatus was largely in response to opposition hostility to social projects funded through ALBANISA (Perla and Cruz-Feliciano 2013). Nevertheless, this arrangement also lends itself to possible forms of bureaucratic corruption, amounting to "a slush fund of $200 million a year, unaudited and unsupervised by the FSLN [party] or the state" (La Botz 2016, 321). The little evidence that does exist makes for a troubling picture. In 2015 ALBANISA's president and vice president noted that the company was holding $189.3 million of Venezuelan debt, due to PDVSA's reneged delivery of promised oil.

Given that ALBANISA always pays its national producers promptly, the company's outstanding debt remains unresolved in the absence of Venezuelan's cooperation (Olivares 2015). Overall, food sovereignty practice does not seem to share much connection with this ALBA initiative. Nicaragua's food exports through ALBANISA (particularly beef, sugar, and coffee beans) are mostly reliant on a small number of large private firms capturing the majority of value-added from processing to the detriment of small or medium-sized suppliers (Michelutti 2012, 6; cf. Martí i Puig and Baumeister 2017). Given the preference toward large-scale producers, it is likely that farm-gate prices for small-scale campesinos are cripplingly low; indeed, many small-scale cooperatives struggle to meet the level of demand generated from purchases across the ALBANISA complex. Thus, state support for Nicaraguan farmers tends to amount to low-interest credit lines in order to invest in productivity, rather than high farm-gate prices (Carrión 2017, 27, 34).

All other EMSAs are located in Venezuela, under the auspices of CVAL, and oriented toward the production of rice, legumes, pork, chicken, fish, and dairy (*Gaceta Oficial* 2010b).[3] Contrary to Chávez's aim to construct a truly "transnational" food company within ALBA, the entire thrust of endogenous development has been effectively *nationalized*, geared toward satisfying the internal consumption needs of Venezuela, with little productive participation from member states.

As I argued in chapter 1, we can better understand the complexities of ALBA's regional development policy by unpacking the relationship between its accumulation regime, mode of regulation, and hegemonic project, which together articulate the processes of material production, institutional construction, and ideological legitimation. Firstly, ALBA's regional *accumulation regime* is dominated by "extractivism," which is heavily integrated into the global division of labor and thus exerts a centrifugal force upon the internal integration of the bloc (Purcell 2016; Vergara-Camus and Kay 2017). This should not be seen in an economically reductionist sense, as if selling abroad automatically undermines regional cohesion. Indeed, the longevity of ALBA would remain seriously in question if its member states *did not* accumulate foreign exchange from extraregional markets. Rather, the forces pulling ALBA in different directions stem from the institutional materiality of *global governance* and the differential integration of member states into specific governance regimes. For instance, one of the principal obstacles to the consolidation of an intraregional trade regime is the simultaneous subsumption of ALBA's states under WTO trade rules and other free trade agreements. While this does not present an absolute limit to regional cooperation, the TCP would have to take on board a much stronger and institutionally binding set of trade rules (Cusack 2019, 96). As one Ecuadorian official noted, "we [ALBA] haven't constructed models of economic and productive complementarity. We don't know how to enhance our capacity jointly, in terms of resources, industrial development... If you want to do an FTA [free trade agreement] everything's ready" (cited in Cusack 2019, 111). Thus, ALBA's pursuit of a more endogenous form of regional development was hampered by a significant level of risk and uncertainty in the absence of more robust regional planning.

Secondly, this shallow institutionalization is a function of ALBA's *mode of regulation*, a result of both the regional accumulation regime *and* the contradictory projection of Venezuela's *national* accumulation regime/mode of regulation onto the regional scale. As noted previously, the operation of ALBA is heavily shaped by Venezuela's oil-based accumulation regime and thus the magnitude of ground rent (as well as the volume of oil) available for regional projects. ALBA's social missions, such as the Venezuela-Cuba oil for doctors program (Barrio Adentro), the far-reaching literacy and health programs (SELA 2013; cf. Artaraz 2011; Muhr 2011), or the Empresas Mixtas Socialistas del ALBA located in Venezuela, were largely dependent on flows of oil (as a direct means of payment) or flows of ground rent (as the valorization of oil in the world market) for their survival. Consequently, the institutional materiality of the ALBA bloc tended to reflect the materiality of the Venezuelan state itself. As we saw at the beginning of this chapter, the Bolivarian state has seen the effective consolidation of power within the executive branch relative to other apparatuses of the state, reminiscent of Poulantzas's notion of "authoritarian statism," though paradoxically one that is embedded in grassroots popular power (Poulantzas 2014, 203–16; Azzellini 2016). Given Venezuela's centrality within ALBA, its institutional materiality was projected onto the regional scale, with "abundant proposals, limited and unstable human resources, multi-agency participation with unclear responsibility, infrequent and irregular oversight, weak accountability, and shallow planning" (Cusack 2019, 39). Despite appeals from Bolivian and Ecuadorian officials for greater consolidation and consistency in policymaking, these requests were never headed by their Venezuelan counterparts (108).

Finally, the specificities of ALBA's accumulation regime and mode of regulation should be read through the prism of its hegemonic project. By and large, ALBA established its raison d'être in the quest for greater regional autonomy from the pressures of U.S.-led neoliberal globalism (ALBA 2004). As such, the discourse of *sovereignty* has occupied a central place in ALBA's legitimation.

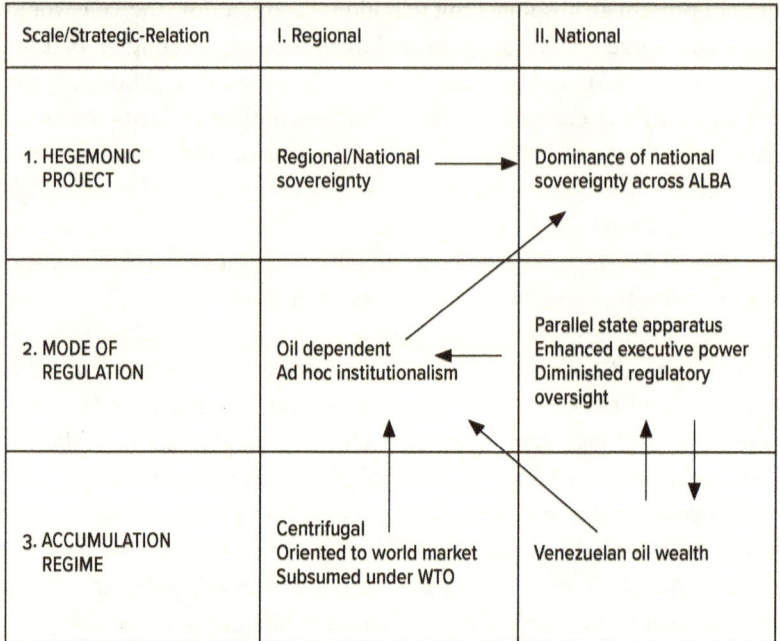

FIGURE 4. Strategic-relational view of ALBA. Author's elaboration.

Yet with declarations exhorting the reclamation of "National and Regional Sovereignty" (ALBA-TCP 2008c), it was never clear how this multiscalar sovereignty would function. In the end, national sovereignty overdetermined the process of regional organization, partly due to the dictates of *endogenous development* but also due to a lack of institutional consolidation and rulemaking at the regional scale (cf. Grugel and Riggirozzi 2012, 15; ALBA-TCP 2012, articles 2.2, 2.6).

This strategic-relational analysis of ALBA has been summarized in figure 4. Clearly, the relations between ALBA's accumulation regime, mode of regulation, and hegemonic project, as well as the lines of political force between its different scales, encompass a complex picture of region-building. There is no linear relationship between a strategic relational element or scalar level (Brand, Görg, and Wisson 2011, 162–63). For instance, Venezuela's accumulation regime and mode of regulation (see cells 3.II, 2.II in figure 4) are mutually reinforcing; as we will see in chapter 5, the magnitude of ground rent does not determine the precise nature of policy (mode of regulation) but rather sets the limits of possibility for a spectrum of policymaking (*strategic selectivity*). Additionally, cell 2.II refers only to Venezuela, in order to narrow down the dominant determinations acting upon the rest of the ALBA space (i.e., all other national modes of regulation within ALBA states exert a negligible effect on the regional scale).

This strategic relational view helps to explain why ALBA's Food Grandnationals exist as a series of nationally constituted factories within Venezuela. In the realm of food policy, the spatial and strategic selectivity of ALBA would gravitate toward Venezuela as a site of investment and agrarian development—relatively import-dependent and with abundant investment funds at its disposal, the Bolivarian state would naturally remain the centerpiece of ALBA's food policies. But this on its own does not explain the failure to maintain other Grandnational projects. Rather, the limits of regional policymaking stem from the lack of organization necessary for brining Chávez's original vision of a transnational company to life, by linking together its member states in cooperative complementarity. And while the ALBANISA complex remains the only food initiative outside of Venezuela, its institutional structure and operation sits uneasily with goals of food sovereignty, as we will see in the next chapter.

In light of the centrality of Venezuelan rentierism, and its specific mode of regulation, in the operation of ALBA, one might say that ALBA itself has taken the form of a "magical region"—festooned with endless declarations and development projects among ALBA's leaders, yet strategically disorganized. The distribution of ground rent tends toward the production of a "spectacle" rather than concrete policy. This is not to say that ALBA's development goals are entirely ephemeral. Rather, the gap between rhetoric and reality can only be accounted for by a relative dissonance created by the power accorded to an accumulation regime underwritten by the capture of extraordinary wealth and a mode of regulation that often works against the organization of the region's wealth in the goal of satisfying regional development goals.

Conclusion

This chapter has analyzed the historical and social sources of ALBA's institutional materiality. From a historical point of view, it is near-impossible to sufficiently understand the antecedents of the ALBA regional space without further exploring the lineaments of the Venezuelan state. Casting a long shadow over the processes of state formation, the production of oil has significantly shaped both the class structures and political discourses constitutive of this "magical state." Under the Bolivarian state, the expansion of state power, particularly concentrated in the executive branch, reflected a peculiar type of "authoritarian statism," which differed substantially from Pérez's initial transformation. Chávez's Fifth Republic saw the strong state tethered to an altered terrain of decentralized political spaces conducive to protagonistic democracy. Combining the strong state with the flowering of popular democracy therefore set the scene for the slow but steady emergence of ALBA's underlying strategic and spatial selectivities.

Our examination of ALBA focused on two specific dimensions that directly relate to the remaining chapters of this book: state-social movement relations embodied within the Council of Social Movements and the political economy of ALBA's Grandnational Concept. While the CSM was a truly novel feature of ALBA's regional project, there remains a marked imbalance between the CSM and the centers of regional policymaking. The political economy of ALBA and its development philosophy in the form of the Grandnational Concept were always heavily shaped by Venezuela's push toward the social economy. In the case of the agricultural sector, cooperative advantage and the new map of goods sought to identify not only the mode of exchange but also a select number of agricultural products around which the new trade regime would be oriented. Yet the contradictory position occupied by some ALBA states with respect to the world market and alternative trade regimes, as well as the underdeveloped institutional capacity of the TCP, has resulted in a relatively small level of trade between member states. The effort to incorporate "endogenous development" within a regionwide production platform was significantly shaped by ALBA's strategic and spatial selectivity, resulting from a complex articulation between its accumulation regime, mode of regulation, and hegemonic project, all of which congeals into the reassertion of *raison d'état*.

As a result of ALBA's particular institutional materiality, the politics of food sovereignty across the ALBA space has remained relatively fragmented, with peasant-led struggles largely concentrated within national contexts. As we will see in the next chapter, one reason for this fragmentation stems from the strategic necessity of confronting the duality of modern sovereignty, condensed within spaces of capitalist production and the capitalist state itself. And yet, the specific balance of class forces within each national context tends to limit the degree to which peasant movements are capable of pushing state institutions toward satisfying their collective demands. As with the ALBA's Council of Social Movements, peasant movements have been kept at a critical distance from the centers of state decision making. As they confronted formidable obstacles at the domestic level, the prospects for scaling up food sovereignty to the regional level became ever distant.

CHAPTER 4

Spaces of Agrarian Struggle

Rights, Territory, and Food Sovereignty in ALBA

Attempting to speak of food sovereignty within the ALBA regional space poses certain challenges. As FS scholars have long pointed out, no two peasant movements are alike, which presents a relative obstacle to forging "unity in diversity" (Desmarais 2007; Desmarais and Wittman 2014; Alonso-Fradejas et al. 2015). Of course, rural communities and movements possess a variety of shared customs, norms, discourses, and organizational strategies, similarities that may stretch across national or even regional scales. Yet a closer look at the diversity of experiences among ALBA states helps bring into focus the contingent and place-specific nature of FS politics.

At one end of the spectrum is Cuba, arguably the most radical example among ALBA states in its pursuit of land reform and the promotion of agroecological farming techniques (Wilson 2016). With the collapse of the Soviet Union in 1991, Cuba lost a significant trade partner in agricultural inputs. The continued U.S. trade embargo (in place since 1958) further prevented the acquisition of key materials from the world market. Facing a reduction of imports for conventional inputs, as well as the numerous ecological consequences of large-scale industrial agriculture, Cuba's peasant organizations, grouped under the National Association of Small Farmers (ANAP), spearheaded the transition to low-input agroecological farming; by 2009, some 60 percent of farmland operated through low external inputs, expanded use of biopesticides, and diversified cropping systems (Reardon and Pérez 2010, 916). Despite these achievements, Cuba remains relatively import-dependent, particularly in terms of cereals, legumes, and meat (Altieri and Funes-Monzote 2012; Costa, Sousa, and Sorzano 2013). While the Cuban state has not passed legislation referring to "food sovereignty," the transformation of the national food system has nevertheless engendered substantive "indicators of food sovereignty" (Reardon and Pérez 2010), through a number of decree laws pertaining to redistribution of state lands for usufruct rights (*Decreto Ley 259*, 2008, 300) as well as the creation of nonagricultural cooperatives engaged in the management of local markets and food distribution networks (*Decreto Ley 305*, 2012, 309). The example of Cuba thus presents a significant (albeit ongoing) transition toward substantial forms of FS politics.

At the other end of the spectrum lies the wider Caribbean subregion, making up a large segment of ALBA's membership (Antigua and Barbuda, Dominica, Grenada, Saint Kitts and Nevis, Saint Lucia, and Saint Vincent and the Grenadines). The paucity of food sovereignty initiatives in the Caribbean speaks to the legacy of colonial agriculture across the subregion. Instead of a preexisting Indigenous peasant culture, subaltern classes "emerg[ed] from diverse experiences on the margins of European colonial enterprise—as squatters, early yeomen, proto-peasantry, deserters or runaways" (Thompson 2019, 96). Somewhat similar to Venezuela, Caribbean nations have undergone significant de-peasantization, with rural populations declining from 36 percent to 17 percent between 1960 and 2000 (Weis 2003, 180; Thompson 2019, 92). The general dissolution of farming as a way of life, increased food imports, and consistent migration of young people to urban centers further undermine the capacity of peasants to mobilize as a political force (Weis 2007, 114). Lastly, the very "imaginary" of sovereignty carries distinctive features within the Caribbean subregion. As Thompson (2019) suggests, the heritage of British colonial rule, in conjunction with the relatively late arrival of national independence, has transmuted the very notion of sovereignty into one that resides squarely within the state, rather than the people-nation (see also Lewis 2013). Thus, the framework of food sovereignty taken up by Caribbean peasant movements tends to become entangled with more firmly entrenched discourses of state-centric sovereignty.

The divergence between Cuba and the wider Caribbean helps to remind us of the radical diversity in experiences among FS movements. In order to provide a sharper empirical frame to the analysis of food sovereignty politics in the ALBA, this chapter compares the cases of Bolivia, Ecuador, Nicaragua, and Venezuela. These examples share a common history in their passing of food sovereignty legislation into their national constitutions, often as a result of previous cycles of peasant mobilization. Yet they are also marked by diverse movement strategies, demands, and domestic contexts. As we will see throughout this chapter, specific configurations of accumulation regimes, national power blocs, and forms of legitimation both work for, and often against, FS protagonists.

The analysis proceeds along three sections. Firstly, I examine one side of sovereignty's hidden edifice, property-power, and the ways in which struggles over property in the context of food sovereignty revolve primarily over struggles for *land ownership* (Vergara-Camus 2014; Borras, Franco, and Suárez 2015). At the same time, property rights become legible through the juridical order with respect to the control of nature, space, and human bodies (Graham 2011), while the power of law, and *law-making*, is necessarily concentrated within the "modern" nation-state. Peasant struggles for land thus correspond to "a form of strategic essentialism that calls upon the idea of [state] sovereignty to claim juridical ground in the short run" while at the same time cultivating "the potential to reformulate the meaning of sovereignty itself in the long run" (McKay, Nehring, and Walsh-Dilley 2014, 1179). Put differently, securing the de jure recognition of peasant rights opens the prospect for the creation of de facto practices and institutions that contribute toward a more substantial food sovereignty regime. Thus, the complexity of law-making often runs through the praxis of *law-breaking* (Brabazon 2017) as a key part of FS struggles.

Secondly, I analyze the dimension of *knowledge-power*, as the other half of sovereignty's edifice, in the context of building new forms of territoriality embedded in forms of political organization and modes of knowledge production. As Blomley (2019, 245) suggests, "territory is not just an outcome of the power relations operative in property, but a means through which such relations are realized." Seen from this angle, while the struggle for property (land) is an integral part of FS politics, landownership is articulated through wider networks of commodification, market relations, and legal recognition. Far from simply an economic space of equal exchange, territory contains "an essentially political character, in that the State tends to monopolize the procedures of the organization of space" (Poulantzas 2014, 104). Consequently, the possession of a "secure" land title may not be enough to guarantee *land security*, which is crucially shaped by a variety of legal, social, and economic power relations (Broegaard 2005). The struggle for FS thus implicates the struggle over *sanctioned knowledge*, as the material content of territorial organization. Through the production of "subversive knowledge" that privileges cooperative and participatory territorial practices (Bidet 2016, 118; cf. Santos 2015, 208), FS protagonists create the potential for alternative food systems beyond the logic of capital.

The politics of territoriality within FS struggles traverses both vertical and horizontal dimensions. Vertical territoriality denotes the strategic engagement with, and transformation of, state institutions that form a series of nested hierarchies of scalar relations. Through this terrain of political struggle, FS protagonists attempt to reconfigure the prevailing power bloc, with the potential to impact higher-scalar levels (regional/global). Horizontal territoriality, on the other hand, points toward the construction of networks of cooperation, exchange, and knowledge production among agrarian actors through which new forms of knowledge-power emerge. Rather than existing in isolation, both vertical and horizontal territoriality are internally related, with transformations in one necessarily shaping the evolution of the other.

Property-Power: Class Struggles in and against the Law

The centrality of rights, law, and state institutions in the broader context of social transformation is highly visible with Latin America's left turn, and with ALBA's member states in particular (cf. Romero 2019). As Fernández (2012) observes, the "new constitutionalism" in Bolivia, Ecuador, and Venezuela departs from the liberal tradition of the individual citizen-subject by extending the juridical field toward collective legal-subjects, social and communal property, and greater emphasis on social participation in public life. Rural populations were key protagonists in the formation of Latin America's new constitutionalism in the context of food sovereignty politics. The election of Evo Morales in Bolivia in 2005 was made possible through mass mobilizations among Indigenous, peasant, and working-class movements that formed a constituent assembly the following year to redraft the country's constitution. Taking inspiration from its Brazilian counterpart (Vergara-Camus 2014; Dunford 2016), Bolivia's Landless Peasant Movement (Movimiento sin Tierra) was instrumental in pushing the state toward the adoption of food sovereignty legislation, principally through widespread occupation of large-scale latifundios (Brabazon 2017).

Ecuador's path to food sovereignty legislation was created by a much wider set of political forces mobilizing around broad-based anti-neoliberal coalitions. Instrumental within this movement were a host of Indigenous and peasant-based groups seeking to reverse the nation's expansive extractivism, as well as redress the disempowerment of the rural classes within an increasingly agro-industrial food system. As in the case of Bolivia, Ecuadorian peasant movements participated in the creation of a new constitution under the government of Rafael Correa, which eventually adopted FS principles into the constitution in 2008 and passed the Organic Law of the Food Sovereignty Regime the following year (Giunta 2014; Peña 2016).

In contrast to these examples, Nicaragua's introduction of food sovereignty legislation did not directly arise on the back of peasant mobilizations and struggles. Following the electoral defeat of the left-wing Sandinista FSLN party in 1990, leading peasant groups, such as the Rural Workers Union (Asociación de Trabajadores del Campo, ATC) and other popular movements, staged numerous land occupations and struggles over property ownership in the context of a complex and fluid land redistribution scheme under the neoliberal Chamorro administration. Yet these popular insurrections quickly lost momentum as the reconcentration of landownership continued, largely to the benefit of medium-sized farms (Martí i Puig and Baumeister 2017).[1] Thereafter, the ATC and the National Farmers and Ranchers Union (La Unión de Agricultores y Ganaderos) began a piecemeal effort to encourage policies and practices of food sovereignty at the local/municipal level through the cultivation of partnerships with local officials and sympathetic allies in the National Assembly. These efforts culminated in a draft proposal for a Law of Food and Nutritional Sovereignty and Security (FNSS) formulated by rural movements and other civil society organizations. With the election of Daniel Ortega in November 2006, the FSLN party integrated the FNSS into national policy (Godek 2015).

The case of Venezuela shares a number of similarities with the preceding examples. Some of Venezuela's most militant rural movements find their historical roots at the end of the 1980s, in the frontier region between Venezuela (Apure) and Colombia (Arauca). The Massacre of Amparo in 1988, in which fourteen Venezuelan fishermen were killed by Venezuelan security forces on the maritime border with Colombia, was a key turning point in the formation of Venezuelan peasant movements (Romero 2016). From that time onwards, and with the collaboration of university student organizations, a new peasant movement began to slowly emerge from self-organized strategies and interventions against large landowners (particularly through land occupations) as well as marches and roadblocks (Settembrino 2012, 87).

While the Venezuelan constitution of 1999 emphasized the construction of "food security" rather than food sovereignty, the revitalization of agriculture was framed through the "privileging and development of internal agriculture" (rbv 1999, article 305). Despite the involvement of peasant movements in the drafting of the new constitution, the legacy of land reforms from the 1960s and the lingering hegemony of the AD and COPEI in the countryside led to a relatively small share of rural votes for the Chávez's MVR party. Yet the Land Law of 2001 and the right-wing counteroffensive in 2002–2003 decisively shifted rural support toward the new Bolivarian state (interview, FNCEZ Guanare, June 10, 2016; cf. Ciccariello-Maher 2013, 207).

With the Organic Law of Lands and Agricultural Development passed in 2001, Venezuela's two principal rural movements—Frente Campesino Revolucionario Simón Bolívar (FCRSB) and the Frente Campesino Revolucionario Ezequiel Zamora (FCREZ) organized over three thousand peasants to claim sixty rural settlements that were deemed "unproductive" or "idle" (McKay 2011, 109). In 2004 the FCRSB and FCREZ came together to form the Frente Nacional Campesina Ezequiel Zamora (Longa and Wahren 2009, 110). Nerson Guerrero, one of the national coordinators for the FNCEZ, describes this group as "a social movement, distinctly popular, [and] very autonomous" (interview, FNCEZ Barinas, July 18, 2015). He estimates that the FNCEZ represents around twenty-five hundred peasant families in Barinas city alone (around four to five people per family), with some one thousand to twelve hundred dedicated militants engaged in permanent agitation and organization.[2] In terms of political organization, the FNCEZ is but one part of a larger cluster of movements under the umbrella group of the Corriente Revolucionaria Bolívar y Zamora, a revolutionary current comprising the Simón Bolívar National Communal Front, Simón Rodríguez Center for Training and Social Study, the FNCEZ, and various popular worker movements (interview, CRBZ Caracas, April 26, 2016).

Across each of the ALBA states examined in this chapter, food sovereignty legislation encountered a number of setbacks and reversals, as each national power bloc attempted to reshape the content of reforms around their economic interests. In Bolivia, right-wing political forces actively moved against Morales's political project, firstly via a recall referendum that was ultimately defeated and latterly through a series of local revolts across the Media Luna region, comprising the departments of Santa Cruz, Beni, Pando, and Tarija in 2008. Through countermobilizations among Morales's social base, Bolivia's landed classes were eventually defeated in their attempt to realign state policy. Yet the confrontation with the landed elite tempered Morales's approach to agrarian reform, resulting in a reconciliation of the landed classes to the state's promotion of an agro-industrial export regime. While the government oversaw 3.9 million hectares redistributed by 2010, much of this was based on retitling, with the majority merely transferred from state-owned land to peasant producers (Webber 2017b, 338). This led to a three-tiered structure of landownership, comprising a "nucleus" of large-scale landowners, a semiperipheral sector of "rich peasants" subsumed under this nucleus, and a third (largely land-poor) peripheral sector providing rural wage labor to the first two tiers (344).

Peasant struggles for land in Ecuador parallel the patterns seen in Bolivia, particularly around Indigenous-led insurrections and land occupations precipitating the emergence of food sovereignty legislation. By 1990 peasant/Indigenous struggles entered a particularly intense period, with the Confederación de Nacionalidades Indígenas del Ecuador embarking on a *levantamiento* (uprising), occupying the iconic Santa Domingo Church in Quito as well as a variety of lands and other buildings (Goodwin 2017, 580–81). While these struggles for land did not lead to significant redistribution, they catalyzed a new cycle of subaltern resistance to neoliberal governance during the 1990s, which provided the groundwork for the election of Rafael Correa in 2006.

However, land reform under the Correa administration was complicated by the relative divisions seen among the country's peasant movements and their differential integration into the state (Martínez Valle 2014, 55–56; Goodwin 2017, 589; Henderson 2018). The largest of Ecuador's peasant organizations, Confederación Nacional de Organizaciones Campesinas, Indígenas y Negras (FENOCIN), is broadly split between small-scale Indigenous producers in the highlands and commercially oriented mestizo peasants on the coast. As I was told by two representatives from FENOCIN, these divergent reproduction strategies led to a relative tension within the organization between competing claims toward the state (interview, FENOCIN Quito, July 25, 2016). The *Plan Tierras* law of 2009 saw modest land redistribution efforts, with 114,500 hectares redistributed to peasant associations and 897,000 hectares formally titled to Indigenous *comunas* (P. Clark 2017, 359). While FENOCIN's Indigenous fractions have attempted to craft further laws pertaining to land redistribution from private latifundios—which in their view remains the sine qua non of food sovereignty (Henderson 2018, 12–13)—the state has concentrated its rural policies on the coastal regions, which received around 80 percent of total land redistribution (Martínez Valle 2014, 57). Ecuador's Ministry of Agriculture (Ministerio de Agricultura y Ganaderia, MAGAP) is thus primarily concerned with integrating peasant producers into traditional production techniques, as well as chemical fertilizer and seed markets dominated by corporate capital (interview, FENOCIN Quito, July 25, 2016).

Although food sovereignty policy under the Ortega presidency did not revolve around land *redistribution*, capitalist elites in Nicaragua aimed to halt the legal proceedings for the institution of the FNSS, particularly over issues pertaining to the prohibition of transgenic materials, a relative increase in state support for small and medium-sized producers, and a renewed push for land titling (Godek 2014, 192).[3] The country's main business lobby group, the Superior Council of Private Enterprise (Consejo Superior de la Empresa Privada, COSEP), vigorously contested the state's food sovereignty legislation through its alliance with the Constitutionalist Liberal Party (Partido Libral Constitucionalista), rallying around traditional bourgeois discourse that equated the health of capital with the health of the nation; as one COSEP representative asserted, the potential threat to agribusiness rendered the law "far from contributing to food sovereignty and food independence" (cited in Godek 2015, 536). Similar to the cases of Bolivia and Ecuador, the FSLN eventually struck a more conciliatory tone with the agrarian elite, particularly in light of the state's subsumption under the CAFTA free trade agreement with the United States (Araújo 2010, 503).

The case of Venezuela, however, differs from Bolivia, Ecuador, and Nicaragua, insofar as the executive branch of the state did not maintain an organic relationship to the landed classes. Facing opposition to the land law from right-wing political forces in the National Assembly, Chávez introduced the Organic Law of the Supreme Tribunal of Justice in 2004, expanding the number of judges from twenty to thirty-two and thus ensuring a more favorable distribution of rulings over land reform (Albertus 2015, 260). As a result, the government gained the upper hand and was able to pass its previously blocked agrarian legislation. The modified law deemed expropriation necessary for the purposes of maintaining "food security" (article 68), in accordance with "public utility and social interest" (article 69) or simply "exceptional circumstances" (article 84) (rbv 2005; cf. Lavelle 2013, 142).[4] Legal discourse concerning land rights therefore shifted somewhat beyond the abstractly verifiable codes of conventional jurisprudence and toward a gray area of (arbitrary) executive right, which was nonetheless couched in legal discourse.

While political struggles over the social content of rights and law played out within the juridical apparatus of the state, they also stretched far beyond it. As another FNCEZ coordinator intimated that while the size of its membership may be growing, it is doing so under conditions of intense class violence on behalf of the old *hacendados* and their allies in the security services (interview, FNCEZ Guanare, June 10, 2016). As I was told, over three hundred peasants had been killed over the past decade, one hundred from the FNCEZ alone. The relative power and autonomy of landed capital in Venezuela, demonstrated by its command over the means of production and means of violence, strikes a sharp resonance with Ciccariello-Maher's description of this class as "local petty sovereigns" (2013, 212). It is difficult to ascertain the precise number of murdered peasants in Venezuela; as others suggest, this is possibly due to the state's reluctance to open legal probes into extrajudicial killings, as some personnel within the government have been tied to executions of peasant leaders over the past two decades (Lopéz-Sánchez and Rodríguez 2014). As a result, not a single landowner has been charged with respect to these killings, while peasants continued to face violent evictions from the land carried out by local fractions of the state apparatus (Ellis 2011; *Correo del Orinoco* 2014; PROVEA 2016; Boothroyd Rojas 2017).

Despite the near constant threat of class violence, Venezuelan peasant movements continued to actively shape new understandings of property and power in the countryside. Yet challenges to maintaining momentum arose once certain victories were secured. Particularly with respect to land reform and redistribution among the peasantry, movement activists encountered some resistance from their social base in pushing forward the broader struggle for agrarian citizenship and political power (interview, FNCEZ Barinas, July 18, 2015). Subsequent to one of the first big FNCSB occupations in 2002 of a cattle ranch owned by the widow of former president Carlos Andrés Pérez, the National Land Institute (Instituto Nacional de Tierras, INTI) had issued a *carta agraria* (land title recognized by the executive branch yet not necessarily cleared through the judicial system) to those who had taken the lands under occupation. Once the land had been divided among peasant families, some had simply disengaged from the movement, partly due to their insistence on maintaining private property for family smallholdings, while a large number of active movement cadres sought to implement systems of collective ownership (O'Brien 2014, 63).[5] Representatives from the Coordinadora Agraria Nacional Ezequiel Zamora—the other main peasant movement alongside the FNCEZ— noted the relative dominance of small-holding private property, which "has barely scratched the surface" in the struggle for a "socialist mode of agrarian life" (interview, CANEZ Apure, June 27, 2016). As I was informed, the "fundamental objective" of CANEZ is the formation of "new relations of production, which should be based on social property in production." In their view, this lack of progress was largely the fault of institutional inertia and specific policies that disfavored collective property ownership (interview, CANEZ Apure, June 27, 2016).

However, it should be emphasized that family farming is not incompatible with collective methods of production. As Bina Agarwal has shown, autonomously chosen collective/cooperative farming among many families engenders a greater longevity compared with top-down collectivization schemes

TABLE 5. Land distribution in Venezuela, 1997/8–2007/8

Size	Units	% of Units	Surface Area (hectares)	% of Surface Area
1997–98				
< 20 ha/s	376,878	75%	1,707,674	6%
20–1,000 ha/s	119,156	24%	14,396,774	48%
>1,000 ha/s	4,945	1%	13,966,744	46%
TOTAL	500,979	100%	30,071,192	100%
2007–08				
< 20 ha/s	295,819	70%	1,444,619	5.335%
20–1,000 ha/s	124,418	29%	14,670,881	54.188%
> 1,000 ha/s	4,019	1%	10,958,380	40.475%
TOTAL	424,256	100%	27,073,880	100%

SOURCES: FAO (1996/7); MPPAT (2007/8)

(Agarwal 2014, 1260–64; Agarwal 2010).[6] For members of the Venezuelan Peasant Collective "Argimiro Gabaldón," individual (privately owned) family plots established under Venezuela's land reform are qualitatively different from mere "individual property" (i.e., land as commodity). Venezuela's land law contains a clause dealing with *noncommodified* family property (rbv 2001a, article 12) and thus maintains an immanent connection to more communal territorial arrangements, aggregated through local communes (interview, Argimiro Gabaldón, May 28, 2016).[7]

Land redistribution during the first years of the agrarian reform process saw some notable achievements. Between 2003 and 2012, around 6.3 million hectares (ha/s) had been "rescued" (*rescatado*), and 7.6 million ha/s regularized (registered) through 91,000 *cartas agrarias* (Gutiérrez 2015, 40). Despite these relative gains, large-scale landholdings remain essentially untouched.

According to the agrarian census of 2007/8, there was a meagre change from the decade previously (see table 5). Both small holdings (< 20 ha/s) and large holdings (> 1000 ha/s) have decreased by 263,055 and 3 million ha/s, respectively, while medium-size holdings increased by 274,107 ha/s. Thus, while large holdings lost out overall by surface area, this represents only 926 units, while there was a staggering loss of 81,059 holdings for small units. Given the decline of medium-sized holdings by 5,262 units, this suggests a relative distribution toward larger size units within the 20–1000h/a range. Nevertheless, as of 2008, just over 40 percent of total agricultural land was still owned by large landowners, which essentially leaves the relative weight of these units untouched. More significantly, there was a net decline in surface area under production by 2,990,404 ha/s, which would suggest a significant abandonment of land during the reform period (cf. Page 2010; Lavelle 2016). Beyond

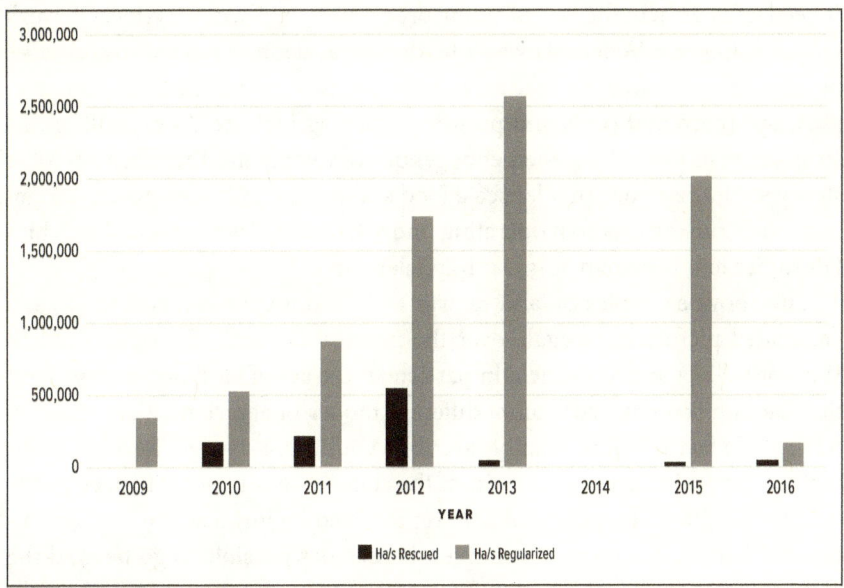

FIGURE 5. Number of hectares rescued/regularized, 2009–16.
SOURCES: PROVEA (2009, 2010, 2011, 2012, 2013, 2015, 2016).
NB: Number of hectares rescued for 2009 not available. Data for 2014 not available.

2008 available data becomes either less descriptive, or simply absent. According to the Ministry of Agriculture and Lands (as summarized in a series of reports from PROVEA), the "rescuing" of land continued beyond 2008, though coming to a virtual halt from 2013 onward (figure 5). Venezuela has witnessed a significant expansion in the legal titling ("regularization") of holdings, which peaked in 2013 at just over 2.5 million. Unfortunately, data beyond 2008 does not provide indication as to the distribution of rescued lands among size of unit, though it is likely that medium-size holdings (20–1000 ha/s) have continued to expand.

Beyond these figures, it is relatively impossible to determine whether large landholdings are privately owned or held by the state under the INTI. It is also difficult to assess the overall distribution of *labor regimes* (relations of production) within specific units. The 1996/1997 agricultural census reported around 211,290 people as "hired permanent workers" (wage laborers), or 21 percent of the economically active population in agriculture in 1997. The most recent available census of 2007–8, meanwhile, contains no data on types of tenancy or differentiation by labor type.[8] Given the relative stagnation in land redistribution, it is likely that production relations continue to be dominated by capital, in either private or state form (cf. Hernández 2009, 93; Deere 2017, 271).

Indeed, after 2011, in the face of falling production in the countryside, Chávez's Gran Misión AgroVenezuela was intended to tackle the problem of shortages by expanding the total surface area under production, increase the main staple crops (corn and rice), and promote urban agriculture. As a result of this stronger push toward state-led endogenous development, there has been the steady shift away from smaller scale food sovereignty initiatives toward large-scale state-run farms, often operating under traditional workplace hierarchies (Enríquez and Newman 2015, 14; Kappeler 2013).

The above examples of land reform within ALBA states reveal the highly variegated picture of struggle over the political content of property rights. With of Bolivia and Venezuela in particular, the act of land occupations and the autonomous construction of different modes of agrarian citizenship signals the de facto/de jure duality inscribed within the struggle for land, transecting the entire strategic terrain of the state—from its outer fringes in the countryside, to its institutional core represented by juridical law and constitutional battles. From these examples, it becomes possible to go beyond the empty abstraction of "the right to have rights" toward a concrete praxis of *the right to create rights* (Santos 2010, 114–16), which (however limited or temporary) subverts the division between manual and intellectual labor congealed within the state and its monopoly on "juridical logic" (Poulantzas 2014, 89). Peasant movements in Ecuador followed a broadly similar path, yet with less tangible results. While Indigenous/peasant mobilizations across the 1990s and early 2000s provided the foundation for Correa's electoral victory, a variety of splits within these groups led to a relative imbalance of class forces within the state's power bloc, leading in turn to limited progress on land reform and food sovereignty legislation.

Movements in Nicaragua, for the most part, did not specifically engage with land occupations or struggles for land redistribution. In the former, issues of land reform and food sovereignty were negotiated through institutional spaces of dialogue and participatory policymaking, even if the decks were stacked against rural actors. In the latter constitutional battles for the formalization of food sovereignty centered on issues pertaining to transgenics and land titling.

Within this struggle over property-power, we find the intersecting determinations of law-making, bourgeois discourse, and dominant modes of capitalist development radically punctuated by bursts of subversive knowledge grounded in law-breaking, popular agrarian discourse, and alternative modes of development. It is to these specific determinations, as the second half of sovereignty's edifice, to which we now turn.

Knowledge-Power I: Vertical Scaling

Despite the "return of the state" under Latin America's left turn (Grugel and Riggirozzi 2012), the crafting of progressive policy within ALBA states has remained deeply entrenched with the legacies of neoliberal restructuring over the previous decade. The expansion of ground rent used toward popular programs and social policy notwithstanding, the redistribution of wealth under Left governments was not appropriated from the private sector; indeed, tax regimes across Latin America's progressive states have been remarkably regressive (North and Clark 2018; Nakatani and Herrera 2008). However, to interpret this mode of regulation as merely a capitulation to capital would miss the inherent contradictions associated with popular hegemonic projects that are, at the same time, sustained through accumulation regimes entangled with the old power bloc. Particularly with respect to Bolivia, Ecuador, Nicaragua, and Venezuela, progressive governments have, as Nelson (2019) puts it, "walked the tightrope" between substantive reform and pragmatic caution in the face of organized bourgeois opposition.

These contradictions have proved decisive for the struggles over food sovereignty across ALBA states, in terms of how the reproduction of national power blocs centered on capital is mediated by the production of a specific knowledge-power comprising the state's institutional materiality. Indeed, in the case of the four ALBA states examined in this chapter, this body of knowledge-power is constituted by a relatively antagonistic mix of popular-progressive discourse on one hand (including the calls for food sovereignty) and the continued technocratic faith in the power of capital to rejuvenate the "nation." In light of this contradictory political terrain, FS protagonists attempt to walk their own tightrope between cooperation/co-optation with/by the state on the one hand and political autonomy that potentially veers toward isolation on the other. Each national context thus presents its own specific power bloc and in turn its own set of challenges for FS politics.

As a result of the strategic partnership between the Bolivian state and agro-industrial capital, the passing of Law 114 in 2011, which outlined a "Productive Revolution" in the service of promoting "food sovereignty," led to the subsumption of small-scale farmers under broader commodity chains (McKay 2018). As we saw above, rather than redistributing land from latifundios, land reform under the Morales government centered on the legal titling of lands to peasant producers embedded within export markets, such as coca, quinoa, and soy (Tilzey 2019, 637). Agrarian policies directed toward smallholders were also shaped by broader global governance institutions, with one of the largest rural development programs—Proyecto de Alianzas Rurales (PAR)—devised by the World Bank in 2005 and officially integrated into the MAS government's development program in 2007. The PAR's multilevel governance structure operates through a specific second-order condensation of class relations across local/national/supranational scales. Significantly, the implementation of World Bank policies through the PAR takes place in relative separation from the Bolivian state apparatus. While formally linked to the Ministry of Rural and Land Development, the PAR's technical staff working within peasant communities report directly to World Bank officials (Córdoba, Jansen, and González 2016, 96).

Through this parallel institutional hierarchy, the PAR has been relatively insulated from popular demands centered around food sovereignty norms, which permitted a greater space for the construction of knowledge-power that "weaves a politicised vision of empowerment [of commodity owner in the market] and a non-relational vision of empowerment together" (Córdoba, Jansen, and González, 93). In light of the dominance of this type of knowledge-power, many food sovereignty initiatives in Bolivia converge with Fabricant's (2012) notion of "hybridized agrarian citizenship"—trapped between a mode of citizenship based on collective organization and agroecological production on one side and the atomized "citizen-individual," dependent on market exchange and monocrop production on the other (cf. Colque, Urioste, and Eyzaguirre, 2015, 110). Agrarian movements have thus fragmented along pro- or antigovernment lines in recent years, with large sections of the Confederación Sindical Unica de Trabajadores Campesinas de Bolivia tightly integrated into the state apparatus (principally through the National Institute of Agrarian Reform, the Ministry of Land and Rural Development, and the regional Comunidad Andina de Naciones regional institution), while other organizations, such as CONAMAQ and CIDOB resigned from the state's "Unity Pact" in 2011. As Webber argues (2017b, 334), the reproduction of agrarian capitalism in Bolivia has thus led to a "decapitation of peasant movements, the containment of independent peasant militancy, rather than a fundamental transformation of the state apparatuses and political economy of the Bolivian countryside" (see also Bottazzi and Rist 2012; McKay 2020).

The Ecuadorian state under the Correa administration was marked by a fragmentation among the peasantry, reflecting divergent class alliances congealed within the state apparatus. While some National Assembly members originating from rural social movements were key supporters of food sovereignty legislation, other political leaders maintained close relationships with domestic agribusiness. Among this latter group, Minister of Production Nataly

Cely was a vocal proponent for the reconstitution of agrarian capitalist development, having previously worked in the Inter-American Development Bank on the promotion of *negocios inclusivos* that connected peasant producers to corporate commodity chains. In her ministerial role under Correa, Cely further integrated this development model into Ecuador's agrarian policy, under the aegis of the Programa de Negocios Inclusivos Rurales within the Ministry of Agriculture (Clark 2017, 356–57). The integration of food sovereignty into the state thus became increasingly subsumed under the logic of transnational capital, particularly in light of Correa's subsequent veto of several articles within the Organic Law of the Food Sovereignty Regime pertaining to the banning of GMOs, land reform, and the production of biofuels (Bellinger and Fakhri 2013, 3).

Nevertheless, peasant movements in Ecuador continued to work across the strategic terrain of the state in order to maintain progress on the institutionalization of FS principles. This primarily took the form of a series of policy-making workshops organized by the Plurnational and Intercultural Conference on Food Sovereignty (Conferencia Plurinacional e Intercultural de Soberanía Alimentaria), which brought together a wide range of agrarian movements, labor unions, NGOs, local officials, and state agencies. As Peña argues, these spaces of knowledge-exchange and policy-formation represented "instances of participatory and deliberative democracy that strengthened the social capital of social organizations while lending legitimacy to the state" (2016, 230). And yet, between social movements and the state, it was the latter that won out over the former. While projecting a seemingly radical political technology in the form of participatory spaces of vertical territoriality, political power remained concentrated within the executive branch of the state apparatus.

This trend could be seen even during the initial stages of Ecuador's food sovereignty legislation, with the introduction of the Mesa Agraria (Agrarian Roundtable) as the peasant movement body tasked with crafting the content of the law. As Romelio Gualán, national president of La Coordinadora Nacional Campesina-Eloy Alfaro, put it, "[the Ministry of Agriculture] gave us the agrarian roundtable just to justify that it is including the opinions of social organizations when in reality it isn't. In terms of food sovereignty, credit and training there still hasn't been a response—the government wants to control everything" (cited in Henderson 2017, 45). State credits largely favored agro-industrial export sectors based on large-scale/intensive cultivation techniques, with the largest beneficiaries situated within the beef (44.6 percent), cacao (6.24 percent) and corn (3.92 percent) sectors (Vega 2017, 16–17; cf. D. Carrión and

Herrera 2012, 99), while more direct credit lines from state budgets to local communities essentially bypassed peasant organizations altogether in an effort to further marginalize organized peasant resistance (Henderson 2017, 46).

The case of Nicaragua, as we saw above, did not center so heavily on issues of land redistribution but around broader policies contained within the FNSS law pertaining to international trade and investment, as well as land registration policy. The constitutional battle over the implementation of the law revolved around the contested meaning and interpretation of food sovereignty as a development discourse. As in the case of Bolivia, this process became further complicated with the involvement of global governance institutions, such as the UN's Food and Agricultural Organization (FAO) (Godek 2014, 201–10). The already-tense negotiations behind Nicaragua's food sovereignty legislation were further compromised by the involvement of FAO technical experts who spoke more often of statist food security rather than food sovereignty.

The relative neglect of food sovereignty principles can be understood through the differential integration of agrarian classes into state-led development policy. Somewhat similar to Venezuela (as we will see subsequently), Nicaragua hosts a sizable cooperative movement, with around 80 percent of smallholder peasants organized into multiscale cooperatives linked through village or community level associations, local unions, and national federations (principally the Federación Nacional de Cooperativas Agroprecuarias y Argroindustriales, FENACOOP) (Metereau 2020, 816–17). However, with the creation of the MEFCCA (Ministerio de la Economía Familiar, Comunitaria, Cooperativa y Asociativa), the state began to subsume other institutional bodies under its control; as García (2017, 220) notes, "this megaministry is not specialized in, nor does it prioritize, rural development."[9] Running parallel to this institutional complex is the network of Consejos de Poder Ciudadano, in which local municipalities and communities maintain direct linkages to the executive branch of the state apparatus. While this institutional connection between communities and the state provides multiple channels of state support, it also effectively bypasses the more politicized peasant movements (like those within FENACOOP) that actively call for the transition to food sovereignty (Martí i Puig and Baumeister 2017, 392; Godek 2021, 97). Overall, the substantive role and participation of social movements and cooperatives has tended to decline over time. While popular social forces in Nicaragua actively participated within ALBA from 2006, by 2008 the Ortega government's closer cooperation with national capitals has seen this role steadily diminish (Carrión 2017, 32–33).

The construction of a new power bloc under the second Ortega administration thus points toward the relative disorganization of the popular classes. As one ALBA official working in Nicaragua described it:

> There was a certain fear [among the FSLN] that the economic empowerment of cooperative [*autogestionario*] movements could in some way fracture the social base of the Sandinista Front if they gained further autonomy. A peasant movement that struggles for recognition over land, health and education is before anything else an identity movement, and, as such, can compete with the identity movement of the "People's President" that the government is pursuing. This decision also has to do with the ideological change in the highest level of the FSLN leadership. The principles of a society under leftist criteria that many social organizations have, such as transforming the productive apparatus, were seen as more radical and less adequate for the historical development of the country. It was believed that private enterprise or the national oligarchy was the one who could modernize the country more easily than the social movements. (Cited in Carrión 2012, 48)

Having been kept at a critical distance from the state apparatus and its assemblage of knowledge-power based on conventional large-scale agriculture ("food security"), peasant movements were relatively powerless to halt the reconstitution of landed capital linked to international markets, as well as the ALBANISA complex (Ripoll 2018).

Perhaps more than any ALBA state (though comparable to Cuba), the vision of multiple sovereignties implicit with a food sovereignty regime finds sharp convergence with Venezuela's political technology of participatory democracy (cf. Menéndez 2013; Schiavoni and Camacaro 2009). Chávez aimed to bring about a new "geometry of power" based on a "socialist geography" that might "break old paradigms" (Chávez 2009, 80; cf. Massey 2009). In transforming the "geopolitical organization of its territory" (Massey 2009, 20), the Bolivarian state expressed a new constellation of knowledge-power that aimed to promote a politics of "humanity and inclusivity" (Menéndez 2013, 233). Venezuela's protagonistic democracy decentralized decision-making power through a variety of spatial scales, from "communal councils" (consejos comunales) to higher level "communes" (comunas) (de Oliviera and Fátima 2016). As stipulated in the Law of Communal Councils, Citizens Assemblies (as grassroots organizations that approve the formation of CCs) maintain the power to designate their own territorial limits for the CC (*Gaceta Oficial* 2006). Peasant movements actively took hold of these nested hierarchical arrangements, starting at the level of the parish, with working groups formed among residents. From within these groups, a delegate team is then sent to the municipal level (composed of representatives from all parishes in the municipality), which in turn moves up toward the (subnational) regional level. According to one national coordinator of the CRBZ, their cadres are active in 260 communes out of the country's 1,500 total, and perhaps even up to 300 (including those that are not officially registered as communes) (interview, CRBZ Caracas, April 26, 2016). The final level of this vertical territoriality consists in the Socialist Presidential Council of Peasants and Fishermen (Consejo Presidencial Socialista de Campesinos y Pescadores), creating a direct line between locally based delegates (voceros) and the executive branch of the state in order to cooperatively plan the transition to food sovereignty (interview, FNCEZ Barinas, July 18, 2015; cf. Lavelle 2016, 151–55). These councils are integrated by municipality with five delegates from each—the state of Portuguesa alone contains seventy such delegates (interview, CANEZ Apure, June 27, 2016).[10] This formal multiplication of sovereignties was further expanded in 2014 through the creation of the Presidential Councils of Popular Power (Consejos Presidenciales del Poder Popular), comprising twelve different councils across a range of issues, including councils for women, youth, workers, Indigenous, peasants and artists (interview, FNCEZ Barinas, July 18, 2015; see also Ladera 2014). While these councils were passed into law a year later, the lack of previous legal standing did not stop the congregation of movement spokespersons with officials at the presidential and vice-presidential level (*Gaceta Oficial Extraordinario* 2015).

This nested hierarchy of political decision making has been fundamental to the broader struggle for territorializing the political content of food sovereignty. However, as with other examples of vertical territoriality among ALBA states, such encounters between popular sectors and the state apparatus carry their own tensions: "Though we might have the structure of a council there may not be substantial participation, perhaps because there is some fear on behalf of the 'boss' [state functionary] that power may be lost" (interview, FNCEZ Barinas, July 18, 2015). The movement's relationship with Elías Jaua at the Ministry of Agriculture and Lands, for instance, fostered a continual flow of contact, meetings, and communication. The subsequent minister, Juan Carlos Loyo, maintained only sporadic contact with the group: "If they miss a meeting, or do not call one, then we must put pressure on them to step up" (interview, FNCEZ Barinas, July 18, 2015).

An added complication to state-peasant relations is the marked complexity of the Bolivarian state itself. With the proliferation of new agencies tasked with the implementation of Venezuela's agrarian reform—most notably for credit, technical assistance, and infrastructure (FONDAS, INDER, BAV, INTI,

CIARA, Misión Che Guevara), agroecology (INIA, INSAI), and marketing (CVAL, MERCAL) (see McKay, Nehrling, and Walsh-Dilley, 2014, 1182)—the problem of institutional redundancy becomes an ever-present danger, with increased propensity for intra-agency conflict and confusion over the distribution of state competencies (Enríquez and Newman 2015; Page 2011; cf. Poulantzas 2014, 155).[11] These types of institutional bottle-necks took a particularly heavy toll on agrarian production in the context of Venezuela's economic crisis; time-lags between the allocation of credit packages and their actual transfer have been a common occurrence, where the time in between incurred a marked rise in factor prices due to inflation, thus rendering the original credit package drastically short of current financial needs (interview, CRBZ Caracas, April 26, 2016).

At a more microfoundational level, the state apparatus remained relatively fractured among political allies of the movement and those opposed to it: "We also had problems under Chávez, well not necessarily with him, but with the people below him, because in this country people are accustomed to a certain way of being; for instance, being the minister of agriculture and lands somehow makes you the 'owner' of the peasants. So, if you are irreverent, they categorize you as 'undisciplined,' or 'counterrevolutionary'" (interview, FNCEZ Guanare, June 10, 2016). As Poulantzas noted, as a social category state personnel "is not a social group existing alongside or above classes: it has a class place and is therefore internally divided" (2014, 154). And while such personnel may be embedded within the formal appearance of a progressive left-wing state, latent forms of hegemonic subjectivities and practices predispose state personnel toward the maintenance of old class alliances (156). As one of the national coordinators of the CRBZ, Mareli Ramírez, put it:

> There are people inside these institutions that have thirty or forty years there and continue to respond to the policies of the Fourth Republic, because they were never convinced of what Chávez said and were never in agreement with the socialist project or perhaps changed because they had other interests. So they thought, "I'm better off with the large landowner who will continue to pay me, rather than a peasant who is going to produce only their ten hectares and is going to be in a collective, and I'm not going to get my share, or I won't benefit because this socialist project is going to fail." (Interview, CRBZ Caracas, April 26, 2016)

Practices of bureaucratic corruption, in the form of clientelist class alliances, cropped up with some frequency during my conversations: "There's a very common saying here among the people: that if you are employed in the public sector and you leave without money, you're an idiot—that is to say, you have to steal in order to make your foundation [*para hacer pilas*]" (interview, FNCEZ Guanare, June 10, 2016; cf. Coronil 1997, 307–8). The Agropatria state company is a particularly glaring example of this type of institutional mismanagement and corruption. The company was born from the expropriation of Agroisleña in 2010, a private monopoly accused of price speculation and charging extortionate interest rates to farmers (Purcell 2017, 305). While the formation of Agropatria was intended to support the production of cheap food for the national market (largely through subsidized agro-chemical inputs), the company is beset by institutional fragmentation, with inadequate links between its various outlets and the central headquarters (MPPAT 2015, 688).[12] There is also a massive deficit in planning and budgeting, which creates huge blind spots that allow the continuance of corruption and waste (ibid). While the company assisted around 594,000 producers in 2013, this figure has dropped to 398,000 in 2015, which covers just 1.4 million ha/s, about half the total area under production (MPPAT 2015, 687; cf. Gutiérrez 2015, 40). Peasants have sporadically protested corruption inside the company, with managers and employees allegedly reselling agricultural inputs in the black market for personal gain (PROVEA 2015, 16).

Similar problems of graft or mismanagement have been seen throughout a string of state firms within the food sector, particularly those associated with ALBA mixed socialist enterprises. The Pesquera Industrial del ALBA (Pescalba), which emerged from a self-organized worker takeover of the previously private company, initially saw positive results in its output and productivity. Yet the company's workforce was soon sidelined by more bureaucratic strata that ignored workers' calls for greater investment in the firm's infrastructure (Lubbock 2018). In 2016 the head of the Leguminosas del ALBA plant was arrested for the contraband sale of 120 tons of beans from the company's storehouses (*Aporrea* 2016a). Representatives from CANEZ, meanwhile, specifically singled out the ALBA-Arroz rice producing factories, which failed to come through on their responsibilities to process raw material from the surrounding fields. One of the fields directly owned by the ALBA-Arroz firm, Caño Seco, had been idle for some time, strewn with abandoned tractors and other machinery. Such means of production, either in the form of land or machines, "do not belong to the peasants, nor to the 'point and circle' that surrounds the ALBA factories, it's their property. They have personnel that are there only to cover their own weekly salaries" (interview, CANEZ Apure, June 27, 2016).[13]

These forms of graft and mismanagement have not gone unanswered by peasant movements. In the early years of Venezuela's agrarian reform, mounting injustices—spanning from the organized violence against peasant producers to the mismanagement and corruption inside key agrarian institutions—eventually led to the Zamora toma Caracas, a ten-thousand-strong peasant march in 2005 organized by the country's leading agrarian movements. This cycle of peasant struggle helped to consolidate a more cohesive state-movement relationship and the eventual formation of vertical territoriality (as we saw above) (Rodríguez 2008, 135). However, as one leader of the Plataforma de Lucha Campesina movement, Andres Alayo, noted, this turning point also marked a significant expansion of state intervention into the agricultural sector, with "the grassroots initiative . . . no longer centre stage" (cited in Marquina 2019).

This resurgence of the state can be traced to the relative failure of Venezuela's agrarian cooperatives. In response to both hyper-urbanization and peasant demands for land redistribution, the state launched its *Vuelta al Campo* (Return to the Countryside) campaign in 2005, which sought to reintegrate urban citizens into small-scale agrarian cooperatives (Fundos Zamoranos). State-led training of newcomers to these cooperatives was hobbled by the overemphasis on ideological formation (the benefits of "cooperativism"), rather than the *building of technique*. Insufficient knowledge-input from established farmers and the lack of bottom-up participation in planning limited the transfer of much needed technical capacity to new cooperatives (Page 2010, 270). Thus, the production of knowledge-power, as a *sanctioned form of knowledge*, was skewed toward upholding statist Bolivarian *ideals*, rather than the *techniques* required for cooperative production.

Yet the relative failure of rural cooperatives was also significantly shaped by the broader contradictions of the rentier-economy. With a large gap between the official and black-market exchange rate, price inflation became a permanent feature of the overall economy, as producers and consumers took flight from the national currency in favor of dollars. In this macroeconomic context, credits to rural cooperatives were provided with nominal interest rates far below the rate of inflation; the real interest rate on these loans went from -3.9 percent to -13.4 (2002–2008), which effectively amounted to the acquisition of free money (Gutiérrez 2015, 42; cf. Purcell 2017). According to several peasant producers I spoke to at the INTi headquarters in Apure, the government's credit policy to cooperatives was poorly supervised, "when this process began, credit was given to anyone with a *cedula* (ID card), and the credibility of peasants fell enormously; there was an infiltration of a lot of people who were not peasants, and had no intention of being so" (interview, INTi Apure, July 11, 2016). Thus, while early experiments in rural cooperatives may have benefited from greater input from established farmers, they were also systematically undermined by highly subsidized state support without proper oversight or monitoring.

With the chronic underperformance of agrarian cooperatives and the eventual drop-off in national production levels from around 2008, government policy began to privilege "flag-ship products" (Enríquez and Newman, 2015). As one participant told me, "You can go to the state looking for credits to grow rice and corn, but not for papaya, xanthosoma [ocumo], yucca, roots and tubers, or passion fruit" (interview, FNCEZ Guanare, June 10, 2016). One of the centerpieces of state-led agro-industrial production is the Centro Técnico Productivo Socialista Florentino. The company was established through a takeover of a privately owned latifundio, deemed by the state to be underutilizing its land and thus eligible for expropriation. A central task of Florentino was the sowing of corn (a key flagship product), with nearby peasant cooperatives contracted to supply raw material for processing at the plant. Yet the operation of the company tended to function through rigid management hierarchies and an elevated importance of technical knowledge wielded by company experts (*los técnicos*). One consequence of this division between manual and intellectual labor was the underperformance of Florentino's corn production in relation to the more successful peasant plots adjacent to the center. This difference in yield was largely due to the accumulated knowledge of corn production among small farmers as well as Florentino workers who possessed an intimate understanding of climate and ecology, which technically trained agronomists working at Florentino lacked (Kappeler 2015, 172–73). As with the case of the *Vuelta al Campo*, the productive organization of the Florentino center consistently pushed grassroots input from center stage.

While forms of knowledge-power, congealed within structures of vertical scaling, constitute a vital component to the construction of new political technologies of food sovereignty, substantial conflicts remain within state-movement relations. The relative reproduction of the manual/intellectual labor divide within state institutions or centers of production limits the integration of alternative forms of knowledge that may well solve the very problems faced by state officials. In light of the systemic contradictions afflicting the broader economy—particularly shortages of inputs, a dysfunctional credit system, and price inflation—many of Venezuela's agrarian movements have sought to overcome these limits through alternative (if not complementary) modes of organization based on the cooperative self-organization.

Knowledge-Power II: Horizontal Scaling

As part of their struggle across the terrain of the state, FS protagonists seek to build alternative modes of popular organization and forms of subversive knowledge in order to shift the relationship of forces across the state apparatus as a whole. It is in this sense that peasant movements often engage with forms of horizontal scaling, as a more autonomous, networked approach to intercommunal knowledge exchange, support, and solidarity. As we saw in chapter 2, the Campesino-a-Campesino methodology became a crucial plank in resisting the predations of the Green Revolution and its destructive effects on the human and ecological landscapes. Over the past thirty years, Latin American peasant movements have extended this method of movement building through the construction of thick networks of political cooperation across borders, forming a veritable "regionalism from below" (see Rosset et al. 2022).

A significant example of regional food sovereignty is found in the network of agroecological schools under the banner Instituto Universitario Latinoamericano de Agroecología. The first of these schools was established in Venezuela in 2006, as the "IALA-Paolo Freire" in the federated state of Barinas. Though first conceived through encounters between social movements and the Venezuelan state, the creation of IALA was established through the radicalization of Venezuela's higher education policies, primarily through the promulgation of a five-year plan for the reformation of higher education, with the explicit aim of guaranteeing "the participation of society in the creation, transformation and socialization of knowledge, [and] to contribute to overcoming the division between manual and intellectual labor" (MPPEU 2008). IALA now boasts a network of agroecology institutes across the Latin American region in Brazil, Ecuador, Paraguay, Argentina, Chile, Nicaragua, and Colombia, providing education in agroecological science, pedagogy, and political thought to young activists and LVC cadres who go on to become the next generation of FS protagonists (Snipstal 2015; McCune, Reardon, and Rosset 2014; Chohan 2017).

Within the national scale, peasant movements often engage with *circuitos cortos de comercialización* (CCCs)—peasant-led markets (*ferias*) that help to short-circuit traditional commodity chains dominated by commercial intermediaries. These autonomous initiatives resemble a type of "nested market" that establishes a set of shared rules and cooperative norms that "help to shape production, processing, distribution and consumption in ways that contrast markedly to those induced by the general commodity markets" (Ploeg, Jingzhong, and Schneider 2012, 166). Forms of horizontal scaling in the shape of CCCs thus help to go some way toward the goal of "controlling the market through organization" (Bidet 2016, 250).

In Bolivia, these markets have become more prominent since the onset of the world food crisis of 2007–8, providing secure outlets for peasant produce and reliable sources of clean and culturally specific foods for "conscientious" consumers (Elías and Devissche 2014, 24–27). According to one survey across the departments of La Paz, Cochabamba, and Trajia, peasant markets are either organized around agroecological products (*ferias ecológicos*) or traditionally produced goods (*ferias tradicionales*), with land-poor peasants (< 2ha/s) predominantly found in the former (Chambilla 2014, 56). While most peasant markets operate along fixed prices, consumers do not face higher prices (albeit not particularly lower prices) compared to those found within supermarket chains (77).[14]

Ecuador hosts its own nationwide network of *ferias*, providing both agroecologically- and traditionally produced food for urban consumers (Houtart 2014, 174). Around half of all producers working through local peasant markets are land poor, working on less than a hectare of land (MAGAP-Heifer 2014, 109). Market prices are not uniformly set, with around 44 percent of producers opting for fixed prices, while the remainder engage in barter exchange with consumers (106). Though peasant markets remain a vital space of commercialization, they remain limited in scope and scale. The two representatives I spoke to from FENOCIN believed there was a lack of state guaranteed channels for linking small-scale production with concentrated urban centers. Consequently, the majority of urban residents in Quito buy their food from large supermarket chains, leading to an undervalued perception of local production: "We don't value what my neighbor producers... and it won't be easy to change this" (interview, FENOCIN Quito, July 25, 2016; see also Lacroix, Chauveau, and Taipe 2013).

Similar to the above examples, FS protagonists in Venezuela have established a series of alternative market networks that help to overcome the organizational deficiencies of state-led distribution, the predations of private market intermediaries, and the problem of inflation (Vaz 2018a). In contrast to Bolivia and Ecuador, the Venezuelan state placed a premium on the formation of public markets that would guarantee access to food for the popular classes.

As a strategic response to the opposition's early counteroffensives, Misión Mercal was created in 2003, establishing thirteen thousand outlets and four thousand *casas de alimentación* (feeding houses) (Purcell 2017, 302; *Gaceta Oficial* 2003). By 2006 some 40 to 47 percent of the population had bought subsidized goods through the Mercal network, with the average discount of food at around 41 to 44 percent (Harnecker 2015, 126n11). The UN's Food and Agriculture Organization praised the government's MERCAL networks as contributing to a marked improvement in food security (Parker 2008, 136). Indeed, the MERCAL networks were so successful that private firms began to lose significant market share. In one sense, the contradictory outcome of policy success was the eventual switch from production to imports among Venezuelan capital, as private firms could no longer compete with state-subsidized food prices (Castro-Aniyar 2013). As we saw in the previous chapter, the private sector's substitution of production for imports created one of the key drivers of price inflation in subsequent years, as hoarding and speculation became the predominant form of accumulation.

And yet, Misión Mercal did not always connect with the wider goals of food sovereignty. Though sporadically linked to local producers, the Mercals increasingly relied on imports to maintain supply, reaching 78 percent of distributed food by 2010. The reliance on imports can be traced to the relative decline in national production in the main staple crop (*maíz*) used for the primary good consumed in the Mercals: the *arepa*. With increased dependence on imports, the Mercal network suffered a 10 percent decrease in supply between 2008 and 2014 (Gutiérrez 2015, 39). In 2016 President Nicolás Maduro called for the reinvigoration of the deteriorating network: "Mercal should be Mercal again, I ask for assistance from fraternal governors, mayors, the FANB [National Bolivarian Armed Forces of Venezuela], for your discipline, your organization, [and the] love for your country" (cited in *Correo del Orinoco* 2016a).

In the face of these severe challenges to national food distribution, a wide variety of civil society actors have begun to expand peasant-led markets across Venezuela, in both rural and urban spaces. Similar to other instances of CCCs, prices are largely set by personal interaction and barter, rather than impersonal market forces (interview, CRBZ Caracas, April 26, 2016). These types of horizontal scaling also connect Venezuela's highly urbanized population with their rural counterparts, providing healthy and affordable food for one group as well as necessary remuneration for the other, as with the La Alpargata Solidaria market in Caracas (Schiavoni 2015, 475–76). More institutionalized rural/urban networks, such as the Pueblo a Pueblo initiative, establish both urban-based autonomous consumer markets as well as involving volunteers from the cities to work on the farms from which they buy their food (interview, Ataroa commune, November 29, 2018).

Beyond the establishment of alternative food markets, Venezuelan peasants construct autonomous forms of horizontal scaling through self-directed territorial networks that both connect peasants and communities across large territories and provide much-needed technical support to underperforming areas of the economy. For Mareli, there is a qualitative difference between community-level politics before and after Chávez's arrival: "Before the Law of the Communes, we simply had neighborhood associations" (interview, CRBZ Caracas, April 26, 2016)—local corpuscular groups that were largely fragmented and unable to achieve significant political weight (see Ellner 1999). From Mareli's perspective, popular power is not formed through some mystical force emanating from Miraflores Palace but is crucially made through autonomous social forces that often create de facto modes of political organization that subsequently become enshrined into de jure law.[15]

A key example of this type of popular organization can be seen in the spectacular growth of autonomous "political territorial corridors" connecting dozens of communal councils, communes, and other movements. The political-territorial corridor of "Agrimiro Gabaldón" in the federated state of Lara comprises several communes (El Maizal, Ataroa, Minas de Buría, and Negro Miguel) and is itself connected to other corridors (Fabricio Ojeda and Negro Miguel) across the neighboring state of Portuguesa (Fréitez and Martínez 2015, 210; Alves et al. 2016, 149). The agrarian commune El Maizal is a striking case in point. The commune emerged in 2009, when Chávez expropriated a two-thousand-acre latifundio, promising the land to the commune for their collective production. Yet no sooner was the land out of private hands did it find its way into the hands of the state. Under the ownership of CVAL, the *comuneros* were offered wage work from the state similar to what they might find under a private landowner. After years of frustration, they finally occupied the land and ejected the state company (Ciccariello-Maher 2016, 140–42). Today, the commune comprises twenty-two communal councils and around nine thousand people across twenty-three hundred hectares (Vaz 2018b). Nine hundred hectares of the twenty-three hundred total consists of "communal property," as a single unit held in common among El Maizal's members. The remainder is divided among roughly eighty different property types and sizes, from medium-sized holdings to small family plots (interview, Ataroa Commune, January 29, 2018).

In 2014 the commune took over twelve high-tech greenhouses from FONDAS and quickly brought these infrastructures back online as they continued their repairs. Later in 2017, El Maizal took over the near-abandoned Porcinos del ALBA processing plant. In cooperation with the ALBA workforce, they soon expanded the number of animals from four hundred to over three thousand and began distributing pork through the Local Committees for Food Distribution and Production (Comité Locale de Abastecimiento y Producción, CLAP) (Vaz 2018b; Kozarek 2018).[16] Through its expansive and efficient communal production, El Maizal develops investment funds into other areas of production, such as beef, dairy, and vegetables, all of which are distributed to members of the commune and the surrounding territories at affordable prices. Additionally, funds are invested into local infrastructures for education, housing, road paving, and credit services for local farmers. In terms of organization, the commune seeks to break down unaccountable institutions associated with state bureaucracies. By maintaining transparent accounts that are open to inspection and auditing by all members of the commune (Kozarek 2018), El Maizal has begun to dissolve the division between manual and intellectual labor characteristic of bourgeois institutions, thus facilitating an "immediate discourse, equally shared by all" (Bidet 2016, 250).

And yet, the relative absence of *agroecological practice* within El Maizal presents a contradiction within food sovereignty initiatives in Venezuela. The adoption of food sovereignty legislation was principally aimed toward breaking the dependence on industrial inputs monopolized by transnational capital. To this end, two separate extraordinary laws were passed in 2008—the Organic Law of Food Security and Sovereignty (rbv 2008a), and the Law of Integral Agricultural Health (LIAH; see rbv 2008b). For the former, the role of "food sovereignty" is explicitly conceived as a radical decentralization of powers to agrarian actors embedded within ecologically sustainable methods of production and self-sufficiency. This policy was to be enacted through "the transformation of the relations of exchange and distribution, from the co-management in planning with the participation of all actors involved in agrarian activity," as well as through "the identification and recognition of the social relations of production and consumption, within the concrete necessities and possibilities of every one of those actors of distinct agrarian chains" (article 4, rbv 2008a, 46–47). As a corollary, the law aimed to substitute "sustainable production" for practices of "intensive monoculture" and excessive market dependence (article 10, 52–53). The LIAH further elaborated the introduction of "agroecology" as a "scientific base of tropical and sustainable agriculture" (article 49, rbv 2008b, 42). And while the OLFSS makes various references to the presence and use of agrochemicals in the process of agrarian production (articles 79, 80, 81, rbv 2008a, 91–92), the LIAH explicitly states the intention to "progressively prevent" (phase out) the use of chemical and toxic agents as well as to prohibit their production and importation (article 56.3, 57.12, rbv 2008b, 45). Finally, training programs and agroecological universities have greatly expanded through initiatives from both above and below (Herrera, Domené-Painenao, and Cruces 2017).

Yet the scaling up of agroecology has encountered a number of obstacles. Undoubtedly, Venezuela has seen an abundance of projects, schools, and policies seeking to support agroecological farming throughout the national food system (rbv 2008a; Herrera Domené-Painenao, and Cruces 2017). And yet, as Giraldo and McCune (2019) point out, the transition to agroecology requires the breakup of large-scale private property as well as significant investment in territorial infrastructures linking rural producers. The relative survival of latifundios within Venezuela (even if under state control) presents one limit to achieving the preconditions for agroecological farming, as do large-scale agrarian communes reliant on farm machinery to maintain high yields. On the other hand, Venezuela's territorial infrastructure remains inadequate. Lack of irrigation, for example, constitutes a major gap in Venezuela's rural infrastructure, which covers only 10 percent of the country's productive land (located across Portuguesa, Barinas, Guanare). The remaining 90 percent relies on a combination of hoses, pipes, lakes, and rivers (interview, CRBZ Caracas, April 26, 2016). This debility stems from an historic neglect of one of agriculture's key infrastructural inputs; the national irrigation system is around forty years old, with very little state maintenance or upgrading. In consequence, peasants face severe downward pressure on production levels: "We were reduced from seven thousand kilos of rice per hectare to three thousand because there was no water, at least in the case of my family" (interview, CRBZ Caracas, April 26, 2016).[17]

Despite the stated goal of moving toward a more ecologically resilient agroecology model, the relative failure of small-scale cooperatives, lack of infrastructural investment, and the challenges of disseminating agroecological techniques have shifted the balance toward traditional methods of large-scale production (particularly the use of agrochemical inputs) at the expense of agroecological approaches (Schiavoni 2015; Lavelle 2016; Enríquez and Newman 2015). The construction of popular political technologies adequate to the making of a food sovereignty regime thus engenders a delicate balancing act between sustainable agricultural production and the necessity of providing for the community and the nation:

> We don't want to live in backwardness [*atraso*] where you cannot use a tractor, or any machine. Yet we cannot become human just through the production of capital, or mere money. The theme of sovereignty and technology has to proceed according to guaranteeing food for humanity, to be human, to live well, more than producing food through the use of combustibles. I think that the key is to produce together with technology and artisanal culture according to guaranteeing food in order to be human. (Interview, NG, July 18, 2015)

My interviewee's sentiment here looks to a more complex bundle of practices that negotiate the conscious use of technologies in order to satisfy human consumption, rather than the accumulation of capital. Yet satisfying peoples' consumption needs necessitates the synthesis of "artisanal culture" (small-scale production) with larger spaces of industrial processing. As Mareli explained, one of the prime reasons for the establishment of the ALBA factories was to link various small-scale operations into the processing stage of the production chain. As she recalled, her family farm (oriented mainly around the production of rice) yields around six tons per hectare (ha) on a ten ha piece of land. Yet processing this crop is a laborious affair in the absence of machinery (six family members threshing six thousand kilograms of rice). While there remains much debate over the place of industrial food production within FS politics (cf. Schiavoni 2016), there is, at the same time, "the need to increase rural incomes through interventions... such as complementary marketing and processing activities" (Altieri and Nicholls 2008, 478; see also Edelman et al. 2014, 925). This broader vision of food sovereignty more closely converges with the perspectives of those I spoke to who worked in industrial centers of production, like the factories established under the ALBA.

Conclusion

The chapter has attempted to track the variable and complex process of food sovereignty politics across the ALBA regional space. While I cannot account for each and every instance of FS politics across this regional canvas, the chapter revealed some of the key dynamics of peasant struggles around questions of rights, territory, and sovereignty. Drawing on the theoretical framework in chapter 1, the comparative analysis of peasant struggles and FS initiatives across four ALBA states—Bolivia, Ecuador, Nicaragua, and Venezuela—brings into focus the shared patterns of struggle over the transformation of property-power and knowledge-power conducive to the "collective appropriation of the market and of organization" (Bidet 2016, 250), in the form of self-directed labor and cooperative territorial governance.

The struggle over the transformation of property-power, specifically through land reform, has seen a mix of advance and retreat (if not stagnation) across all four cases. The participation of peasant movements in the creation of FS legislation constitutes a powerful example of how agrarian actors have worked toward "the development of practices of citizenship that enable people to demand and secure rights *for themselves*" (Dunford 2015, 2, emphasis in original), often through the creation of de facto rights that are later transformed into de jure law. And yet, the class content of FS legislation remains a potential threat to the power of agrarian elites seeking to maintain traditional hierarchies within national food systems. As such, ALBA's "post-liberal" states each, in their own way, walked a tightrope between transforming social relations of power on the one hand and engaging (or even cooperating) with agents and institutions organized within the old power bloc on the other.

The production of new modes of knowledge-power, as well as self-organized networks of knowledge-exchange and political organization, all constitute distinct moments of vertical and horizontal scaling that remain inseparable dimensions of the political technology of food sovereignty. Despite the qualified opening of state institutions to the participation of agrarian actors, the institutional materiality of ALBA's member states remained relatively entrenched within modes of knowledge-power conducive to large-scale capitalist agriculture. In many instances, the partial integration of national development plans within global governance institutions formed a significant barrier to the transformation of national food systems, with dire consequences for the empowerment of FS actors. The formation of agrarian cooperatives, particularly in Nicaragua and Venezuela, provided one avenue for cooperation among the state and rural classes, yet in each case movement-state relations were overdetermined by the prevailing accumulation regimes within each national space. With the exception of Cuba, the development of participatory democracy and grassroots empowerment has gone the furthest in Venezuela. Yet the fragmentation within the state apparatus, coupled with the contradictions of national policymaking, tends to work against the consolidation of a system of nested hierarchies that complement, rather than counteract, each other.

As a natural response to these challenges, various modes of horizontal scaling offer a potential escape route from the strictures of state power, even if they are always conditioned by it. The horizontal organization of production, distribution, and marketing among self-directed communities forms the basis of knowledge-power adequate to a food sovereignty regime. In many ways, the construction of political-territorial corridors in Venezuela provides the closest example to this type of transformation, fusing the reconfiguration of property-power and knowledge-power into a synergistic mode of organizing across rural and urban spaces. In the case of El Maizal and other agrarian communes, overcoming the economic alienation associated with the manual/intellectual labor divide typical of wage-work goes hand in hand with weaving spaces of production into a concrete *popular political technology*, which helps to "dismantle centralised-privatised power" away from both capital and the state (Fréitez and Martínez 2015, 210). Struggles for food sovereignty in Venezuela have thus begun to slowly transform the elements of property-power and knowledge-power into spaces of democratically self-directed labor and cooperative territorial governance that move through a wider chain of peasant production and industrial processing. As noted above, it was within this vision of an integrated food system informed by popular participation that the ALBA factories were created. And yet, these spaces of production within Venezuela have encountered a variety of tensions and contradictions determined by the unique political economy of oil rentierism.

CHAPTER 5

The Political Economy of ALBA-Arroz

Class Struggles across the "Point and Circle"

On April 8, 2016, an article published in Portuguesa's local newspaper, *Ultima Hora*, reported that the flagship ALBA-Arroz production site, Píritu II, had been occupied by the workforce the day before. Having ejected then-acting president of ALBA-Arroz, Arturo Aponte, workers demanded the reactivation of production at the plant, which had reportedly sunk below 80 percent capacity. Among other complaints, the ALBA union representative, Tirso García, cited the lack of raw material inputs from the local countryside, neglect of factory machinery, and the lack of transport facilities for the workforce (Palencia 2016). The ALBA union had called upon Minister of Agriculture and Lands Wilmar Castro Soteldo to enter negotiations with the workers to rectify the situation. As indicated by the secretary of the ALBA union Héctor López, the identified deficiencies had also caused a complete paralysis in the supply of rice to the local communal councils (Hurtado 2016).

This chapter unpacks the complex and contradictory dynamics that led one of the few concrete examples of ALBA's food sovereignty initiatives to a virtual standstill. Drawing on firsthand interviews with workers at both the coordinator and factory-floor level, as well as members of the neighboring communal council in the municipality of Payara, the chapter aims to shed light on the ways in which ALBA's Grandnational Concept became severely compromised by Venezuela's contradictory political economy. The onset of economic crisis and the debilities of factory management adversely impacted the surrounding community the factory system was designed to serve. The case of ALBA-Arroz presents a key example of Chávez's vision of the "point and circle," a new political geography centered on a series of socialist production sites (points) working in cooperation with self-organized communities (circles). However, broader structural macroeconomic forces, and the clash of class strategies seeking to manage them, ultimately dissolved the organic links between the factory point and communal circle.

Empresas Mixtas Socialistas del ALBA-Arroz: Origins and Challenges

ALBA's Empresas Mixtas Socialistas del ALBA emerged from the signing of a joint Cuban-Venezuelan accord in 2007. That year, a binational survey and investigation—carried out by a Cuban team of seven and two Venezuelan participants—established possible locations for the ALBA-Arroz factories. ALBA-Arroz was later signed into Venezuelan law on July 16, 2007, and finalized the following November (*Gaceta Oficial* 2007a; *Gaceta Oficial* 2007b). The first installations came in 2008, with the Unidad Primaria de Producción Socialista "Río Guárico" (Guárico) and the Píritu I and Payara plants (Portuguesa). The latter two installations together comprise a potential production capacity of around eighty tons of processed rice per day with a workforce of eighty-five employees, employing technology acquired through a joint agreement with Brazil (Depablos 2009).

ALBA-Arroz's central production site, Píritu II, emerged from a state expropriation of the "Santa Ana Parabolizado" plant, also in the state of Portuguesa, from the U.S. agroindustrial firm Cargill. The expropriation came after government inspections found Cargill in violation of price control regulations through the modification of its rice products (i.e., switching from Type-1 white rice to precooked rice) and failure to mark its packaging with regulated prices, made worse by the discovery of eighteen thousand tons of regulated white rice sitting in its warehouses (in violation of laws against hoarding) (Suggett 2009b).

In 2010 these EMSAs were transferred from the Ministry of Agriculture and Lands to the CVAL, under the rationale that "it is essential for the policies of agroindustry and agriculture to establish a system of functional centralisation for the organization of state-led guarantees of food security and sovereignty, as well as the just satisfaction of the needs of the people in order to improve production of those products of primary necessity and of a strategic character" (*Gaceta Oficial* 2010b).

Under the auspices of CVAL, the entire "food chain"—from primary production and processing to distribution and consumption—would fall under the "model of socialist management" (*Gaceta Oficial* 2010b, 14). This "socialist" model of agrarian development crystallized under "functional centralisation" within CVAL, which often spontaneously directed factories to redirect supplies of consumer goods to particular strategic outlets within the PDVAL or MERCAL networks (interview, Píritu II, May 11, 2016). As of 2015, ALBA-Arroz maintained an operating budget of Bs 86,478,742, the highest of all the EMSAs (MPPAL 2015, 42).

As we saw in chapter 3, the formation of EMSAs reflects Venezuela's wider push toward the creation of socialist production units (SPUs), which numbered between one to three thousand by 2009. Like the ALBA-Arroz factories, SPUs are organized around a "triple subsidy": provision of above-average wages, locally sourced inputs from surrounding territory at above market prices, and sale of goods at below-market prices (Larrabure 2013). As the bilateral partner, Cuba was to receive a fixed volume of eight thousand tons of rice annually (MPPAT 2012, 648; MPPAT 2013, 620). And yet, the realization of ALBA's principles, embodied in the "socialization of the means of production" and "proactive workers" (ALBA-TCP 2012; MPPAT 2013, 646), has been subject to numerous obstacles, tensions, and contradictions as a result of Venezuela's unique sociopolitical context.

Losing in Order to Win?
Systemic Contradictions of the Social Economy

When I sat down with the coordinator at the Píritu II plant, it was immediately clear that the problems faced by the ALBA factories stem from the same systemic mechanisms afflicting the entire country. With a loss of $10 billion in oil revenue between 2015 and 2016 alone (OPEC 2017, 20), the reduction in ground rent severely impacted the firm's production capacity, due to the misaligned cost/sale ratio:

> A kilo of paddy, which is shelled rice, was bought at 17Bs from the direct producer.... But for us to produce a kilo of finished rice, we need two kilos of paddy. So that comes to 34Bs. And yet, we were selling at 25Bs, which is the regulated price... So we are simply working under a loss. We have to pay for man-hours, packing material, electricity, and gasoline, not to mention maintaining the machinery... It's as if something costs 10 Euros to produce, and you sell it at 5. (Interview, Píritu II, May 11, 2016)

The rate of inflation, meanwhile, added considerable cost to the price of inputs. At the Píritu I plant, the cost of maintaining the industrial rubber roller used during the hulling process was 30,000Bs at the beginning of 2016; by July that year, the cost rose to 170,000Bs. However, these sums were (at the time) relatively small. As I was told, the main concern was the restoration of the milling equipment, which had been badly worn out yet could be fixed for a relatively small sum (interview, Píritu I, May 13, 2016). Nevertheless, the central concern was how price inflation complicated production plans; the time it takes to analyze the necessary values for a given purchase often undermines the very same process, as by the time a solution is obtained, the values no longer hold (interview, Píritu III workers, June 30, 2016).

Interwoven with these problems were wider issues with national infrastructure. From 2002 the state had taken on a much larger role in the electricity sector, generating around 90 percent of national output (Massabié 2008, 193). As a consequence of state regulations, virtually all state-run energy entities operate without profits due to increased energy consumption and subsidized prices, which can only be sustained through the transfer of ground rent. Yet chronic underinvestment has led to an increase in power failures, from eight in 1994 to eighty-four in 2005 (196). The Guri hydroelectric dam, which generates around 70 percent of the country's electricity, is also highly vulnerable to drought conditions. During a severe drought during the summer of 2016, the Guri facility experienced a major drop off in supply, which led to emergency measures of nationwide rationing (Koerner 2016a). As a result, virtually every

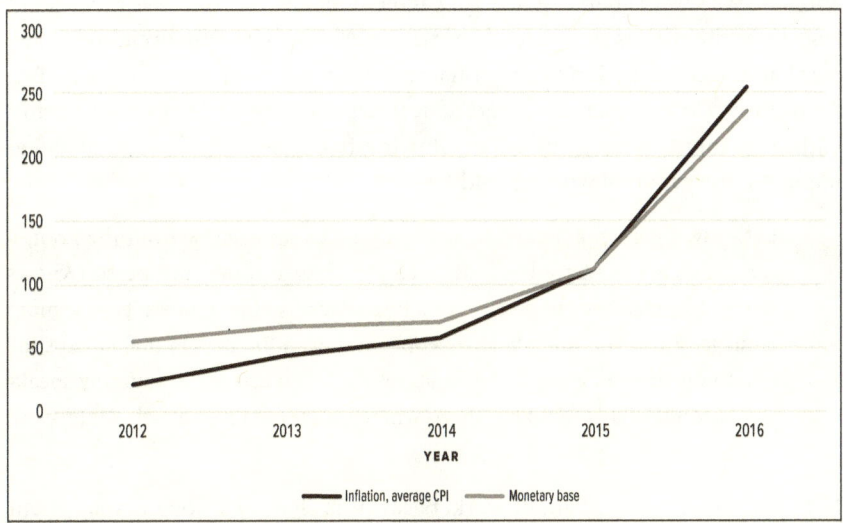

FIGURE 6. Growth of inflation (average CPI) and monetary base, percentage (2012–16).
SOURCE: IMF, Banco Central de Venezuela

business sector—from manufacturing to retail—became subject to closures and planned downtime. The Píritu I plant reported an average of four hours per day in downtime due to electricity shortages, which reduced production capacity from 1.3 million kilos to 3.5–5,000 kilos annually (interview Píritu I, May 13, 2015; interview Píritu II, May 11, 2016).

The broader goals of endogenous development and the "social economy" have therefore been severely impeded by this complex array of crises. The government response has merely aggravated the situation through the printing of inorganic money and the monetization of state budget deficits, which (in combination with reduced production capacity and purchasing power across industry as a whole) feeds into an inflationary spiral (Sutherland 2018; Dachevsky and Kornblihtt 2017; see also figure 6). Yet even with the enormous challenge of runaway inflation most of my conversations with the ALBA workers centered on the *politics of production* within the factories themselves, imbricated with the wider bureaucratic structures of the Venezuelan state apparatus.

Despotic Power in the Social Economy

In seeking to go beyond neoliberal regionalism, the ALBA elevated the principles of the *economía social* onto the regional plane (Schaposnik and Pardo 2015). As we saw in chapter 3, the 2012 agreement aimed to achieve the "socialization of the means of production" within ALBA's Grandnationals as a key plank in the construction of a regional socialism. And yet, the reality of ALBA-Arroz more closely resembled hierarchical structures typical of capitalist firms, with little input or communication flowing from the shop floor to management. As one group of workers told me,

> Let's say a person assigned to sweeping picks up a screw from the floor, a screw that should have been attached to a fixture above, this person knows the problem, and so the screw could be replaced so that it doesn't cause more damage. But if you don't talk to people, not even the person that sweeps the floor, how are you going to know about the fallen screw? Structurally speaking, in terms of this company, this is where we are administratively. (Interview, Píritu II workers, June 28, 2016)

Even the supervisory strata of workers saw this rigidity among management layers as a significant obstacle: "When you are a president you have to talk with the workers, with the commune, with the people, because you work in a socialist company, and you have to have this conviction because you're a socialist." As I was later told, the previous president was "egocentric": "He was a despot, and we are not used to working in this way" (interview, Píritu I, May 13, 2016). Instead of approaching problems through the utilization of a workforce that attains its knowledge through the everyday experience of production, the problems afflicting ALBA-Arroz network were "solved" through the simple rotation of personnel at the top level of management, particularly the factory president. The Ministry of Agriculture and Lands identified this problem of near-permanent management rotation early on (MPPAT 2012, 650; 2013, 622). To the workforce, however, the situation appeared as nothing less than the operation of bureaucracy, inefficient planning, and often outright corruption and fraud: "There is a very famous saying here: *'No me des, ponme donde hay'* [Don't give it to me, put me where it is]" (interview, Píritu II workers, June 28, 2016).[1] The problem of communication did not stop at the factory gates:

> We are managing information here that varies a great deal from the information that they have above [in state ministries]. For example, they will be thinking that we are producing at 80 or 90 percent capacity, whereas we are more like 10 percent.... Until recently the "situation room" [*sala situacional*] in the Republic of Venezuela didn't know anything.[2] I even spoke to a friend of mine who works in these circles, and they haven't been to these sites since 2012... As far as the situation room is concerned, we don't exist. (Interview, Píritu I, May 13, 2016)

For some workers, the problem was rooted in a certain pattern of clientelist state management: "The question is whether the process completes as it should, and that there is no favoritism or nepotism, or because you know a minister which means that the plants are always reported as 'perfect'" (interview, Píritu III workers, June 6, 2016). This critical distance between the workforce and the state apparatus also led to a paradoxical reduction of factory operation. At the Píritu III plant, used for storing and the preliminary conditioning of raw product,

> we used to receive anything: cereals, corn, rice, whatever comes, we were ready and we could process all of it, but they passed us on to ALBA-Arroz, and they limited us, that you have to concentrate purely on rice, whereas right now, Venezuela is passing through a huge crisis, and we cannot put a limit on what we do. Already we have shortages of flour, of pasta, sugar, of everything. We cannot be married to just one product; we must be open to everything. There are peasants that are producing corn, there's corn in the fields,

and there is a paralyzed plant that is capable of receiving corn. Why don't we receive corn? Bureaucracy! (Interview, Píritu III workers, June 30, 2016)

And yet, the levels of plant utilization could easily be returned to their previous status through the simple process of switching sieves and filters for sifting particular grains (interview, Píritu III workers, June 30, 2016). In light of these obstacles, the ALBA workers were uncertain as to the next stage of ALBA-Arroz:

> I don't know how this president [of the factory] is going to do. We have proposed to lend services to other clients, that they will transfer us to another ministry, or even transfer the company to the workers because we know how to work and to generate our own investments necessary to pay our workforce without being dependent on any ministry. So far, they have told us nothing, and we continue to wait, and even looking for clients in the meantime so that we get enough product to carry on... without having to wait for the government to pay for everything. That would be one way, that they give us the opportunity to generate our own investments by means of simply working the plant as such... The knowledge that we have, the practical skills that we have, knowing how to manage practically everything. This is the key. (Interview, Píritu III workers, June 30, 2016)

Self-Management Deflected: The Struggle against Statism

In my conversation with the coordinator at the Píritu I plant, I asked whether ALBA-Arroz had ever been organized under the principle of *autogestion* (self-management), as a central component to Venezuela's and ALBA's vision of the social economy. The answer was quite straightforward: "No, never. We are completely centralized" (interview, Píritu I, May 13, 2016). Yet it was firmly believed that the workforce was capable of moving toward self-management:

> The point is that everyone already knows what to do. There is no need for someone to come from the outside and tell me what to do, and I certainly don't have to go with a whip to supervisors telling them what to do with their work teams. Here, everyone works within their area, with conviction and in order to get the job done... So I think that if they were to put us in a position of self-management, I think we would have the capacity to do it. (Interview, Píritu I, May 13, 2016)

This understanding was also shared among other shop floor workers:

> Chávez used to say, "You don't have to wait for me to tell you what to do, if you already know what to do"... I mean you don't have to be someone from NASA to fix a machine. (Interview, Píritu III workers, June 30, 2016)

> We know that this company does not move without the workers. The workers are those that operate this plant, without the workers the machinery doesn't move, the equipment doesn't move, but we still need a management structure inside this plant, to maintain an order. (Interview, Píritu I workers, June 29, 2016)

Despite the advantages of self-management, the immediate change in the relations of production, and in the structure of ownership and control over the plant, was not the top priority for those working at the ALBA-Arroz factories: "In this moment we are not looking to be self-managing, but in the long term it certainly could be" (interview, Píritu I, May 13, 2016). The severity of the economic crisis and the desire to bring the factory back into production seemed to top all other considerations. If anything, the main priority revolved around the acquisition of competent management personnel, those with specific training and knowledge in the area of rice production, rather than the imposition of "military men" as company presidents (interview, Píritu I workers, June 29, 2016). Coordinators at the Píritu I plant had similar conclusions about the strategic necessity of acquiring high-level personnel with the necessary skills and knowledge:

> The presidents that come here, none of them come with the same preparation, nor do they know much about processing rice... So, the presidents are not so clear about how the system really works, as they are administrative types, like management is, as is the industrialization department. They don't have knowledge of this, and a lot of them come because they know someone, because they have influence with some ministry, or the president of CVAL. (Interview, Píritu I, May 13, 2016)

Workers on the shop floor, meanwhile, were skeptical about the prospects of moving toward self-management:

> There was a time when Chávez said, "You are going to be the owners of these companies, so that your work becomes self-sustainable," but what we have now is another protocol, from above, ministers, vice-presidents; this is the fear

that exists. Perhaps they believe that things are going to change from chavista to opposition, this is the internal political conflict... (Interview, Píritu III workers, June 30, 2016)

They won't allow it [transition toward self-management] because those who have control will not relinquish it. Even though they are asphyxiating you and strangling you, and they know that what they are doing to you is bad, they are not going to let go of you, because it's about power. When one has power, it's very difficult to let it go. We imagine that what you suggest is an alternative, because we have suggested the same ourselves. But do you believe that those above are going to say, "I'm going to give 300 million Bs to the workers at ALBA-Arroz and that they shall administer, buy the raw material, pay wages, that they will have this company there, and I will do nothing here?" You know that this is not going to happen, because you are talking about losing control, and losing power. (Interview, Píritu II workers, June 28, 2016)

I asked whether there was anything they (as workers) could do to remedy the situation or even struggle against recalcitrant forces that may stand in the way of the transition to self-management:

We have tried, but what do they send us? National Guard, SEBIN, PTJ, CICPC, police

Against you?

Of course.

So what can you do?

Cry.

Do you think there is any way Chávez's dream can be saved from below?

We can achieve this change inside a new structure of socialism; it is possible. But they will have to change the oxygen; they will have to admit that they were wrong and rectify their mistakes; or we are going to do what you are talking about, we are going to create a type of self-management, something that should be autonomous, to begin to capture ideas, but something that is real. (Interview, Píritu II, June 28, 2016)

Food Sovereignty Scales Up:
Opportunities and Challenges of Industrialism

In light of ALBA's promotion of food sovereignty within its Grandnational Concept, I was curious to know more about how the workforce understood this concept and how it impacted upon factory organization. Many of the immediate answers were more strongly aligned to the earlier strategic priority among FS protagonists: "assuring that the people have access to food, and to try and bring it to them directly, without the use of intermediaries" (interview Píritu III, June 30, 2016). As another coordinator from the ALBA factory in Payara noted, the goal was "to guarantee every Venezuelan or every family their food, that no one is left out, from the poorest to the richest, and that there is a distribution to all without exception, and that this food comes at a just price, or a real price—a just price for the Venezuelan, which should also be a just price for the industry" (interview, Payara, July 6, 2016). Yet it was also made clear that this vision of secure food supplies was not based simply upon imports but on the cooperative integration between farmers and factories:

> I think that it is to the small producers where they [the government] have to come and say, "Keep going, continue the struggle, we'll continue to help you, we will finance whatever shortfalls you have, whether its technical assistance or whatever. Why did you stop farming those lands? Instead, you should increase the amount of lands you produce." Here for me is where the ultimate foundation lies, in stopping the importation of food, and thus where lies the triumph of food sovereignty and food security of the country—in the countryside. The factories, those that process, are merely a fixture, because if the fields don't bring me raw material, what am I going to process? It is here, in the countryside, in the fields, where the true strength of food sovereignty consists, in partnership with the small, medium, and large producers. (Interview, Píritu I, May 13, 2016)

As the coordinator at the Payara plant explained, peasant producers had ample access to credit, tools, technical assistance, and legal support. Through the proposed partnership with the state, distributed credit would be returned through payments in kind:

> Before the revolution, it was the same but this time through the private firms. However, according to government studies, the private sector did not cover every producer, but rather favored the large producers, with the small peasantry left out.... So what was Chávez's vision? To try to capture all of those people

that could sow any type of crop for the struggle for food sovereignty. As *comandante* Chávez put it, "*Ven a mí que tengo flor.*"[3] That was the vision, to help the small and large producer, and to bring them to the state industries, through the state, with the expectation that those in receipt of government help would in turn sell their product to the same people. (Interview, Payara, July 6, 2016)[4]

Despite this envisaged partnership between peasant production and factory processing, ALBA-Arroz suffered from a deficit of raw materials from the surrounding fields. As the Ministry for Agriculture and Lands annual reports show, the decline of technical assistance and surface area used for the production of raw material (rice paddy) has been a continuous problem (see tables 6, 7, 8). I wondered initially whether this was due to the traditional problem of rural flight and whether there was enough labor in the countryside capable of meeting industrial demand. However, I was told firmly that the agricultural labor force had not moved at all and are still producing their plots as nor-

TABLE 6. ALBA-Arroz, results of Annual Project (2012)

Goal (2012)	Goals Executed	Shortfall	Percentage of Goal Achieved
Acquisition of rice paddy (60,000t)	42,707	17,293	71%
Production of finished rice (30,000t)	15,441	14,559	51%
Recuperation of Productive Capacity at ALBA-Arroz[a]	3	6	33%
Comprehensive technical service to sowing rice (14,941 ha/s)	4,613	10,328	31%
Export Rice to the Republic of Cuba (8,000t)	0	8,000	0%
Sow rice on fields of ALBA-Arroz (11,800 ha/s)	4,225	7,575	36%

a: unit of measure not given.
SOURCE: MPPAT (2012), author's elaboration and abridgement.

TABLE 7. ALBA-Arroz, results of Annual Project (2013)

Goal (2013)	Goals Executed	Shortfall	Percentage of Goal Achieved
Acquisition of rice paddy (54,000t)	37,712	21,228	61%
Production of finished rice (27,000t)	19,800	7,200	73%
Comprehensive technical service to sowing rice (11,800 ha/s)	1,880	9,920	16%
Export rice to the Republic of Cuba (8,000t)	0	8,000	0%
Sow rice on fields of ALBA-Arroz (4,215 ha/s)	3,168	1,047	75%

SOURCE: MPPAT (2013), author's elaboration and abridgement.

TABLE 8. ALBA-Arroz, results of Annual Project (2014)

Goal (2014)	Goals Executed	Shortfall	Percentage of Goal Achieved
Acquisition of rice paddy (60,000t)	25,006	34,994	42%
Production of finished rice (30,000t)	12,229	17,771	41%
Export Rice of the Republic of Cuba (8,000t)	0	8,000	0%
Sow rice on fields of ALBA-Arroz (4,000 ha/s)	994	3,006	25%

SOURCE: MPPAT (2014), author's elaboration and abridgement.

mal, even if under precarious conditions (interview, Payara, June 30, 2016). In one respect, difficult conditions (relatively low, state-mandated farm-gate prices coupled with inflationary input costs) led many farmers to switch out of rice production and move toward nonregulated products in order to cross-subsidize their remaining losses from rice (interview, Píritu II, May 11, 2016; see also Purcell 2017, 309). Whatever rice does remain is often sold to the private sector. As I was informed, private companies typically buy at 100–120Bs per kilo of paddy against the government's 70Bs (interview, Píritu I, May 13, 2016). In effect, this price war between the state and private sector complicates the third dimension of the "triple subsidy": with the private sector in command of higher farm-gate prices, the final product will most likely be sold well above the regulated price.

As a result of these contradictions, rice production took a precipitous decline between 2014 and 2015 (see figure 7). While reduced land area of cultivation was a major problem, it was not the only cause. Indeed, for 2008–9 and 2011–12, total hectares under use for rice production actually increased by 738ha/s and 5,493ha/s (respectively), while total yield *decreased* by 116,693 tons and 24,184 tons, respectively (see figure 8). These negative correlations are therefore shaped by other factors beyond land use. Unlike that of corn (*maíz*), the production of rice is prone to a number of complications that impact crop development, such as weeds, viruses, bacteria, fungi, and a large variety of underbrush, many of which are resistant to chemicals due to the rapid rate of genetic mutation (Interview, Píritu II, May 11, 2016).[5] Interestingly, and somewhat inconsistently with the general approach to food sovereignty, the use of transgenics was invoked by one participant as a potential solution to the problems of rice cultivation: "We have laws against transgenics, though transgenics are not necessarily bad, you just have to know how to use them" (interview, Píritu II, May 11, 2016). The main concern with such techniques was

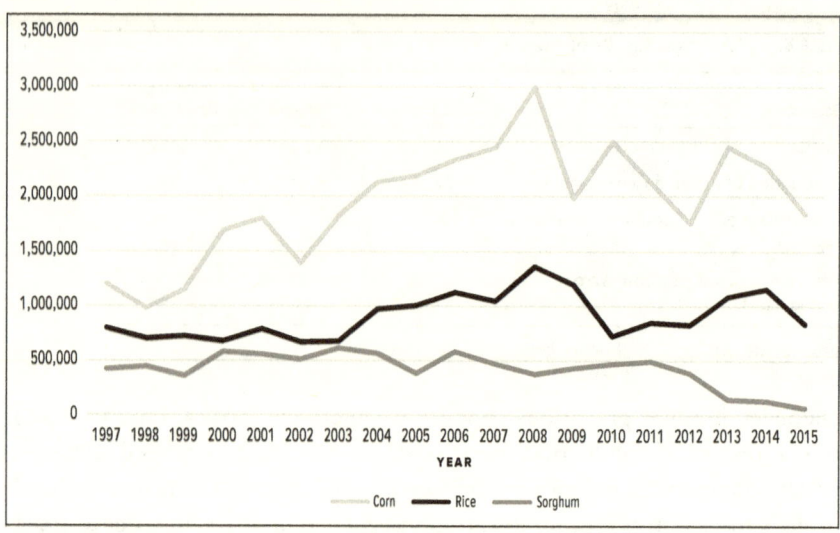

FIGURE 7. Production volumes (metric tons) of rice, corn, and sorghum.
SOURCE: FEDEAGRO

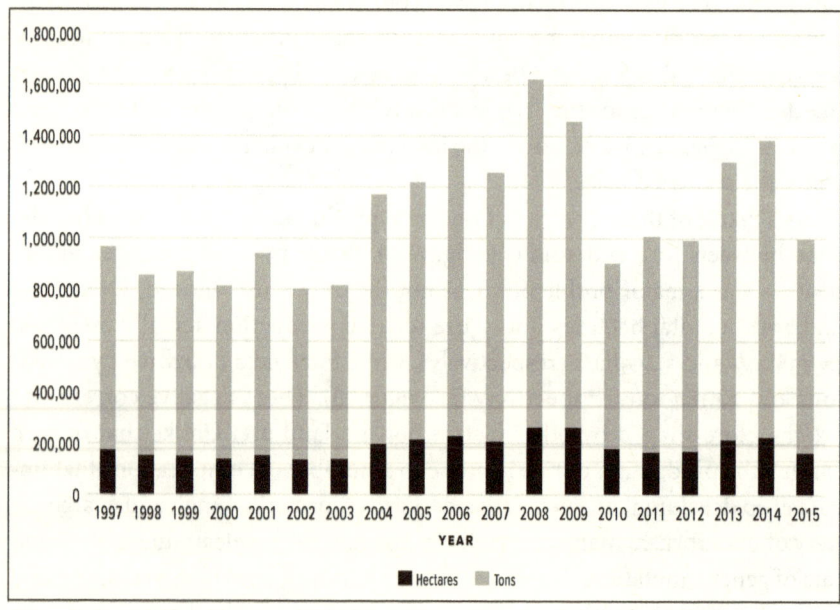

FIGURE 8. Ratios of surface area (hectares) to yield (metric tons) of rice production.
SOURCE: FEDEAGRO

rather the pattern of ownership and control over their distribution, not necessarily the agroecological impact: "Our agriculture is very depressed. This is because everything that is brought to the process is imported: the chemicals, seeds, transgenics.... The problem is that Monsanto manages the Roundup molecule and has a strain of soy that is resistant to Roundup. They manage the monopoly, and this company has effectively monopolized the economy of the country" (interview, Píritu II, May 11, 2016).

Foreign monopolization became a major challenge for Venezuelan agriculture in the face of lower inputs of labor on the land. As the coordinator at Píritu II explained, his time spent in Haiti, Cuba, and Iran revealed a mode of agrarian development based more intensively on labor inputs: "It's a rice that is distinctly natural and without chemical inputs." Venezuela's smaller agrarian population, in contrast, is compensated by industrial inputs and methods, such as tractors, which lead to "problems of compactification ... which has degraded the soil" (interview, Píritu II, May 11, 2016). In light of these challenges, in was understood that the peasantry could not immediately switch out of more conventional farming practices:

> You might say to the small producer, "We're going to stop using agrochemicals." But the producer comes from a very old culture that has been applying these inputs for decades. So you could say, "We're going to substitute chemicals with agroecological inputs," but the producer will say, "Well, let's do a test and see the result." The thing is, they prefer quick results. In the case of insecticides and other chemicals that are stronger, the producers can see the results, above all in economic savings.... To incentivize these practices [of agroecology] will take time, but it can be done. You can incentivize it by saying that ecologically there is less damage to the environment, it's going to have better strength in germination for the crops, the food grown will be cleaner, and you can suggest this to the producer because they are primarily the ones who will be consuming their own food. It's very much an iterative process, little by little. But people put into practice only that which accords to their circumstances, to the way they are living. (Interview, Píritu I, June 29, 2016)

These comments reflect the broader challenges in the transition from more traditional agricultural practices dominated by capital to agroecological methods that facilitate more autonomous and sustainable farming. As Schiavoni puts it, there is always a (creative) tension between *building and dismantling*, "dual processes [that] are inherently relational" (2019, 195). Entrenched usage of agrochemical inputs among Venezuelan campesinos is thus inherently related to the wider agro-industrial complex, lack of state support, and the dominance of state-sanctioned knowledge-power (i.e., bureaucratism, top-down decision making). As the workers at Píritu I emphasized, moving toward food sovereignty implies an iterative process of building cooperation between those working across the social economy, in both the factory and field.

Factory Points and Communal Circles: The Political Geography of Chavismo

Despite the severity of their situation, many workers (particularly those in supervisory positions) remained loyal to the state (interview, Píritu II, May 11, 2016). However, these sentiments were most clearly articulated through the communal discourse of chavismo. Like any living political ideology, chavismo cannot be reduced to a singular identity, nor derived from a single source; rather, it emerges both as an organic self-identity among popular sectors as an expression of their "constituent power" and from the state-led hegemonic project that constructed the Venezuelan people as a "collective actor" (cf. Ciccariello-Maher 2013, 15–16; Carosio 2017, 105–6). This deeper understanding of chavismo carries a sharp resonance with the political content of food sovereignty—as the building of collective power through everyday actions and discourses among heterogenous groups. And yet, the very substance of this popular hegemonic project remains vulnerable to the ongoing struggle across the strategic terrain of the state over who maintains the power to control and the power to decide.

As a key example of this tension within chavismo, workers at ALBA-Arroz spoke of the "Point and Circle" initiative—"an idea handed down to us by our president Hugo Chávez Frías, to be closer to the people and to help them in any way we can" (interview, Píritu III, June 30, 2016). This initiative was seen as a way to transform the social landscape in the service of building socialism, though without necessarily expropriating the private sector in its entirety (i.e., manufacturing, medical services, education etc.). Rather, the emphasis was placed upon specific locales (e.g., a state-run factory) acting as springboards for the molecular process of transforming values, consciousness, and cooperative practices.

While the ALBA-Arroz factories were initially formed as a "point" around which the surrounding communities would organize, some years later the process began to encounter serious problems:

> Since about 2013, we've seen a diminishment in this type of political formation [the Point and Circle]. We don't know if this was lost by those that were

in the company as such, those who lead, but it was degenerating, and in turn this had a bearing on the community because when we started in 2007 the presence of the plant and the workers toward the communities was protagonistic; it helped, for instance, toward a nutritional census, and it helped us to estimate what the community needed in terms of food supply.... But even before the onset of the economic situation we have now, we had stopped seeing the government helping the communities. And this disinterest was seen many times in the ways in which communities started to look at us with suspicion, because we had stopped helping them, and so the community had started to feel mistreated. A lot of times the community said, "Before they gave us a bag of food and now they don't need us, they're already in power." (Interview, Píritu III, June 30, 2013)

I was curious to understand more about the tensions and conflicts that emerged from this breakdown in cooperative governance. To my surprise, I would be given an opportunity to see firsthand how the circle confronts the point. During my conversation with the coordinator at the Payara plant, he spoke about the close collaboration with surrounding communities in the distribution of rice from the factory. While periodically checking his watch in anticipation of another meeting, he remarked:

Right now, I am waiting for the communal council because they are managing thirty tons of rice for the town of Payara. And that's what we are doing, we are bringing the vanguard in direct contact with the people: company to people, communities, peasant councils, communal councils, and communes. This is the alliance we have that helps guarantee food sovereignty and to combat the economic war that has befallen this country. (Interview, Payara, July 6, 2016)

"We Believe in This Process":
The Circle Confronts the Point

As I was returning from the meeting with the coordinator at the Payara plant, I had the good fortune of sharing a cab with someone from the local communal council. Hearing about my meeting with the coordinator, she told me that her council had been in lengthy negotiations with the factory and other local officials on the delivery rice and other products. "You should come to our meeting with the mayor's office in the square," she said.

Two days later, when I arrived at the Parish of Payara, the small plaza was quiet, with only the sound of birds singing and a small number of elderly gentlemen sitting on benches, chatting about this and that. Just a few minutes later, the plaza was bustling with people from the community, eagerly awaiting the arrival of the official from the mayor's office. A major problem had arisen concerning the supply of food to the community through the CLAP, a state-led initiative that directly connected the country's food imports and national production to self-managing committees in every communal council.

The "dispatch" (lower-level official) from the mayor's office had arrived at the plaza. As she sat on a bench, surrounded by dozens of disgruntled people almost talking over each other as they expressed their frustration, the meeting was now well under way. The main problem appeared to be the late delivery of rice form the ALBA-Arroz Payara plant to the local community. The people were unclear as to why they could not pay the factory directly for the allotted rice, rather than rely on the mayor's office to make an electronic cash transfer. Some spoke of the frustration of seeing trucks of rice moving through the parish of Payara, only to be distributed to other locales. The representative of the mayor's office weakly protested, "We are responsible for the whole municipality [Páez], not just the parish [Payara]." Yet people felt as if they were being overlooked. As one man protested, "We're going to be like they say in the United State: 'Venezuela is the backyard.' Well, we're like the backyard of Acarigua!"[6] There were clear sympathies with the community of Acarigua, acknowledging its large size; it was merely an official commitment from the mayor's office that was missing, which the community felt they deserved. At the root of this conflict was the question of who held authority to dispatch the rice from the Payara factory. Apparently, a misunderstanding had arisen as to whether or not a transfer of funds had actually reached the factory, which held up the delivery of rice. Unable to reach an agreement on the facts, the official advised the community to go directly to the factory to speak with the coordinator (field notes, Payara, July 8, 2016).

Suddenly, the crowd dissipated, with two dozen people piling into a pick-up truck. Unsure of precisely what was happening, I followed the people boarding the truck, and asked them where they were headed. "We're going to ALBA-Arroz," a woman said, her arm extended out, and pulled me onto the back of the truck. As we sped off down the road, the people seemed almost jubilant, laughing and joking, as if their collective power might somehow compensate for their dire situation.

About twenty or so people crammed themselves into the coordinator's office. After a few minutes of excited conversing, the coordinator calmed the room to explain the situation. As he said, the problem came down to verifying the transfer of funds to the factory, which had to be secured before the dispatch of rice could take place. If the transfer was made with cash payments, the process would be considerably quicker compared to credit transfer, which could take up to forty-eight hours to clear. Yet the ultimate problem came down to the lack of an agreed accord between the mayor's office and the community in terms of whose dispatch "codes" would manage the order.

As the coordinator explained, he was powerless to dispatch a single grain of rice unless the name and ID number of a designated driver and truck was received from the mayor's office. According to the Venezuelan national logistics system for food storage and transport, every producer must submit a request to for a "unique mobilization guide" (*guía única de movilización*) and in turn receive the details of the allocated driver and vehicle. While the coordinator referred to the "SADA guide" (from the Superintendencia Nacional de Silos Almacenes y Depósitos Agrícolas), SADA was replaced in 2015 by the Superintendencia Nacional de Gestión Agroalimentaria, SUNAGRO) (MINPPAL 2015, 23). Without the receipt of a guide from SUNAGRO, the coordinator could neither verify who was driving away with perhaps the most valuable commodity in Venezuela (food), nor confirm whether the dispatched truck possessed the carrying capacity of the product load. This cumbersome and relatively inefficient system tends to incur major time lags between requests and the receipt of the guides for food producers (Ortiz, Cañameras, and Malavé 2016). While people from Payara were exasperated by the lack of clarity on the issue, the coordinator was more sanguine, assuring them that if they held a meeting with the mayor to sign an accord, their problems would be solved: "If we just work together—mayor, community, company—we can achieve a lot," he insisted (field notes, Payara, July 8, 2016).

Two days later, I met up with three of the (CC) voceros—all women—for the Comuna Agroindustrial "Payara Socialista," of which they are a part. As one of Portuguesa's 142 communes, the Payara Socialista commune was signed into legislation on July 25, 2015.[7] Of the fourteen different communal councils that it comprises, those within the CC adjacent to the ALBA Payara plant were directly involved in the negotiations with the ALBA-Arroz factory, in cooperation with other spokespersons from the commune (interview, CC Payara, July 10, 2016).

As I was told, the point and circle structure of Payara initially followed the "communal route," in which the ALBA factory dispatched rice to every communal council twice a month, though later changing its remit to dispatch it to the Payara Socialista commune to later distribute to all fourteen CCs. Each sector of the commune collected money from the residents, deposited funds into the factory's bank account, and communicated with the factory administration at the time of dispatch. Sometime after, however, the "communal route was severed with the introduction of the Estado Mayor de Alimentación" (interview, CC Payara, July 10, 2016). Created at the beginning of 2016, in the context of President Maduro's "Bolivarian Economic Agenda" that sought to strengthen the "fourteen motors of production" as a means of overcoming the economic crisis, the Estado Mayor represents a type of bureaucratic strata that mediates the distribution of food toward the local CLAPs and CCs (*Aporrea* 2016b). This layer comprises various functionaries from across the state's different fractions, from governors to the various ministries and state companies involved in the national food chain. With this stratified system of authority, ALBA-Arroz Payara receives its orders via authorization codes emitted from the mayor's office, rather than the communes. As a result, higher-level institutions may prioritize the delivery of food to one locale at the expense of another for political reasons. Part of the reason for the neglect of Payara, the voceros claimed, is that its residents were not involved in the widespread protests in 2014 and 2016 over the economic crisis throughout the country, which typically took the form of street barricades and violent clashes between protesters, civilians, and security forces (see *Venezuelanalysis* 2017). "Here we are peaceful, maybe too peaceful . . . because if we engaged in these protests, they would pay attention to us. But we don't do that here."

Yet the voceros were not hostile to state institutions per se: "What we want is to help the mayor, so he can help us . . . As a commune, we want to take some of the work from the mayor so that we can also help ourselves." One of the main points of contention was securing a signed agreement from the mayor's office to reinstate the commune's code as the true point of authority for the distribution of food. As one of the voceros noted, echoing the sentiments expressed by the workers at the ALBA-Arroz factories, "To be clear, when we formed our commune—and this is no secret—the governor and the mayor never wanted us to become a commune. From the beginning, they were afraid of us, because I think they believed that we were going to take away all their power. That's why they have done very little to help us; they've never wanted to help us" (interview, CC Payara, July 10, 2016). This feeling of distrust between the grassroots and higher-level institutions was reinforced by the pattern of state-community relations in the context of electoral cycles: "For example, you're a candidate running for office, and we the community organize in order to turn out the vote for you. Then you win, change your telephone number, buy a car, and forget about everyone. When there's elections, they are here. But when they win, they just call us lowly campesinos and give us nothing, even though we got them elected" (interview, CC Payara, July 10, 2016).

Despite the enormous obstacles facing the commune, communal power continues to guide grassroots strategy: "We continue to struggle because we believe in this process. We believe in Chávez's project, because he left us this project that continues today. But a lot of the people are demotivated, because we don't see change." The desire for political autonomy springs not only from a deep commitment to the values of chavismo but also from the community's material potential:

> Payara has to become independent from the mayor and governor.... Imagine it: this entire zone is agricultural—sugar, rice, sunflowers, all these products. But all this surplus is simply taken, like a tax, and we don't see the benefits. Imagine this space as like a "tube" [*tubo*], material comes in this end and comes out this end, but that it stays within the Parrish—Payara would be transformed! This is the direction of development we see for the future of Payara, and that's why we continue the fight, so we can improve the quality of life for everyone." (Interview, CC Payara, July 10, 2016)

Antinomies of the State-Capitalist "Alliance"

The protracted struggle between the commune and the factory in Payara provides a condensed example of Venezuela's contradictory social economy under conditions of economic and political crisis. The coordinator at the Payara plant had his own view as to the source of this crisis:

> What happens is that there is a culture here, where no one is accustomed to gaining 30 percent or 20 percent, but rather everyone is seeking 100 percent gain. Have you ever eaten an empanada?
>
> *Sure.*
>
> How much do you pay for it?
>
> *About 300Bs*
>
> And how much is a kilo of flour?
>
> *No idea*
>
> A kilo of flour is 180Bs and an empanada they sell you is around 200 to 300. You know how many empanadas you can get out of a kilo of flour? Almost twenty? This is the problem that we have, of consciousness—that we are not accustomed, like those developing countries that profit some given percent, like 20 or 30, but here no. Here everyone wants to profit 150 percent. Or take another example, a tomato; ask here how much a tomato is, they are

going to say to you 600Bs, but go to Acarigua and its 800. There is just no uniformity of prices; everyone manages the price differently. So there is no equilibrium among prices in this economy and that has an impact on inflation.... No one has had the consciousness to adapt to profiting only a certain percent ... so this is one of the wars that the government is battling. To battle this inflation, we should make 30 percent the maximum margin for foreign companies. (Interview, Payara, July 6, 2016)

I asked him about the impact of Venezuela's exchange rate system, to which he merely replied that it was the work of "the economists" to find a solution so that "not this social group or that social group wins, but that everyone wins." He also referred to government measures in early 2016 that opened up a wider space of participation for the private sector in state policymaking. While the existence of a "tactical alliance" between the government and certain fractions of Venezuelan capital had been in place since the oil lockout in 2002–3 (Marín and Ellner 2015), the Maduro administration placed a renewed emphasis on the formation of new alliances with the private sector in order to battle the nationwide economic crisis. In February 2016 Maduro appointed Miguel Pérez Abad, a former businessman and ex-president of the business lobby (representing small and medium sized firms), to the vice-presidency for productive economy, replacing the left-wing political economist Luis Salas (Koerner 2016b). Subsequently, Abad noted that more than 90 percent of the private sector had been in dialogue with the government, carried out through weekly meetings at the National Economic Council (Lorca 2016). One prominent and recent example in the state of Portuguesa (surely in the mind of the Payara coordinator) was the establishment of a partnership between local private producers and the CLAPs to supply more than 250 tons of food. As Secretary for Food Security and Sovereignty in Portuguesa Akalapeizime Castro noted at the time, the alliance was based upon the participation of "responsible businessmen that receive raw material from the Corporation of Agricultural Supply and Service (CASA), and in turn dispatches us part of their final product" (cited in AVN 2016). This thawing of state-business relations also garnered widespread support, with a 75 percent approval rating of the government's dialogue with the private sector (Alavarado 2016) and 74 percent approval of a common strategy of price setting with private businesses (*Correo del Orinoco* 2016b). As the coordinator continued,

It's not only us that has problems in the area of rice, the private companies have felt it and have lowered production margins—I have friends in the private companies; we have shared ideas and we will solve the problem together, not only the state... If we come together and don't lose perspective, we are going to be able to have a better country... He who thinks that he is simply harming the state [by engaging in hoarding or price speculation] is in fact harming the entire country.... Obviously we have to work with a supply and demand, but we are going to work with the supply and demand where everyone wins, win-win, where the business man wins and the consumer wins, through the 30 percent [profit] cap, which would be my recommendation—because there is no real price, it turns into a speculative price, and then you have mega inflation which simply misaligns the whole economy. (Interview, Payara, July 6, 2016)

Here, the coordinator referred to the 2011 Law for the Control of Fair Costs, Prices, and Profits that stipulates a 30 percent profit cap for companies and commercial intermediaries across the board (Robertson 2013; 2014; see also *Gaceta Oficial* 2014), the profit cap was not so much a line in the sand between the state and the private sector but rather the basis through which cooperative relations and economic recovery would go hand in hand:[8]

We have to respect the rules of the game, that this percentage [of profit margin] is maintained and that we solve things internally. If one has to form a structure of costs, we're going to do it together. You're not going to make one, and I make another... Even if you are against the State, you should not want that economy to fail. We always have to look at the well-being of the collective, we cannot have individualist thought; we have to think in the collective so that the country can prosper. (Interview, Payara, July 6, 2016)

What emerged from our conversation was the notion of a loyal "national bourgeoisie"—a political outlook characteristic of postwar ISI development, in which a forward-looking capitalist class would (in the words of the Payara coordinator) "look at the wellbeing of the collective." And yet, this idea has always proved to be highly contradictory in practice. As Chibber (2005, 162) points out, during Latin America's ISI period, "state managers... labored under the impression that, since their agenda was devoted to strengthening national capitalism, it would elicit the support of national capitalists." Yet the specific conditions of national development across Latin American states, particularly the prevalence of tight domestic markets and firms' monopoly power, militated against innovation and upgrading, which eventually led to a stagnant rate of accumulation (150).

In the case of Venezuela, this trend was especially pronounced. As we saw in chapter 3, the ISI policies of the 1960s and '70s offered enormous protection to Venezuelan firms and easy access to credit; they also spawned the concomitant tendency for the formation of oligopolies that dominated the national market. With tight domestic markets and easy credit, Venezuelan capital lacked the incentive to specialize in one sector or maximize their organizational capacity. Instead, the risks involved with diversification into many different sectors could be tolerated given that product markets were locked in, with prices set unilaterally by firms rather than the market (Enright, Frances, and Saavedra 1996, 282–23; Werz 1990, 193; Coronil 1997, 248). Under such conditions, the state failed to implement its directives toward strategic sectors and price controls.

State-capital relations under Chávez, meanwhile, assumed a similar form to the ISI period, only this time the source of tension was between the antichavista fraction of Venezuelan capital and the more "responsible" allied bloc that accepted the 30 percent profit cap. In a sense, the limits and contradictions of Venezuela's "socialist" development path can be traced to this "reactive" strategy of keeping hostile capitalist fractions at bay, rather than fostering a new, socialist-oriented business class (Ellner 2019, 172–73). By 2016 the Venezuelan state was, perhaps out of tactical desperation, leaning more heavily toward the participation of the private sector in kick-staring production. As Miguel Pérez Abad proclaimed in May 2017 (this time as head of the Banco Bicentenario, one of Venezuela's leading public banks), the 1999 constitution, as well as the (then-proposed) new Constituent Assembly, guarantees the right to private property in the means of production, "as an instrument of democracy" (cited in *Noticia al Dia* 2017). However, the standoff between the state and domestic capital continued. As Abad noted elsewhere, "In 2016 practically not a single dollar was given to the private sector, they are working with their own effort" (cited in Marco 2017). While the decline of hard currency distribution was largely due to falling oil revenues, Abad's lament crucially overlooks the bottlenecks and inefficiencies of the national currency system even when dollars are abundant, including expatriation of hard currency, overseas asset purchasing, hoarding, and *bachaqueando*, or outright fraud through ghost imports (cf. Dachevsky and Kornblihtt 2017; Yaffe 2015). Thus, whether in the form of individual appropriations of ground rent or through speculative practices based on commercial exchange, individual firms pursue merely the accumulation of capital (through whatever means necessary), rather than production for the "public good."

Lower-level workers at the Payara plant, on the other hand, did not share the same optimism as their coordinator on the strategic partnership with the private sector:

Even with the salaries that we have, our wages aren't enough. And so, there is not enough to cover all of the demand that there is. Despite everything the government wanted to do, that is to say, to sell to the people at a just and economical price, we simply don't have enough companies created for this particular system because they created some, but the majority of the companies are capitalist, at least the companies operating at the national level. (Interview, Payara workers, July 1, 2016)

On average, lower-level workers were far more skeptical toward the state and political officials, expressing perception of an ossified discourse among the bureaucracy and the inability to adapt to political circumstances:

If you analyze this system, but look at the discourse, it's always the same: economic war, *los gringos*, the invasion, imperialism, and people dying of hunger... The system can change, but we have to change the ideas, to generate new ideas, our form of thought, and our form of evolving... You cannot keep people entrapped in the same discourse we've had for ten years, because we're living in a different reality. You cannot pretend that the people are with you because you gave them a bag of food, with a litre of oil, some flour, beans, and butter—this is not supplying the people. You have to find alternatives so that Venezuelans can dress themselves. Venezuelans have the same clothes they've had for the last eleven years! (Interview, Píritu II, June 28, 2016)

Perhaps unsurprisingly, opinions on the nature and resolution of the country's economic crisis varied among participants, particularly on whether the private sector, and indeed the state, could be counted on for solving the country's problems. For the workers at Payara, state-led firms (such as those within the ALBA network) represented a possible alternative, or even rival, to capitalist enterprises, albeit only if the balance of economic forces tipped toward the public sector. From the workers' perspective, only the relative dominance of state-led firms operating with calibrated levels of profit and investments funds could break the economic deadlock.

From Occupation to Re-Normalization

At the time of my visits to the ALBA factories, the Unión Socialista Bolivariana de Trabajadores de Arroz del Alba was in negotiations with the president of CVAL and other officials. As one of the union voceros noted, it was important for all the workers to maintain constant contact across all factory sites, "so we can speak with one voice." Yet there was also a level of pragmatism involved in their strategies: "Our demands have to be something more or less equilibrated, and what you ask should be according with the reality of the company and the reality of the country, because we cannot ask for something below what is necessary in order to satisfy the workforce" (interview, Píritu I, May 15, 2016). Central to these negotiations was the establishment of a new price structure:

> Rice at the competitive price is almost 470Bs. So, we have petitioned CVAL to increase the price to at least 130Bs, for us to be able to be profitable, and to be sustainable as a company. The problem is that the costs vary a lot, for example packing bags used to cost 8Bs and now they cost around 120Bs . . . and you can't maintain a company like this, because when we have to invest in certain services, like fixing the boilers, this costs millions. You have to do this every six months, and if you don't you're going to seriously damage your machinery. (Interview Píritu II, May 11, 2016)

Having read the most recently published price regulations from the Superintendencia Nacional para la Defensa de los Derechos Socioeconómicos—in which the maximum selling price for white rice grade 1 was now 120Bs—I wondered whether this readjustment had fully taken on board the grievances of the workforce. After all, the purchase price of two kilos of rice paddy was 140Bs, which already puts the cost of production above the new (higher) sale price. "Yes, we are losing, but this company was not created to gain" (interview, Píritu II, June 21, 2016). Somewhat taken aback by the seemingly straightforward answer, I asked whether this once again threatens the sustainability of the company:

> Sure, but what is the sustainability that should be inside this company? To look for an alternative product to sell. Remember that white rice, table rice, has something that is called subproduct. And those products also are commercialized because they sell as concentrated foods, so you compensate one thing for another; the price that you are losing with packaged rice, you are compensating it with the subproduct or you compensate it like we are producing rice crackers. . . but we cannot close the percentage of the people, which is at 120Bs, because this company was created with this objective: to be self-sustainable but never at the detriment of the people in the street. (Interview, Píritu II, July 21, 2016)

It was not made entirely clear whether or not the sum of derivative products and their sale was enough to offset the losses incurred through the sale of white rice, as I was told that hard data were off limits. What remains central, however, is the remarkable change of tone between my first and second encounter with the coordinators at Píritu II. Just before my second visit to the factory, the company had resumed operations, this time under a new ALBA-Arroz president, also a military man, whom I met quite unexpectedly during our second interview. From one angle, it appeared as if the immediate goals of the workers had been met with the relaunching of factory operations. And yet, as I shook the coordinator's hand for the last time and walked out of the factory, I wondered whether or not the workers' struggle had all been in vain; in the end, it seemed as if the nature and operation of the ALBA-Arroz factories had reverted to what they had been the day before the occupation.

Conclusion

This chapter has traced the problems and contradictions afflicting the ALBA-Arroz factories, which impart a series of ruptures across the entire terrain of rights, territory, and (food) sovereignty. With the statization of property rights, the division of manual/intellectual labor continues, and thus sovereign power is maintained under the "state capitalist." But what exactly does the combination of rights, territory, and sovereignty in ALBA-Arroz tell us about the politics of production within a "socialist" factory?

One way into this question is through Michael Burawoy's typology of industrial regimes. In comparing factory organization within Western and Soviet society, Burawoy distinguishes between "hegemonic" and "bureaucratic despotism" regimes, respectively. During the "Fordist" era, the expansion of welfare and state-regulated bargaining (unionization) meant that capital had to *persuade* labor-effort, rather than simply coerce it (Burawoy 1985, 124–26). Under "bureaucratic despotism," in contrast, the prevalence of central planning, rather than market-mediated price signals, leads to the rise of "planners ... [as] ... a class of teleological—that is, purposeful—redistributors" (159). Under "soft budget" constraints, relaxed by state support, workers' remuneration is tied to the completion of production quotas and thus the successful operation of the firm as a whole.

As Burawoy further shows, these distinct factory regimes entail their own forms of class struggle. As we saw in chapter 1, the relative separation of the economic from the political under capitalism leads to the relative obscurity of exploitation; that is, exploitation perfectly coincides with production and is masked by it through the "equality" of exchange in the form of a money-wage. Workers are thus predisposed to hitch their fortunes to the success of the firm and in turn direct their struggles within the confines of the firm rather than across the political field of struggle. Under state socialism, on the other hand, wages emerge not from profits but from state discretion, while appropriation and distribution emerge from state dictates—hence, workers must be coerced into producing surplus through systems of compensation corresponding directly to work-effort (Burawoy 1985, 195). In this way, "enterprise struggles are immediately struggles against the state" (196).

Finally, the subjective disposition of workers under hegemonic regimes tends to correspond to an individualized bond with capital rather than with other workers; under bureaucratic despotism, class identity prevails, posed against a relatively antagonistic class of bureaucratic planners. In Burawoy's view, these conditions of state socialist factory regimes also tend toward the struggle for self-management; both the weak organic integration (hegemony) with the exploiting class and the general lack of confidence in the teleological power of central planners predispose workers to seize factory operations entirely (197). Consequently, the emergence of "socialism from below" is more likely to appear under conditions of "bureaucratic despotism."

Burawoy's framework helps to bring some focus to the specific politics of production within ALBA-Arroz, combining features of both hegemonic and bureaucratic regimes. In terms of the former, the reproduction of labor was mediated through a set of stable wages due to institutionalized bargaining rules, with workers continuing to receive payment during moments of downtime and for the period of occupation itself and the workforce tended to display a higher loyalty to the survival of the firm itself. Meanwhile, the orientation of the workers' struggle did not turn toward the immediate seizure of the means of production and a new system of self-management.

Yet there were also traces of bureaucratic despotism lurking within these socialist factories. Operations are mediated through central planning rather than through competition and the movement of price signals; the work plans are formulated from above (at the state level in terms of product mix and price formation); the broader economic environment is constrained by supply squeezes, in which various types of inputs are generally scarce; and finally, the form of class struggle that took place behind the factory gates penetrated the entire strategic field of the state and in turn ensnared higher levels of the state bureaucracy into the process of dispute settlement.

The combination of these contradictory elements reveals a form of worker subjectivity and agency that brings together relative job security and loyalty to the firm, yet is mediated not through the labor-capital relation but a *labor-state relation*. As a result of this structural bind, workers were stuck between a rock and a hard place—with a positive affect toward the general social values of chavismo and the desire to produce for society on the one hand, and their subsumption under an authoritarian statist regime that further seeks to separate manual and intellectual labor on the other. The result of this bind is merely the reproduction of an inefficient and bureaucratically controlled factory system that marginalizes its greatest asset—the general intellect of the workforce.

In this way, the property-power of the state is ultimately left unchallenged, which in turn severely curtails the possibility of elevating worker-directed knowledge-power over the production process. The example of the frayed Point and Circle strategy similarly indicts the broader political goal of constructing a "communal state." While state discourse has long highlighted the commune as the "fundamental structural cell of the communal state" (*Gaceta Oficial Extraordinario* 2010, 11), the case of the Payara Socialista commune and its struggle against bureaucratic forces is indicative of the rocky and winding road toward popular power.

The story of Payara Socialista is not meant to be representative of popular power across Venezuela; nor is it an in-depth examination of the micropolitics of self-organization within Venezuela's communal spaces. Rather, it serves to illustrate how the contested construction of food sovereignty—as a mode of producing, distributing, and consuming food under principles of equality and empowerment—faces myriad challenges from established centers of power. Only with the true socialization (rather than *statization*) of property-power and knowledge-power, and thus a substantial transition toward *food sovereignty*, would we find not only "a change in state power, but also substantial modification in the relations of production and the state apparatus" (Poulantzas 2014, 175).

Nevertheless, some days before my departure from Venezuela, it emerged that the ALBA workers' vocero, Juan Vicente Perdomo, had filed a lawsuit against the state over the transparency of a procedure pertaining to the possible transferal or shutdown of the factory. As Perdomo claimed, the state did not negotiate with or include the workers in this process, in violation of articles 92 and 142 of the Organic Law of Work (Carrillo 2016). Whether or not the ALBA-Arroz factories will be returned to the private sector remains to be seen. What is now certain, in light of the Maduro administration's order for their liquidation, is that the ALBA-Arroz factories are no longer part of the dream of a "posthegemonic region," or even a national "social economy."

CONCLUSION

For over a century, the terms of socialist revolution have been hotly debated. The first great interimperialist war (World War I) brought to the surface a number of divisions within the international socialist movement—whether to support militarist nationalism or oppose it, whether to seek liberal democratic solutions or overturn the bourgeois order completely. The Bolshevik revolution embodied the impulse to oppose and overturn, only to see the dream of workers' power "degenerate" into a militarized state-capitalist bureaucracy. Over the course of the twentieth century, the Global South was marked by a world historical shift toward emancipatory horizons that, in the end, never truly materialized. The struggle for socialism, as both an answer to the injustices of capitalism and the predations of Western imperialism, eventually succumbed to the pressures of postcolonial state-building and economic dependency. Almost without exception, anticolonial liberation transformed into a top-down form of "socialism" invested in state-driven capitalist development. As the revolutionary horizon receded, many began to speak of the infeasibility of socialism, not only as a theoretical impossibility but by historical fiat. As Francis Fukuyama famously proclaimed, the collapse of the Soviet bloc in 1991 had suddenly brought an end to history, leaving "one contender standing in the ring... Liberal Democracy" (Fukuyama 1992, 42). The coterminous expansion of neoliberalism thus created, for a time, a sense of euphoria as the rising tides of globalization would lift all boats. The ex-communist turned Mexican politician Jorge Castañeda (1993) claimed that with the fall of the Soviet Union, utopia was now "unarmed." The Latin American Left could no longer sell the virtues of socialism to the people; rather, as Castañeda claimed, they now had an unprecedented opportunity to realize their ideals through liberal democracy and market freedom.

And yet, this faith in free markets and political moderation was itself utopian. Neoliberal reform merely sacrificed social cohesion and political equality for modest economic growth. In attempting to lead civil society into a brave new world of liberal democracy, political elites quickly found that their best laid plans were fomenting the very social forces that would eventually lead to their undoing. Indeed, the contradictions of neoliberal capitalism have intensified to such a degree that even in the United States it is no longer taboo to speak of socialism as a viable form of politics. As can be seen in the increasing prominence of socialist politicians such as Alexandria Ocasio-Cortes and Bernie Sanders to the popularization of socialist ideas in the pages of *Teen Vogue*, Fukuyama's liberal utopia has all but evaporated.

Latin America's left turn and the call for twenty-first century socialism thus provide a number of lessons to be drawn in the context of socialism's (relative) revival. In the post-Soviet era, radical social forces across the region embodied the creation of an*other* politics, which, as Sara Motta suggests, was not constricted by unions or political parties but forged in a "politics of knowledge that begins from the ground up and builds from the realities of popular politics in community struggles, movement organizing, and everyday life" (2014, 25). While the new social movements across the continent sought to disengage from traditional political institutions, their desire to roll back the violence of neoliberalism would eventually come full circle, through a tentative embrace with the (anti-neoliberal) state.

The strategic marriage between radical movements and progressive states during Latin America's left turn may have seemed like the best of all possible worlds. But it also fomented the inherent tension between what Hal Draper once described as the "two souls" of socialism: one that is "*handed down* to the grateful masses in one form or another" and the other that is "*realized* ... through self-emancipation of activized masses in motion" (1966, 4, emphasis in original). Making sense of the Latin American Left cannot be achieved through simplistic constructions of bad states and good social movements, or vice versa. Rather, the limits and possibilities of socialist horizons in contemporary Latin America (and beyond) can only be assessed on the basis of how these two souls became intertwined and the political-economic challenges they faced on the road to constructing "socialism in the twenty-first century."

This book has offered a modest contribution to the broader history and debate over socialist transformation, through a so far underexplored aspect of Latin America's only example of "socialist internationalism" in the twenty-first century. While the novelty of the ALBA has certainly not gone unnoticed, its attempt to regionalize food sovereignty deserves much greater attention, not because of what was achieved, but the opposite. In many ways, the regionalization of food sovereignty should have been ALBA's most far-reaching initiative, both economically and politically. The 2007–8 world food crisis led to a series of regional proposals—from food security and sovereignty accords to the construction of Grandnational Enterprises—all of which carried the potential to deepen socioeconomic relations between member states and bring about new forms of political empowerment among grassroots actors. Chávez's calls to radicalize this regional institution through the inclusion of transnational social forces found a natural ally in Latin America's already expansive and well-organized peasant movements.

And yet, food sovereignty movements across the region have not enjoyed the protagonistic role promised to them by ALBA's Council of Social Movements. Meanwhile, coordinated agrarian development policy between ALBA states has barely seen the light of day. The few initiatives to emerge struggled to survive the moment they were born. And most initiatives that did survive operated entirely within, and produced for, the Venezuelan market. In accounting for these limits and contradictions, this book has offered a more critical approach to the politics of food sovereignty through a systematic analysis of class struggle, state power, and regional institutions. In doing so, I hope to have brought some clarity to the ways in which the two souls of socialism fused, and eventually fissured, within the ALBA as it attempted to build a regional food sovereignty regime. The remainder of this conclusion retraces the different chapters of the book, each of which contributes to the rich and multilayered tapestry of food sovereignty politics within ALBA. I conclude with a final reflection on the prospects for radical politics in the region today.

Rights, Territory, and (Food) Sovereignty

This book put forward an alternative Marxian approach to tackling the "sovereignty problem" in food sovereignty studies, as a means of providing one answer to the question of who or what is sovereign within struggles for food sovereignty. In chapter 1, I argued that the substance of sovereign power consists of the historically specific combination of *rights and territory*—as a series of claims, duties, and benefits that determine the contested control over resources and human labor, as well as the spatial organization of society's material and mental content. During the precapitalist era, rights and duties were expressed through relations of "sovereignty and dependence," as Marx put it, signifying the real political control of exploiters over the direct producers. Under the capitalist mode of production, however, an entire series of splits and separations marked out the epoch of "modernity." Separating producers from their land and means of production engenders the simultaneous separation of state from civil society and politics from economics. However, once we step inside the hidden abode of production, the once-separated binaries of politics/economics and law/terror are violently thrown together. Workers' complete dispossession renders them entirely dependent upon the sovereignty of property, selling their mind and body to capital as it attempts to quench its insatiable thirst for surplus value. Likewise, the sovereignty of the state is not given through an abstract principle but stems from the material reality of exclusion, from other states outside its frontiers, and from its own population within them. Borrowing from Jacques Bidet, I argue that one half of sovereignty's edifice crystallizes into property-power, derived from the monopolization of the means of production and intellectual labor, that straddles the legal/extralegal domain.

As a necessary determination of rights, the second half of sovereignty is *territory*, insofar as rights become *place specific*. The modern discourse of rights is largely distinguished by its *universal* character, with the figure of *humanity* as the foundational referent. However, in the absence of a universal (world) state, the "Rights of Man" have always had to reconcile themselves with the rights of (national) citizens (Galli 2010, 60). Similarly, the liberal tradition has always viewed the terrain of rights within nation-states as universally held by its inhabitants, in which territory "is not conceived of as the 'property' of the... sovereign authority, but as 'belonging' in some sense to all the people" (Moore 2001, 142). And yet, the very production of territory and its spatial organization is not equally shared by all. Rather than viewing territory as an abstract entity, a more critical account converges with the concept of political technology—as an ensemble of "dispositions, manoeuvres, tactics, techniques, [and] functionings" (Foucault 1977, 26), all of which constitute a knowledge-power condensed with a particular space. In this sense, both capital and the state employ a series of disciplinary devices in order to pacify, fragment, terrify, or persuade—from factory despotism to the welfare state. Though constructed with different ends in mind—one concerned with the production of surplus value, the other with the production of political order—in each case both capital and the state mobilize knowledge-power as a sanctioned form of calculation, measurement, abstract design, and corporeal control.

My approach to sovereignty, as a terrain of multiple sites of sovereign power, thus lends itself to a homologous reading of Nicos Poulantzas's theory of the capitalist state. While the modern state is certainly embodied by particular institutional loci—in government buildings and ministries—its presence can be felt throughout society, reaching all the way down into the relations of production themselves. The materiality of the capitalist state, expressed primarily by its monopolization of intellectual labor, confers a level of technique capable of disciplining the body politic, organizing the dominant classes into a "power bloc," and disorganizing the dominated classes by keeping them at a critical distance from the state's decision-making centers. Extending this framework to the regional scale, I mobilized Bob Jessop's "strategic relational approach" in order to disentangle the ways in which accumulation regimes, modes of regulation, and hegemonic projects intersect across a variety of political scales. From this critical Marxian perspective, then, the *politics of food sovereignty* can be understood as a radical challenge to the privileges of property-power/knowledge-power within capitalist society, grounded within political struggles over who has the right and ability to decide *what to produce, for whom to produce, and how to produce* (Carchedi 2011, 9). As a corollary to my deconstruction of sovereign power, FS implies the fundamental transformation of property-power and knowledge-power toward the interests of the popular classes through self-directed labor and the cooperative organization of territory.

Chapter 2 explored the historical sociology of international regionalism and the material-geographical conditions that gave rise to the epoch of "continental history." The global expansion of capitalism and the technological frontiers it created across the colonial world engendered not merely an industrial revolution but a *spatial revolution*. The continent-sized island of the United States held up a mirror to the capitalist world, showing a future based upon the territorialization of regional-sized spheres of influence. Latin American leaders were only too aware of the necessity of uniting their continent for the sake of survival in a world of continental powers. Yet the uneven development across the region, as well as its subordinate position within the international division of labor, continued to frustrate the ambitions of regional development. As one of the more recent examples of this historic project, the ALBA similarly based itself on the idea of international cooperation and shared development in order to survive in a world of regions. And yet, its subsequent development would encounter the very same problems faced by previous regional projects.

In order to parse the specificity of ALBA's operation and contradictions, chapter 3 charted the rise of the magical state in Venezuela and its impact on the making of ALBA. If the abundance of oil wealth predisposed the Venezuelan state to conjure spectacular illusions of national development, the centrality of the Bolivarian republic within the ALBA gave rise to a type of magical region. This is not to say that ALBA achieved nothing; regional leaders used their material wealth for the sake of elevating the quality of life for their people through healthcare, housing, education, and cheap energy. More concrete regional development projects, however, proved more challenging than the mere redistribution of oil wealth. The relatively sporadic and uncoordinated mode of regulation at the regional level left a variety of initiatives as mere proposals. Finally, the hegemonic project of the ALBA space, premised on the discursive trope of *sovereignty*, was always pulled in two directions—between the nation and region—at precisely the time when international organization, and hence *regional sovereignty*, was needed most. Of course, building a regional sovereign space is no easy task, and it would be foolish to criticise ALBA's member states for not constructing a regional "state" at the first instance. In any event, the end result was a mere aggregation of states, rather than a consolidated regional "bloc."

Chapter 4 provided a comparative analysis of food sovereignty struggles across several ALBA states. From a Poulantzian perspective, FS protagonists did not simply appeal to state power for protection or fully embrace absolute autonomy; rather, they articulated a much broader struggle across the strategic terrain of the state (see McKay, Nehring, and Walsh-Dilley 2014). In all of these cases, rural actors gained leverage over state institutions (often on the back of previous cycles of struggle) in order to integrate the values of food sovereignty into national legislation. While most ALBA states undertook new policies of land redistribution, others attempted to bring FS protagonists into spaces of decision making over the direction of rural development. Nevertheless, in all of these examples, progressive states ended up walking a tightrope between the elevation of popular power and the entrenched resistance among the dominant classes against popular reforms (Nelson 2019). Seen through the lens of property-power and knowledge-power, FS protagonists faced steep challenges to transforming the configuration of large-scale private property on the land, relatively impenetrable state institutions, and a matrix of knowledge-power valorizing capitalist development. While each country contained its own unique mix of class configurations and institutional complexes, their shared characteristics speak to a general problem of challenging the capitalist state, which distributes rights precisely to *augment* (not diminish) its powers of control (Trauger 2014).

Bringing further focus to the microfoundations of class struggle within a space of "socialist" production, my exploration of the ALBA-Arroz factories in chapter 5 offered some insight into not only the politics of production within Venezuela's "social economy" but also the specific political technologies of chavismo. Whether rightly or wrongly (cf. Schiavoni 2017), the FS protagonists I spoke to invariably viewed industrial processing centers as crucial nodes in the nation's food system, providing not only the necessary scale for strategic goods but new spaces of production in which the values of twenty-first century socialism—principally worker ownership and control—might take root. On this latter aspect, however, the principles of ALBA's Economic Space (2012), which called for the socialization of the means of production, remain far removed from the politics of production at ALBA-Arroz. The division between manual and intellectual labor within these factories was made worse by the fact that bureaucratic management layers had very little "intellectual" resources to begin with. The embodied knowledge within the workforce was therefore constrained by the extension of state power into a regime of factory despotism. This pattern can be similarly seen with respect to the factory-community relations in Payara. The "communal route" connecting "circles" of popular power to the factory "point" eventually succumbed to the pressures of bureaucratisation.

The End of the Progressive Cycle in Latin America? Ruptures, Continuities, and New Horizons

Twelve years after ALBA's 2008 summit enshrining the regionalization of food sovereignty, the Venezuelan Minister of Foreign Affairs, Jorge Arreaza, took the (virtual) podium at the Tenth Economic Council meeting. By this time, the regional picture was one of unprecedented crisis. The ALBA had, for all intents and purposes, ceased to function. Petrocaribe had terminated oil exports to member countries (with the exception of Cuba) due to a precipitous drop in oil output (Dobson 2019; Marquina 2020). Meanwhile, the COVID-19 pandemic that swept through the wider region laid bare the structural vulnerabilities of all Latin American states, scrambling to cope with crumbling health care systems and declining food security (ALBA-TCP 2020; cf. Attwood et al. 2020). Just as they did in 2008, ALBA officials saw the global crisis of 2020 as a warning sign. Without the relaunching of ALBA's socioeconomic ambitions, its peoples would be left vulnerable to the irrationalities of the capitalist world system. To meet this challenge, Arreaza called on member states to relaunch the ALBA Food Program in an effort to strengthen the entire food chain, "from seeds to fertilizers, to food, food distribution, and prices" (cited in *Telesur English* 2020).

And yet, as we have seen throughout this book, the challenges currently facing ALBA go much deeper. After two decades of progressive politics throughout the region, the relative drop in world commodity prices put an end to the "commodity consensus." As a result, the turn away from progressive governments has left ALBA smaller and potentially more isolated that it was a decade ago. As Maduro remarked at ALBA's Misión Cultura in November 2018, "The correlation of forces is not friendly. . . . I call on the ALBA's leadership to prepare and unite more than ever to show that justice is inherent in the ideas of XXI Century Socialism" (cited in *Telesur English* 2018). Arreaza's call to relaunch ALBA's food initiatives clearly sought to make good on this call to arms. However, as the Caracas-based activist Ambar García told me, the solution to ALBA's woes will not come from leaders above, but from people below: "If the social movements do not assume the necessary critique for repoliticizing the process . . . then we will not be talking about ALBA in three years" (interview, ALBA TV Caracas, June 20, 2016).

If Ambar's statement was somewhat pessimistic, her sentiment was well placed. Since the collapse in global commodity prices in 2014 and the partial return of right-wing parties across the region the following year, it has been commonplace to speak of the "end of the progressive cycle" in Latin America (e.g., Main and Codas 2016; Schavelzon 2015). Yet the relative fragility of the Latin American right should give caution to the idea of a long-term "conservative wave." Indeed, in an attempt to relaunch the utopia of neoliberal "reason," the conservative wave has come crashing against the rocks of reality. In Argentina, the center-left Alberto Fernández defeated Mauricio Macri in 2019; Peru saw its first campesino president with the election of Pedro Castillo in 2021 on the back of a vibrant anti-neoliberal ticket; a year later the former Colombian *guerrillero* Gustavo Petro became the first leftist president in the country's history, alongside the historic election of an Afro-Colombian feminist activist, Francia Márquez, as vice-president; finally, in the same year, the mass protests in Chile against rising cost of living carved out a new space for the election of long-time student movement activist Gabriel Boric (McNelly 2022, 100–102).

However, as Verónica Gago and Diego Sztulwark (2016) suggest, positing the beginning and end of political "cycles" obscures the ways in which radical ruptures fuse with historical continuities. The relative wax and wane of left-wing politics in the region should not be measured according to electoral fortunes but read through the relative imbalance between the two souls of socialism. Despite their differences, the material foundation of leftist governments during the first progressive wave rested on redistribution of resource rents as a means of reproducing their hegemony. The eventual unravelling of this political compact led to the fraying of these two souls and degenerated into increasingly authoritarian modes of governance, reflecting the condensation of political crises emerging from the transformation of class relations and economic rhythms of a particular conjuncture (Poulantzas 2014, 206, 211; cf. Tilzey 2019).

Perhaps nowhere were these contradictions more acute than in Venezuela, the beating heart of the ALBA. As state-led agrarian development projects increasingly filled the vacuum left behind by underperforming cooperatives, the multiple sovereignties envisaged by food sovereignty politics was gradually substituted with a more centralized form of sovereign power condensed within the state itself. Even more successful forms of communal agriculture, like the El Maizal commune, found themselves in confrontation with a hostile state apparatus.[1] It seems apposite to note in the same year Maduro took to the airwaves to extoll the virtues of socialism, with special reference to the centennial anniversary of the Bolshevik revolution (*Correo del Orinoco* 2017). If history was not entirely repeating itself, there was certainly more than an uncomfortable similarity between the degeneration of the workers' state in Russia and the turn to authoritarian statism in Venezuela. As the former minister for communes and social movements Reinaldo Iturriza argued, over the course of its lifetime, chavismo has been irrevocably "brutalized," firstly by right-wing opposition forces and latterly through the substitution of bureaucratic "officialism" for the communal "subject of struggle." Within this moment of political crisis, the "strategic horizon begins to blur. In such circumstances, officialism plays the role of the messenger" (Iturriza 2016, 183).

When one of the representatives of the El Maizal commune, Ángel Prado, was asked about the current splits within the chavista movement, his answer was telling: "I think there is some political exhaustion, worn out politicians that have no initiative anymore. There are many politicians that might be over the hill, perhaps they believed that Chavismo was going to die with Chávez, or that Maduro was going to be overthrown" (cited in Vaz 2018c). And yet, despite the blurring of revolutionary horizons across Latin America, the reconfigurations of national governments and regional institutions cannot extinguish the radical social forces that seek to build new forms of popular sovereignty from below. As the coordinator for the social movements at the ALBA headquarters, Rubén Pereira, put it to me, "Chávez used to say: 'Presidents die, governments pass, but the people remain.'" From this perspective, even with the passing of institutions and political regimes, the struggle for food sovereignty, and for the idea of an independent Latin America, will live on in the hearts and minds of those who continue to fight for a better world.

NOTES

INTRODUCTION

1. The acronym of ALBA means "dawn" (*alba*) in Spanish. This regional initiative would go on to be renamed the Bolivarian Alliance for the Peoples of our America. Later, in 2006, the name was expanded to include TCP (Tratado de Comercio de los Pueblos—Peoples' Trade Treaty).

2. The Indigenous origins of the *conuco* can be traced back to the Taino peoples of the Caribbean Islands, who had crafted an intricate system of agroecological production across a rugged and mountainous landscape. These small spaces of production were subsequently used by slaves as well as low-wage laborers as subsistence plots within *hacienda* plantations (see Gill 2023; Felicien, Schiavoni and Romero 2018; Hoffman 2003). While maintaining a connection to this deeper history, in contemporary Venezuela, the *conuco* refers to small patios or gardens used by residents as a supplement to their wider consumption.

3. Relations of exploitation refer to the social relationship between the group of non-producers who make a claim upon, and appropriate, part or all of the output of the direct producers.

4. As Peter Thomas points out, this understanding of the state as *constitutive* of the relations of production was already present within Gramsci's broader oeuvre (Thomas 2011, 286–87). Moreover, much of Gramsci's early writing (before the famed *Prison Notebooks*) emphasizes the centrality of workers councils and rural struggles in the making of socialist politics (Gramsci 1977, 1978). But these aspects of Gramsci's work have been largely lost to contemporary Gramscian scholarship in Latin America. More to the point, Gramsci's political writings present a more journalistic patina designed for agitation rather than in-depth analysis. For all these reasons, Poulantzas offers a more robust framework for thinking through the capitalist state in the context of food sovereignty.

5. The root of the "Bolivarian" Republic stems from the Venezuelan independence leader, Simón Bolívar, whose image was (re)molded by Chávez's hegemonic project into a projection of Venezuela's political independence and national transformation (Conway 2003, 156–58).

6. While the characteristics of these institutions will be more fully explored in chapters 3 and 4, the policy of endogenous development refers to the state-guided strategic

priority of strengthening domestic production, which maximizes the use of nonscarce local resources as well as nurturing more inclusive forms of employment and social production. As a corollary to this development model, the expansion of communal councils (*consejos comunales*), communes (*comunas*), and cooperatives (*nucléos endogenos*) provided spaces of participatory management of political and economic projects among local communities.

7. As a poignant example of this radical fluctuation, just one year after the right-wing Bolivian coup new elections brought left-wing candidate Luis Acre to the presidency. Acre subsequently proclaimed Bolivia's intention to rejoin the ALBA-TCP (*Bolivia Digital* 2021).

8. While the CANEZ was formed in 2003 by Chávez in order to unite the country's disparate rural movements, the FNCEZ took a more independent route, emerging in 2004 from the fusion of two previous peasant groupings. The CRBZ is an umbrella movement, comprising the Simón Bolívar National Communal Front, Simón Rodríguez Center for Training and Social Study, the FNCEZ, and various worker movements. Finally, the Universidad Argimiro Gabaldón is an autonomous peasant movement and pedagogical network among various peasant families across the Venezuelan *llanos*—the agricultural center of the country. These groups were chosen in light of their significant weight within peasant politics in the country, a discussion of which comprises a substantial part of chapter 4.

9. One additional Skype interview took place with a member of the Ataroa commune in the Venezuelan federated state of Lara, in November 2018. I am most grateful for their clarifications and insights into the many facets of Venezuela's complex landscape of food politics.

10. Though Ecuador is host to a variety of agrarian movements, the Federacíon Nacional de Trabajadores Agroindustriales Campesinas e Indígenas Libres del Ecuador (FENACLE) is one of the country's largest groupings (along with FENOCIN). I was unsuccessful in my efforts to locate the FENACLE offices in Quito (the few leads I had to go on produced little result), which is why FENOCIN is the only Ecuadorian organization represented in this book.

CHAPTER 1. The Hidden Edifice of (Food) Sovereignty

1. Though Marx himself makes an immediate qualification: "This does not prevent the same economic basis—the same in its major conditions—from displaying endless variations and gradations in its appearance, as the result of innumerable different empirical circumstances, natural conditions, racial relations, historical influences acting from outside, etc. and these can only be understood by analysing these empirically given conditions (Marx 1991, 927–28).

2. The production of surplus-value may take place in one of two ways. Absolute surplus-value corresponds to the lengthening of the working day, with all other conditions remaining as before and thus pumping more surplus labor time out of workers. Relative surplus-value emerges from the reduction of the necessary labor time required for the reproduction of labor, whether through increasing the intensity of work, enhancing the productive powers of labor, or through the cheapening of wage goods (see Marx 1982, 432–33).

3. Anticipating Morris Cohen's critique almost a century earlier, sections of the U.S. working class denounced capital's "sovereign control over the prices of labor," as a result of their utter dispossession and dependence on employers (cited in Tomlins 1993, 10).

4. The notion of the "selectivity" of action was not well brought out in Poulantzas's work, where it is at best implicitly acknowledged. One of the few references to it makes note of the "*non-decision making*" of dominant actors, which "applies not only to the hard core of the relations of production, but also to spheres that go far beyond it" (Poulantzas 2014, 194). In essence, Poulantzas refers to the bounded rationality of agents, the universal gap between agent knowledge and objective conditions. Nevertheless, the notion of selectivity qua agential property was never fully worked out and will be further discussed in this chapter.

5. By "immediate discourse," Bidet refers to interindividual relations presupposing an immediate equality between individuals. Under capitalist modernity, immediate discourse between individuals is always mediated by the market and organization, which is ultimately instrumentalized into their two "class factors" (property-power/knowledge-power). The "horizon" of emancipation, for Bidet, is therefore a return to the basis of immediate discourse—"'communism' or radical democracy"—via the "popular assimilation of both these 'mediations' [market/organization]" (Bidet 2016, 250).

CHAPTER 2. Capitalist Geopolitics and the Rise of "Continental History"

1. The Rio Pact of 1947 and the subsequent Bogotá summit of 1948 would culminate in the Organization of American States (OAS), which effectively embodied the institutional expression of U.S. imperial domination within the region (van der Pijl 2006, 180).

2. The "closing" of the frontier represents a significant structural barrier to Latin America's traditional mode of agricultural growth, in which for the years 1948–1964, "two-thirds of the increase in [agricultural] output stemmed from bringing new land under cultivation" (Street 1987, 203).

3. The peak of trade union density, as one proxy for working class size, was around 22 percent during the height of the ISI period, compared to about 13 percent in the 1990s (Spronk 2013, 80).

CHAPTER 3. From Magical State to Magical Region

1. However, during this time, the weight of the oil industry did not produce inflationary effects because profits were mostly repatriated (McBeth 2002, 115). Indeed, by Löwy's estimation, during the first seven years of AD government rule, some $504 million had been expatriated, "an amount that was equal to almost half of the total income of US investment in Latin America" (Löwy 1981, 182–83).

2. This account stems from Luis Miquilena, one of Chávez's political mentors and key figure in the MVR, who later became somewhat critical of Chávez's approach (Brading 2014, 56).

3. These enterprises are (respectively): Empresa Mixta Socialista Arroz del ALBA; Empresa Mixta Socialista Leguminosas del ALBA; Empresa Mixta Socialista Porcinos del ALBA; Empresa Mixta Socialista Avícola del ALBA; Empresa Mixta Socialista Pesquera del ALBA; and Empresa Mixta Socialista Lacteos del ALBA. There is also one other

EMSA stipulated in the same *Gaceta Oficial*, oriented around the production of timber—Empresa Mixta Socialista Maderas del ALBA. The only other Venezuelan-based food EMSA not contained in this decree is the ALBA-Cacao company, which was signed into law a few months earlier (*Gaceta Oficial* 2010a).

CHAPTER 4. Spaces of Agrarian Struggle

1. A significant exception to this trend was the long-term struggle among coffee workers within the department of Matagalpa to wrest back control of their lands from the Nicaraguan coffee consortium, CONSAGRA-AGRESAMI, which had dispossessed farm workers through debt traps and evictions. The subsequent La Tunas accords, which sought to resolve the plight of the farm workers, were convened in response to widespread protests and street barricades among dispossessed coffee workers and their families (see Wilson 2015).

2. However, it is generally understood that FNCEZ comprises about fifteen thousand peasant families nationwide (Ciccariello-Maher 2013, 202).

3. According to government sources, around 60,439 land titles were registered between 2007 and 2013 (García 2017, 216).

4. Expropriations of privately owned lands centered on those exceeding average-size holdings, whose yield was 80 percent or less of its maximum potential (Lavell 2016, 81).

5. According to O'Brien's account, which is derived from participant interviews among members of the Símon Bolívar communal city, it is apparently this split that led to the formation of the FNCEZ among those advocating collective property.

6. This form of peasant organization has worked particularly well in Cuba over the past two decades (Gürcan 2014).

7. This contrasts quite radically with Ecuador's land reform, in which peasant lands remained commodified and thus potentially alienable through market mechanisms (Giunta 2014, 1219).

8. Enríquez and Newman (2015, 16), however, provide their own proxy for wage-labor in Venezuelan agriculture, as the difference between (a) the "Economically Active Population in Agriculture and Hunting" and (b) the number of those who own their own land. By this estimation, then, the number of agricultural wage-laborers in 2008 would be 580,269, which is just over half of all people in agriculture: (A)-(B), (990,974−410,705) (INE 2015; MPPAT 2007/8). This rise in wage labor compared with a decade earlier would be consistent with the relative drop in small holdings in favor of medium-size units.

9. The two main institutions tasked with coordinating policies for agrarian cooperatives—INFOCOOP and CONACOOP—have now been transferred under the authority of the MEFCCA.

10. It is reported that, nationwide, there are 736 peasant delegates for this council, working across five work commissions (*El Universal* 2014).

11. These institutions are, respectively: Development Fund for Socialist Agriculture, Rural Development Institute, Agricultural Bank of Venezuela, National Land Institute, Foundation for Training and Innovation for Rural Development, National Institute of Agricultural Research, National Institute of Integral Agricultural Health, Venezuelan Food Corporation, and Food Markets (Mercado de Alimentos). The problem of institutional redundancy was acknowledged in January 2020, when Nicolás Maduro an-

nounced the consolidation and centralization of agrarian credit institutions under a new "Social Fund for Production" (VTV 2020).

12. Similar problems of organization can be seen in Bolivia's Empresa de Apoyo a la Producción de Alimentos, an institution that routinely fails in its mission to support small farmers with inputs and market access with just prices (McKay 2018, 416).

13. The "point and circle" refers to a specific political geography of Venezuela's social economy, which we will see further in chapter 5.

14. Precisely which actor fixes these prices depends on the type of market in question. "Rural markets," located within peasant communities, tend to have prices fixed by commercial intermediaries, whereas "promoted markets," located in urban/periurban spaces, offer prices determined by producers themselves. It is this latter type of market that provides the greatest scope for "short-circuited commercialisation" (Elías and Devisscher 2014, 28).

15. This transition between de facto and de jure agency in fact sharply dovetails with the sentiment carried in the original 2007 constitutional reform referendum, which refers to popular power as "not born of suffrage nor any election, but out of the condition of the human groups that are organized as the base of the population" (cited in Spanakos and Pantoulas 2016, 8).

16. The CLAPs were created after chavismo's electoral defeat of 2015 in the National Assembly, which was perceived by party cadres to be a result of the long lines outside supermarkets. The initiative was intended to bring food bags (*combos*) to residents directly through PSUV officials and activists working with communal councils (Ellner 2019).

17. This area of investment is one that has been clearly recognized by rural development agencies in Venezuela, which has led to the implementation of a four-year plan (marked "Phase 1") for the radical rehabilitation of the nation's irrigation system (MPPAT/INDER 2015). As LeRoy et al. (2022) show, self-managed irrigation systems in Mérida display highly adaptive institutional arrangements, allowing residents and users to effectively respond to unforeseen challenges in water management.

CHAPTER 5. The Political Economy of ALBA-Arroz

1. The above translation represents a more precise reflection of the Spanish phrase quoted. However, in the context of the conversation, the fuller meaning would roughly translate to: "Don't just give me stolen funds, put me at the source and I can steal it for myself."

2. This refers to a type of operational HQ at the top echelons of the state, across a series of political departments and levels, from electoral, military, to economic sectors.

3. This expression, derived from a popular card game in Latin America, *Truco*, refers to a player carrying three of a kind, or a winning hand. Chávez often used this phrase in the context of land expropriations.

4. The expectation of a contractually reciprocal relationship between peasant producers and the state was seen as a way out of a common problem in which producers would receive state aid in order to complete a harvest and simply sell their product to the private sector (interview, Agua Blanca workers, June 30, 2016).

5. The material resilience of corn helps to partly explain why production levels have seen a secular increase for the past fifteen years, as seen in figure 8.

6. Acarigua is the capital city of Páez municipality.

7. By this date, around 1,195 communes had been created across the country (Azzellini 2016, 244).

8. Yet with the onset of the first cycle of protests in 2014, the profit cap was largely moot, in light of the government's attempted reconciliation with the business sector (Ellner 2019, 172).

CONCLUSION

1. A stunning example of the state's degeneration into authoritarian statism came during the mayoral elections in 2017, when the representative of El Maizal, Ángel Prado, was actively blocked from running by the country's National Electoral Council. Despite gaining more than seven thousand signatures from the community in line with electoral registration rules, Prado was excluded from the ballot, leaving the PSUV candidate, Jean Ortiz, victorious (Boothroyd Rojas 2017).

REFERENCES

Adelman, Jeremy. 2009. *Sovereignty and Revolution in the Iberian Atlantic*. Princeton: Princeton University Press.
Agarwal, Bina. 2010. "Rethinking Agricultural Production Collectivities." *Economic and Political Weekly* 45 (9): 69–78.
———. 2014. "Food Sovereignty, Food Security and Democratic Choice: Critical Contradictions, Difficult Conciliations." *Journal of Peasant Studies* 41 (6): 1247–68.
———. 2016. *Gender Challenges*. Vol. 2, *Property, Family, and the State*. New Delhi: Oxford University Press.
Aguirre, Jessica, and Elizabeth Cooper. 2010. "Evo Morales, Climate Change, and the Paradoxes of a Social-Movement Presidency." *Latin American Perspectives* 37 (4): 238–44.
Akram-Lodhi, A. Haroon. 2007. "Land, Markets and Neoliberal Enclosure: An Agrarian Political Economy Perspective." *Third World Quarterly* 28 (8): 1437–56.
Alavarado, Maria. 2016. "75% de los venezolanos cree que el gobierno nacional debe dialogar con los empresarios." *Correo del Orinoco*, May 29, 2016. http://www.correo delorinoco.gob.ve/nacionales/75-venezolanos-cree-que-gobierno-nacional-debe-dialogar-empresarios/.
ALBA. 2004. "Declaración conjunta Venezuela-Cuba." I Summit, Havana, Cuba, December 14, 2004. http://www.portalalba.org/index.php/alba/documentos/1221-2004-12-14-i-cumbre-la-habana-cuba-declaracion-conjunta-venezuela-cuba.
ALBA-TCP. 2007. "Proyectos grannacionales." V Summit, Tintorero, Venezuela, April 28–29, 2007. http://www.portalalba.org/index.php/alba/documentos/1228-2007-04-28-y-29-v-cumbre-tintorero-venezuela-proyectos-grannacionales.
———. 2008a. "Acuerdo para la implementación de programas de cooperación en materia de soberanía y seguridad alimentaria." I Extraordinary Summit, Caracas, Venezuela, April 23, 2008. https://portalalba.org/documentos-alba/acuerdo-para-la-implementacion-de-programas-de-cooperacion-en-materia-de-soberania-y-seguridad-alimentaria/.
———. 2008b. "Declaración política." VI Summit, Caracas, Venezuela, January 26, 2008. http://www.portalalba.org/index.php/alba/documentos/1236-2008-01-26-vi-cumbre-caracas-venezuela-declaracion-politica.

———. 2008c. "Conceptualización de proyecto y empresa grannacional den el marco del ALBA." VI Summit, Caracas, Venezuela, January 26, 2008. http://www.portalalba.org/index.php/alba/documentos/1232-2008-01-26-vi-cumbre-caracas-venezuela-conceptualizacion-de-proyecto-y-empresa-grannacional-en-el-marco-del-alba.

———. 2009a. "Acuerdo para la constitución de una empresa grannacional de alimentos." IV Extraordinary Summit, Caracas, Venezuela, February 2, 2009. http://www.portalalba.org/index.php/alba/documentos/1247-2009-02-02-iv-cumbre-extraordinaria-caracas-venezuela-acuerdo-para-la-constitucion-de-una-empresa-grannacional-de-alimentos-en-el-marco-de-petrocaribe-y-el-alba.

———. 2009b. "Acuerdo de seguridad y sobernía alimentaria." IV Extraordinary Summit, Caracas, Venezuela. February 2, 2009. http://www.portalalba.org/index.php/alba/documentos/1248-2009-02-02-iv-cumbre-extraordinaria-caracas-venezuela-acuerdo-de-seguridad-y-soberania-alimentaria-de-los-paises-miembros-de-petrocaribe-y-el-alba-alba-alimentos.

———. 2010a. *Construyendo un mundo pluripolar: Cumbres 2004–2010*. October 2010.

———. 2010b. "Manifiesto bicentenario de Caracas." IX Summit, Caracas, Venezuela, April 19, 2010. http://www.portalalba.org/index.php/alba/documentos/1307-2010-04-19-ix-cumbre-caracas-venezuela-manifiesto-bicentenario-de-caracas.

———. 2012. "Acuerdo para la constitución del espacio económico del ALBA-TCP (ECOALBA-TCP)." XI Summit, Caracas, Venezuela, February 4–5, 2012. http://www.portalalba.org/index.php/alba/documentos/1305-2012-02-04-y-05-xi-cumbre-caracas-venezuela-acuerdo-para-la-constitucion-del-espacio-economico-del-alba-tcp-ecoalba-tcp.

———. 2013. "Cumbre de movimientos sociales del ALBA." XII Summit, Guayaquil, Ecuador, July 29–30, 2013. http://www.portalalba.org/index.php/alba/documentos/1329-2013-07-30-xii-cumbre-guayaquil-ecuador-cumbre-de-movimientos-sociales-del-alba-29-y-30-de-julio-de-2013.

———. 2020. "Declaración conjunta del XX consejo político y X consejo de complementación económica del ALBA-TCP." http://mppre.gob.ve/discurso/declaracion-conjunta-consejo-politico-alba-tcp/.

Albertus, Michael. 2015. *Autocracy and Redistribution: The Politics of Land Reform*. Cambridge: Cambridge University Press.

Alkon, Alison Hope. 2012. *Black, White, and Green: Farmers Markets, Race, and the Green Economy*. Athens: University of Georgia Press.

Alkon, Alison Hope, and Julian Agyeman. 2011. *Cultivating Food Justice: Race, Class, and Sustainability*. Cambridge, Mass.: MIT Press.

Alonso-Fradejas, Alberto, Saturnino Borras, Todd Holmes, Eric Holt-Giménez, and Martha Jane Robbins. 2015. "Food Sovereignty: Convergence and Contradictions, Conditions and Challenges." *Third World Quarterly* 36 (3): 431–48.

Altieri, Miguel A., and Fernando R. Funes-Monzote. 2012. "The Paradox of Cuban Agriculture." *Monthly Review* 63 (8): 23–33. https://monthlyreview.org/2012/01/01/the-paradox-of-cuban-agriculture/.

Altieri, Miguel A., and Clara I. Nicholls. 2008. "Scaling up Agroecological Approaches for Food Sovereignty in Latin America." *Development* 51(4): 472–80.

Alvarez, Angel. 2004. "State Reform before and after Chávez's Election." In *Venezuelan Politics in the Chavez Era: Class, Polarization, and Conflict*, edited by Steve Ellner and Daniel Hellinger, 147–61. London: Lynne Rienner Publishers.

Alves, Johanna Marianny, Rebeca Gregson, Anit Quintero, María Claudia Rossell, María Eugenia Fréitez, eds. 2016. *Comunalizar el poder: Claves para la construcción del socialismo comunal*. Caracas: rbv.

América Economica. 2011. "Venezuela Y Bolivia acuerdan crear Empresa Grannacional de Producción de Alimentos." January 4, 2011. http://www.americaeconomia.com/economia-mercados/comercio/venezuela-y-bolivia-acuerdan-crear-empresa-grannacional-de-produccion-de-.

Anderson, Elizabeth S. 2017. *Private Government: How Employers Rule Our Lives (and Why We Don't Talk about It)*. Princeton: Princeton University Press.

Anderson, Perry. 1974a. *Lineages of the Absolutist State*. London: New Left Books.

———. 1974b. *Passages from Antiquity to Feudalism*. London: New Left Books.

Angosto-Ferrández, Luis Fernando, ed. 2014. *Democracy, Revolution and Geopolitics in Latin America: Venezuela and the International Politics of Discontent*. London: Routledge.

Aponte-García, Maribel. 2011. "Intra-Regional Trade and Grandnational Enterprises in the Bolivarian Alliance: Conceptual Framework, Methodology and Preliminary Analysis." *International Journal of Cuban Studies* 3 (2/3): 181–97.

———. 2014. *El nuevo regionalismo estratégico. Los primeros diez años del* ALBA-TCP. Buenos Aires: CLACSO.

Aponte-García, Maribel, ed. 2015. *El ALBA-TCP: Origen y fruto del nuevo regionalismo latinoamericano y caribeño*. Buenos Aires: CLACSO.

Aporrea. 2016a. "Ministerio Público acusó a Gerente General de Leguminosas del Alba por contrabando de 120 toneladas de caraotas en Yaracuy." May 11, 2016. https://www.aporrea.org/ddhh/n290458.html.

———. 2016b. "Agenda Económica Bolivariana es la estrategia del pueblo trabajador para consolidar el futuro." February 21, 2016. https://www.aporrea.org/actualidad/n286170.html. https://www.aporrea.org/actualidad/n309811.html.

Araújo, Saulo. 2010. "The Promise and Challenges of Food Sovereignty Policies in Latin America." *Yale Human Rights and Development Law Journal* 13: 493–506.

Arditi, Benjamin. 2008. "Arguments about the Left Turns in Latin America: A Post-Liberal Politics?" *Latin American Research Review* 43 (3): 59–81.

Arrighi, Giovanni. 2006. *The Long Twentieth Century: Money, Power, and the Origins of Our Times*. London: Verso.

Artaraz, Kepa. 2011. "New Latin American Networks of Solidarity? ALBA's contribution to Bolivia's National Development Plan (2006–10)." *Global Social Policy* 11 (1): 88–105.

Atasoy, Yildiz, ed. 2009. *Hegemonic Transitions, the State and Crisis in Neoliberal Capitalism*, New York: Routledge.

Attwood, James, Valentina Fuentes, Jonathan Gilbert, and Michael D. McDonald. 2020. "No Meat, No Milk, No Bread: Hunger Crisis Rocks Latin America." *Bloomberg*, September 28, 2020. https://www.bloomberg.com/news/features/2020-09-28/no-meat-no-milk-no-bread-hunger-crisis-rocks-latin-america.

AVN. 2016. "Alianza Pública-Privada Fortalece en Portuguesa venta de alimentos casa a casa." June 6, 2016. http://www.avn.info.ve/contenido/alianza-p%C3%BAblica-privada-fortalece-portuguesa-venta-alimentos-casa-casa.

Azzellini, Dario. 2009. "Venezuela's Solidarity Economy: Collective Ownership, Expropriation, and Workers Self-Management." *Working USA* 12 (2): 171–91.

———. 2015. "Venezuela's Social Transformation and Growing Class Struggle." In *Crisis and Contradiction: Marxist Perspectives on Latin America in the Global Political Economy*, edited by Susan J. Spronk and Jeffery R. Webber, 138–62. Leiden: Brill.

———. 2016. *Communes and Workers' Control in Venezuela: Building 21st Century Socialism from Below*. Leiden: Brill.

Bakewell, Peter. 2002. "Conquest after the Conquest: The Rise of Spanish Domination in America." In *Spain, Europe and the Atlantic World: Essays in Honour of John H. Elliot*, edited by Richard L. Kagen and Geoffrey Parker, 296–315. Cambridge: Cambridge University Press.

Barkan, Joshua. 2013. *Corporate Sovereignty: Law and Government under Capitalism*. Minneapolis: University of Minnesota Press.

Barton, Jonathan R. 1997. *A Political Geography of Latin America*. New York: Routledge.

Bauman, Zygmunt. 1987. *Legislators and Interpreters: On Modernity, Post-Modernity, and Intellectuals*. Cambridge: Polity Press.

Bebbington, Anthony. 2009. "The New Extraction: Rewriting the Political Ecology of the Andes?" *NACLA Report on the Americas* 42 (5): 12–20.

Bebbington, Anthony, and Graham Thiele. 1993. *Non-Governmental Organizations and the State in Latin America: Rethinking Roles in Sustainable Agricultural Development*. New York: Routledge.

Belém Lopes, Dawisson, and Carlos Aurélio Pimenta de Faria. 2016. "When Foreign Policy Meets Social Demands in Latin America." *Contexto Internacional* 38 (1): 11–53.

Bellinger, Nathan, and Michael Fakhri. 2013. "The Intersection between Food Sovereignty and Law." *Natural Resources and Environment* 28: 45–49.

Benton, Lauren. 2010. *A Search for Sovereignty: Law and Geography in European Empires 1400–1900*. Cambridge: Cambridge University Press.

Bergad, Laird W. 2007. *The Comparative Histories of Slavery in Brazil, Cuba, and the United States*. Cambridge: Cambridge University Press.

Berlant, Lauren. 2011. *Cruel Optimism*. Durham, N.C.: Duke University Press.

Berringer, Tatiana, and Mariana Davi Ferreira. 2022. "Power Blocs and Regional Organizations in Latin America: A Poulantzian Perspective." *Revista Brasileira de Política Internacional* 65 (1): 1–16.

Berringer, Tatiana, and Anna Kowalczyk. 2017. "As burguesias brasileira e chilena e os dilemas da integração regional." *Estudos Internacionais: Revista de relações Internacionais da PUC Minas* 5 (1): 47–62.

Betances, Emelio, and Carlos Figueroa Ibarra, eds. 2016. *Popular Sovereignty and Constituent Power in Latin America*. New York: Palgrave.

Bethell, Tom. 1998. *The Noblest Triumph: Property and Prosperity through the Ages*. New York: St. Martin's Griffin.

Bhandar, Brenna. 2018. *The Colonial Lives of Property: Law, Land, and Racial Regimes of Ownership*. Durham, N.C.: Duke University Press.

Bidet, Jacques. 2016. *Foucault with Marx*. London: Zed.
Bistoletti, Ezequiel Luis. 2019. *The Power Struggles over the Post-Neoliberal Social Security System Reforms in Venezuela and Ecuador*. New York: Springer.
Blomley, Nicolas. 2015. "The Territory of Property." *Progress in Human Geography* 40 (5): 593–609.
———. 2019. "The Territorialisation of Property in Land: Space, Power and Practice." *Territory, Politics, Governance* 7 (2): 233–49.
Boito, Armando, and Tatiana Berringer. 2014. "Social Classes, Neodevelopmentalism, and Brazilian Foreign Policy under Presidents Lula and Dilma." *Latin American Perspectives* 41 (5): 94–109.
Bolivia Digital. 2021. "Bolivia retoma su participación plena en el ALBA-TCP, CELAC y UNASUR." February 2, 2021. https://www.ahoraelpueblo.bo/bolivia-retoma-su-participacion-plena-en-el-alba-tpc-celac-y-unasur/.
Bonilla, Frank. 1970. *The Politics of Change in Venezuela*. Vol. 2, *The Failure of Elites*. Cambridge, Mass.: MIT Press.
Bonilla, Yarimar. 2015. *Non-Sovereign Futures: French Caribbean Politics in the Wake of Disenchantment*. London: University of London.
Boothroyd Rojas, Ruth. 2017. "Commune Activist Refused Permission by ANC to Stand as Mayor." *Venezuelanalysis*, November 29, 2017. https://venezuelanalysis.com/news/13524.
Borgucci, Emmanuel, and Jennifer Fuenmayor. 2013. "Antecedentes del debilitamiento institucional en Venezuela durante el gobierno de Luis Herrera Campins." *Espiral: Estudios sobre Estado y Sociedad* 20 (56): 171–95.
Borras, Saturnino M., Jr., Jennifer C. Franco, and Sofía Monslave Suárez. 2015. "Land and Food Sovereignty." *Third World Quarterly* 36 (3): 600–617.
Botão, Gustavo. 2022. "Poulantzas e o regionalismo latino-americano." *Cadernos Cemarx* 16:2–19.
Bottazzi, Patrick, and Stephan Rist. 2012. "Changing Land Rights Means Changing Society: The Sociopolitical Effects of Agrarian Reforms under the Government of Evo Morales: Effects of Agrarian Reforms under the Government of Evo Morales." *Journal of Agrarian Change* 12 (4): 528–51.
Brabazon, Honor. 2017. "Occupying Legality: The Subversive Use of Law in Latin American Occupation Movements." *Bulletin of Latin American Research* 36 (1): 21–35.
Brading, Ryan. 2013. *Populism in Venezuela*. New York: Routledge.
———. 2014. "From Passive to Radical Revolution in Venezuela's Populist Project." *Latin American Perspectives* 41 (6): 48–64.
Branch, Jordan. 2010. "'Colonial Reflection' and Territoriality: The Peripheral Origins of Sovereign Statehood." *European Journal of International Relations* 18 (2): 277–97.
———. 2017. "Territory as an Institution: Spatial Ideas, Practices and Technologies." *Territory, Politics, Governance* 5 (2): 131–44.
Brand, Ulrich, Christoph Görg, and Markus Wissen. 2010. "Second-Order Condensations of Society Power Relations: Environmental Politics and the Internationalization of the State from a Neo-Poulantzian Perspective." *Antipode* 43 (1): 149–75.
Brandt, Loren. 1993. "Interwar Japanese Agriculture: Revisionist Views on the Impact

of the Colonial Rice Policy and the Labor-Surplus Hypothesis." *Explorations in Economic History* 30: 259–93.

Bratsis, Peter. 2016. *Everyday Life and the State.* New York: Routledge.

Bringel, Breno, and Alfredo Falero. 2016. "Movimientos sociales, gobiernos progresistas y estado en América Latina: Transiciones, conflictos y mediaciones." *Caderno CRH* 29:27–45.

Broadhead, Lee-Anne, and Robert Morrison. 2012. "'Peace Based on Social Justice': The ALBA Alternative to Corporate Globalization." *New Global Studies* 6 (2): 1–28.

Broegaard, Rikke J. 2005. "Land Tenure Insecurity and Inequality in Nicaragua." *Development and Change* 36 (5): 845–64.

Brown, Jonathan. 1985. "Why Foreign Oil Companies Shifted Their Production from Mexico to Venezuela during the 1920s." *American Historical Review* 90 (2): 362–85.

Bulmer-Thomas, Victor. 2003. *The Economic History of Latin America since Independence.* Cambridge: Cambridge University Press.

Burawoy, Michael. 1985. *The Politics of Production: Factory Regimes under Capitalism and Socialism.* London: Verso.

Burch, Kurt. 1998. *Property and the Making of the International System.* Boulder: Lynne Rienner.

Burges, Sean W. 2005. "Bounded by the Reality of Trade: Practical Limits to a South American Region." *Cambridge Review of International Affairs* 18 (3): 437–54.

———. 2007. "Building a Global Southern Coalition: The Competing Approaches of Brazil's Lula and Venezuela's Chávez." *Third World Quarterly* 28 (7): 1343–58.

Bushnell, Amy, T. 2002. "Gates, Patterns, and Peripheries: The Field of Frontier Latin America." In Daniels and Kennedy, *Negotiated Empires*, 15–28.

Bye, Vegard. 1979. "Nationalization of Oil in Venezuela: Re-Defined Dependence and Legitimization of Imperialism." *Journal of Peace Research* 16 (1): 57–78.

Califano, Andrea. 2015. "Las empresas grannacionales: Algunas notas aclaratorias." In Aponte-García, *El ALBA-TCP*, 109–46.

Canfield, Matthew. 2022. "The Ideology of Innovation: Philanthropy and Racial Capitalism in Global Food Governance." *Journal of Peasant Studies* DOI: 10.1080/03066150.2022.2099739.

Cannon, Barry. 2004. "Venezuela, April 2002: Coup or Popular Rebellion? The Myth of a United Venezuela." *Bulletin of Latin American Research* 23 (3): 285–302.

Carchedi, Guglielmo. 2011. *Behind the Crisis: Marx's Dialectics of Value and Knowledge.* Leiden: Brill.

Carlson, Chris. 2017. "Latifundio and the Logic of Underdevelopment: The Case of Venezuela's Sur Del Lago." *Journal of Peasant Studies* 44 (1): 286–308.

Carosio, Alba. 2017. "El chavismo como movimiento y pensamiento político." In *Chavismo: Genealogía de una pasión política,* edited by Alba Carosio, Indhira Libertad Rodríguez, and Leonardo Bracamonte, 105–20. Buenos Aires: CLASCO.

Carranza, Mario E. 2006. "Clinging Together: Mercosur's Ambitious External Agenda, Its Internal Crisis, and the Future of Regional Economic Integration in South America." *Review of International Political Economy* 13 (5): 802–29.

Carrillo, Zulay. 2016. "Supresión de Empresa Socialista mantiene a trabajadores en

Zozobra." *Noticias Calabozo*, July 29, 2016. http://www.noticiascalabozo.com.ve/supresion-empresa-socialista-mantiene-trabajadores-zozobra/.

Carrión, Diego, and Stalin Herrera. 2012. *Ecuador rural del siglo XXI: Soberanía alimentaria, inversión pública y política agraria*. Quito: IEE.

Carrión, Gloria F. 2012. *El acuerdo de Asociación con la Unión Europea y el ALBA: Dinámicas político-económicas en Nicaragua*. Managua: Nitlapan-UCA.

———. 2017. "State-Society and Donor Relations: The Political Economy of Domestic Resource Mobilization in Nicaragua." UNRISD Working Paper no. 2017-2, UNRISD, Geneva.

Carty, Victoria. 2006. "Transnational Labor Mobilizing in Two Mexican Maquiladoras." In Johnston and Almeida, *Latin American Social Movements*, 215–30. Oxford: Rowman and Littlefield.

Castañeda, Jorge G. 1993. *Utopia Unarmed: The Latin American Left after the Cold War*. New York: Vintage.

Castro-Aniyar, Daniel. 2013. "La seguridad alimentaria en Venezuela. 1. Una evaluación de los sub-objetivos suficiencia, acceso, disponibilidad y estabilidad. Período 1999–2012." *Revista Venezolana de Ciencia y Tecnología de Alimentos* 4 (1): 63–100.

Cederlöf, Gustav, and Donald V. Kingsbury. 2019. "On Petrocaribe: Petropolitics, Energopower, and Post-neoliberal Development in the Caribbean Energy Region." *Political Geography* 72: 124–33.

Chambilla, Hugo. 2014. "Ferias Ecológicas en Bolivia: Dinamizando la Agricultura Sustentable." In *Del productor al consumidor: Una alternativa comercial para la agricultura familiar*, edited by Marc Devissche and Bishelly Elías, 33–100. La Paz: Agrónomos y Veterinarios sin Fronteras.

Chao, Sophie. 2022. "Gastrocolonialism: The Intersections of Race, Food and Development in West Papau." *International Journal Human Rights* 26 (5): 811–32.

Chaplin, Joyce E. 2001. *Subject Matter: Technology, the Body, and Science on the Anglo-American Frontier, 1500–1676*. Cambridge, Mass.: Harvard University Press.

Chávez, Hugo. 2009. *Comunas, Propiedad y Socialismo*. Caracas: MPPCI.

Chibber, Vivek. 2005. "Reviving the Developmental State? The Myth of the 'National Bourgeoisie.'" In *Socialist Register 2005: The Empire Reloaded*, edited by Leo Panitch and Colin Leys, 144–65. London: Merlin Press.

Chohan, Jaskiran Kaur. 2017. "Reclaiming the Food System: Agroecological Pedagogy and the IALA María Cano." *Alternautas. (Re)Searching Development: The Abya Yala Chapter*. 4 (2): 13–26. http://www.alternautas.net/blog/2017/8/17/reclaiming-the-food-system-agroecological-pedagogy-and-the-iala-mara-cano.

Ciccantell, Paul. 2001. "NAFTA and the Reconstruction of US Hegemony: The Raw Materials Foundations of Economic competitiveness." *Canadian Journal of Sociology* 26 (1): 47–65.

Ciccariello-Maher, George. 2013. *We Created Chávez: A People's History of the Venezuelan Revolution*. Durham, N.C.: Duke University Press.

———. 2016. *Building the Commune: Radical Democracy in Venezuela*. London: Verso.

Claeys, Patricia. 2012. "The Creation of New Rights by the Food Sovereignty Movement: The Challenge of Institutionalizing Subversion." *Sociology* 46 (5): 844–60.

Clare, Nick, Victoria Habermehl, and Liz Mason-Deese. 2018. "Territories in Contestation: Relational Power in Latin America." *Territory, Politics, Governance* 6 (3): 302–21.

Clark, Christopher. 2020. "State, Market, and Popular Sovereignty in Agrarian North America: The United States, 1850–1920." In *Remaking North American Sovereignty: State Transformation in the 1860s*, edited by Jewel L. Spangler and Frank Towers, 177–99. New York: Fordham University Press.

Clark, Patrick. 2017. "Neo-Developmentalism and a 'Vía Campesina' for Rural Development: Unreconciled Projects in Ecuador's Citizen's Revolution." *Journal of Agrarian Change* 17 (2): 348–64.

Clark, Timothy. D. 2017. "Rethinking Chile's 'Chicago Boys': Neoliberal Technocrats or Revolutionary Vanguard?" *Third World Quarterly* 38 (6): 1350–65.

Cocks, Peter. 1980. "Toward a Marxist Theory of European Integration." *International Organization* 34 (1): 1–40.

Cohen, Morris R. 1927. "Property and Sovereignty." *Cornell Law Review* 13 (1): 8–30.

Coker, Trudie. 2001. "Globalization and Corporatism: The Growth and Decay of Organized Labor in Venezuela 1990–1998." *International Labor and Working-Class History* 60: 180–202.

Colás, Alejandro. 2022. "Food, Multiplicity and Imperialism: Patterns of Domination and Subversion in the Modern International System." *Cooperation and Conflict* 57 (3): 384–401.

Collingham, Lizzie. 2015. "The Human Fuel: Food as a Global Commodity and Local Scarcity." In *The Cambridge History of the Second World War*, vol. 3, *Total War: Economy, Society and Culture*, edited by Michael Geyer and Adam Tooze, 149–73. Cambridge: Cambridge University Press.

———. 2018. *The Hungry Empire: How Britain's Quest for Food Shaped the Modern World*. London: Vintage.

Colque, Gonzalo, Miguel Urioste, and José Luis Eyzaguirre. 2015. *Marginalización de la agricultura campesina e indígena: Dinámicas locales, seguridad y soberanía alimentaria*. La Paz: Fundación TIERRA.

Comninel, George C. 2012. "Feudalism." In *The Elgar Companion to Marxist Economics*, edited by Ben Fine, Alfredo Saad-Filho, and Marco Boffo, 131–37. Cheltenham: Edward Elgar Publishing.

Conversi, Daniele. 2016. "Sovereignty in a Changing World: From Westphalia to Food Sovereignty." *Globalizations* 13 (4): 484–98.

Conway, Christopher B. 2003. *The Cult of Bolívar in Latin American Literature*. Gainesville: University of Florida Press.

Córdoba, Diana, Kees Jansen, and Carolina González. 2017. "Empowerment through Articulations between Post-Neoliberal Politics and Neoliberalism: Value Chain Alliances in Bolivia." *Canadian Journal of Development Studies/Revue canadienne d'études du développement* 38 (1): 91–110.

Coronil, Fernando. 1997. *The Magical State. Nature, Money, and Modernity in Venezuela*. Chicago: Chicago University Press.

Coronil, Fernando, and Julie Skurski. 1982. "Reproducing Dependency: Auto Industry Policy and Petrodollar Circulation in Venezuela." *International Organization* 36 (1): 61–94.

Correo del Orinoco. 2014. "Maduro Pide al TSJ corregir 'la inaudita decisión' de retirar carta agraria a comuna de El Maizal." December 12, 2014. http://www.correodelorinoco.gob.ve/impacto/maduro-pide-al-tsj-corregir-la-inaudita-decision-retirar-carta-agraria-a-comuna-maizal/.

———. 2016a. "Gobierno Nacional ordena reestructurar Mercal y Pdval para que retome su objectivo principal." February 17, 2016. http://www.correodelorinoco.gob.ve/gobierno-nacional-ordena-reestructurar-mercal-y-pdval-para-que-retome-su-objetivo-principal/.

———. 2016b. "74 % de los venezolanos apoya que gobierno establezca precios en común acuerdo con sector privado." June 12, 2016. http://www.correodelorinoco.gob.ve/nacionales/74-venezolanos-apoya-que-gobierno-establezca-precios-comun-acuerdo-sector-privado/.

———. 2017. "Presidente Maduro: El socialismo es un asunto de la humanidad entera," November 12, 2017. http://www.correodelorinoco.gob.ve/presidente-maduro-el-socialismo-es-un-asunto-de-la-humanidad-entera/.

Costa, Abel Gamboa, Roberto González Sousa, and Angelina Herrera Sorzano. 2013. "Soberanía y seguridad alimentaria en Cuba: políticas públicas necesarias para reducir la dependencia alimentaria." *Agrisost* 19 (3): 1–14.

Costoya, Manuel. 2011. "Politics of Trade in Post-Neoliberal Latin America: The Case of Bolivia." *Bulletin of Latin American Research* 30 (1): 80–95.

Crosby, Alfred. 1997. *The Measure of Reality: Quantification and Western Society, 1200–1600*. Cambridge: Cambridge University Press.

Cuestas-Caza, Javier. 2018. "Sumak Kawsay Is Not Buen Vivir," *Alternautas* 5 (1): 49–62.

Cusack, Asa K. 2019. *Venezuela, ALBA, and the Limits of Postneoliberal Regionalism in Latin America and the Caribbean*. New York: Palgrave.

Cutler, Alice, and Yasmine Brien. 2013. "Global Struggles for Climate Justice and the ALBA-TCP Council of Social Movements: An Activist Perspective." In Muhr, *Counter-Globalization and Socialism in the 21st Century*, 219–35.

Dachevsky, Fernando, and Juan Kornblihtt. 2017. "The Reproduction and Crisis of Capitalism in Venezuela under Chavismo." *Latin American Perspectives* 44 (1): 78–93.

Daigle, Michelle. 2019. "Tracing the Terrain of Indigenous Food Sovereignty." *Journal of Peasant Studies* 46 (2): 297–315.

Daniels, Christine, and Michael V. Kennedy, eds. 2002. *Negotiated Empires: Centers and Peripheries in the Americas, 1500–1820*. New York: Routledge.

Dargatz, Anja, and Moira Zuazo, eds. 2012. *Democracias en transformación: ¿Qué hay de nuevo en los nuevos Estados andinos?* Ecuador: FES-ILDIS.

Das, Veena, and Deborah Poole, eds. 2004. *Anthropology in the Margins of the State*. Oxford: Oxford University Press.

Davis, Mike. 1999. *Prisoners of the American Dream: Politics and Economy in the History of the US Working Class*. London: Verso.

Davis, Sasha. 2020. *Islands and Oceans: Reimagining Sovereignty and Social Change*. Athens: University of Georgia Press.

Decreto Ley, 259. 2008. "Sobre la entrega de tierras estatales ociosas en usufructo." *Gaceta Oficial de la Republica de Cuba*, July 11, 2008. https://www.fao.org/faolex/results/details/fr/c/LEX-FAOC082664/.

Decreto Ley, 305. 2012. "Ley de las cooperativas no agropecuarias." *Gaceta Oficial de la Republica de Cuba*, December 11, 2012. https://www.ecolex.org/details/legislation/decreto-no-309-reglamento-de-las-cooperativas-no-agropecuarias-de-primer-grado-lex-faoc133485/.

Deere, Carmen Diana. 2017. "Women's Land Rights, Rural Social Movements, and the State in the 21st Century Latin American Agrarian Reforms." *Journal of Agrarian Change* 17 (2): 258–78.

Deere, Carmen Diana, and F. S. Royce, eds. 2009. *Rural Social Movements in Latin America: Organizing for Sustainable Livelihoods*. Gainsville: University of Florida Press.

Delaney, David. 2005. *Territory: A Short Introduction*. Malden, Mass.: Blackwell.

Demirović, Alex. 2010. "Materialist State Theory and the Transnationalization of the Capitalist State." *Antipode* 43 (1): 38–59.

———. 2019. "The Capitalist State, Hegemony, and the Democratic Transformation towards Socialism." In *The End of the Democratic State: Nicos Poulantzas, a Marxism for the 21st Century*, edited by Jean-Numa Duncange and Razmig Keycheyan and translated by David Broder, 43–60. New York: Palgrave.

De la Cruz, Rafael. 2011. "The Experience of Decentralization and Local Development in Latin America." In *The Local Alternative: Decentralization and Economic Development*, edited by Rafael de la Cruz, Carlos Pineda Mannheim, and Caroline Poschle, 39–56. New York: Palgrave.

De Oliveira, Pinho, and María Fátima. 2016. "Los consejos comunales y la gerencia social comunitaria." *Apuntes Universitarios* 6 (1): 9–21.

Depablos, Karina. 2009. "Empresa Mixta Socialista Arroz Del ALBA: Naciones unidas para garantizar la soberanía alimentaria." *Sistema Bolivariano de Comunication e Information*, March 10, 2009. http://www.alopresidente.gob.ve/info/6/1095/empresa_mixta_socialista.html.

Derham, Michael. 2010. *Politics in Venezuela: Explaining Hugo Chávez*. Oxford: Peter Lang.

Desmarais, Annette A. 2007. *La Vía Campesina: Globalization and the Power of Peasants*. Halifax, N.S.: Fernwood.

Desmarais, A. A., and H. Wittman. 2014. "Farmers, Foodies and First Nations: Getting to Food Sovereignty in Canada." *Journal of Peasant Studies* 41 (6): 1153–73.

Devlin, Robert, and Antoni Estevadeordal. 2001. "What's New in the New Regionalism in the Americas?" In *Regional Integration in Latin America and the Caribbean: The Political Economy of Open Regionalism*, edited by Victor Bulmer-Thomas, 17–44. London: Institute of Latin American Studies.

Di John, Jonathan. 2005. "Economic Liberalization, Political Instability, and State Capacity in Venezuela." *International Political Science Review / Revue Internationale de Science Politique* 26 (1): 107–24.

Dobb, M. 1946. *Studies in the Development of Capitalism*. New York: International Publishers.

Dobson, Paul. 2019. "ALBA Summit: Venezuela Promises to Relauch PetroCaribe in 2020." *Venezuelanalysis*, December 16, 2019. https://venezuelanalysis.com/news/14745.

Domené-Painenao, Olga, and Francisco F. Herrera. 2019. "Situated Agroecology: Massification and Reclaiming University Programs in Venezuela." *Agroecology and Sustainable Food Systems* 43 (7/8): 936–53.
Draper, Hal. 1966. *The Two Souls of Socialism*. Pamphlet no. 3. Berkley: Independent Socialist Committee.
Duncan, Colin. 1996. *The Centrality of Agriculture: Between Humankind and the Rest of Nature*. Montreal: McGill-Queen's University Press.
Dunford, Robin. 2015. "Human Rights and Collective Emancipation: The Politics of Food Sovereignty." *Review of International Studies* 41 (2): 239–61.
———. 2016. *The Politics of Transnational Peasant Struggle.*
Resistance, Rights and Democracy. London: Rowman and Littlefield.
Dussel, Enrique D. 2008. *Twenty Theses on Politics*. Translated by George Ciccariello-Maher. Durham, N.C.: Duke University Press.
Edelman, Marc. 2014. "Food Sovereignty: Forgotten Genealogies and Future Regulatory Challenges." *Journal of Peasant Studies* 41 (6): 959–78.
Edelman, Marc, Tony Weis, Amita Baviskar, Saturnino M. Borras Jr., Eric Holt-Giménez, Deniz Kandiyoti, and Wendy Wolford. 2014. "Introduction: Critical Perspectives on Food Sovereignty." *Journal of Peasant Studies* 41 (6): 911–31.
Elden, Stuart. 2013. *The Birth of Territory*. Chicago: University of Chicago Press.
Eley, Geoff. 2002. *Forging Democracy: The History of the Left in Europe, 1850–2000*. Oxford: Oxford University Press.
Elías, Bishelly, and Marc Devissche. 2014. "Prescindir del intermediario: Un sueño campesino." In *Del productor al consumidor: Una alternativa comercial para la agricultura familiar*, edited by Elías and Devissche, 17–32. La Paz: Agrónomos y Veterinarios sin Fronteras.
Ellis, Edward. 2011. "Murder of the Campesinos." *Guardian*, October 2, 2011, https://www.theguardian.com/commentisfree/2011/oct/02/venezuela-land-rights-chavez-farmers.
Ellner, Steve. 1993. *Organized Labor in Venezuela. 1958–1991: Behaviour and Concerns in a Democratic Setting*. Wilmington, Del.: SR Books.
———. 1999. "Obstacles to the Consolidation of the Venezuelan Neighbourhood Movement: National and Local Cleavages." *Journal of Latin American Studies* 31 (1): 75–97.
———. 2008. *Rethinking Venezuelan Politics: Class, Conflict, and the Chávez Phenomenon*. Boulder: Lynne Rienner.
———. 2017. "Implications of Marxist State Theory and How They Play Out in Venezuela." *Historical Materialism* 25 (2): 29–62.
———. 2019. "Class Strategies in Chavista Venezuela: Pragmatic and Populist Policies in a Broader Context." *Latin American Perspectives* 46 (1): 167–89.
Ellner, Steve, and Miguel Tinker Salas. 2007. *Venezuela: Hugo Chávez and the Decline of an "Exceptional Democracy."* Boulder: Rowman and Littlefield.
El Mundo. 2013. "Venezuela y Bolivia acuerdan crear fábrica de producción de alimentos." May 26, 2013. http://www.elmundo.com.ve/noticias/economia/internacional/venezuela-y-bolivia-acuerdan-crear-fabrica-de-prod.aspx.
El Troudi, Haiman, and Juan Carlos Monedero. 2006. *Empresas de producción social: Instrumento para el socialismo del siglo XXI*. Caracas: Centro Miranda International.

El Universal. 2007. "Chávez inaugura procesadora de soya en Anzoátegui." March 22, 2007. http://www.eluniversal.com/2007/03/22/imp_eco_ava_chavez-inaugura-proc_22A847467.shtml.

Emerson, R. Guy. 2013. "Institutionalisation a Radical Region? The Bolivarian Alliance for the Peoples of Our America." *Journal of Iberian and Latin American Research* 19 (2): 194–210.

Enright, Michael, Antonio Frances, and Edith Scott Saavedra. 1996. *Venezuela: The Challenge of Competitiveness*. New York: Palgrave.

Enríquez, Laura, and Simeon Newman. 2015. "The Conflicted State and Agrarian Transformation in Pink Tide Venezuela." *Journal of Agrarian Change* 16 (4): 594–626.

Epstein, Charlotte. 2021. *The Birth of the State: The Place of the Body in Crafting Modern Politics*. Oxford: Oxford University Press.

Escobar, Arturo. 2020. *Pluriversal Politics: The Real and the Possible*. Durham, N.C.: Duke University Press.

Fabricant, Nicole. 2012. *Mobilizing Bolivia's Displaced: Indigenous Politics and the Struggle over Land*. Chapel Hill: University of North Carolina Press.

Fairbrother, Malcolm. 2009. "The Divergent Roles of Political and Economic Elites in NAFTA Countries." In Atasoy, *Hegemonic Transitions*, 147–65.

Fawcett, Louise. 2005. "The Origins and Development of the Regional Idea in the Americas." In *Regionalism and Governance in the Americas: Continental Drift*, edited by Louise Fawcett and Monica Serrano, 25–51. New York: Palgrave.

Fernández, Albert Noguera. 2012. "What Do We Mean When We Talk about 'Critical Constitutionalism'? Some Reflections on the New Latin American Constitutions." In *New Constitutionalism in Latin America: Promises and Practices*, edited by Detlef Nolte and Almut Schilling-Vacaflor, 99–122. Surrey: Ashgate.

Fernández, Argel. 2012. "Extrabajadores de procesadora estatal de leche exigen reenganache." *El Tiempo*, August 23, 2012. https://issuu.com/eltiempovenezuela/docs/120823045048-92cb90e053c1426aba7b0a91a174be74.

Figueroa-Helland, Leonardo, Cassidy Thomas, and Abigail Aguilera. 2018. "Decolonizing Food Systems: Food Sovereignty, Indigenous Revitalization, and Agroecology as Counter-Hegemonic Movements." *Perspectives on Global Development and Technology* 17:173–201.

Fitzgerald, Deborah. 2003. *Every Farm a Factory: The Industrial Ideal in American Agriculture*. New Haven: Yale University Press.

Food and Agriculture Organisation (FAO). 1996/7. "Agricultural Census 1996/97." http://www.fao.org/fileadmin/templates/ess/documents/world_census_of_agriculture/main_results_by_country/2000venezrevised.pdf.

———. 2014. "Developing Sustainable Food Value Chains. Guiding Principles." http://www.fao.org/publications/card/en/c/aa9b41cf-ea96-4927-a730-ab51dcfcbb91.

———. 2015. *The State of Food Insecurity in the World*. FAO: Rome.

Foster, John Bellamy. 2000. *Marx's Ecology: Materialism and Nature*. New York: Monthly Review.

Foucault, Michel. 1977. *Discipline and Punish: The Birth of the Prison*. New York: Pantheon.

———. 1978. *The History of Sexuality, Vol. 1*. Translated by Robert Hurley. New York: Pantheon.
———. 1982. "The Subject and Power." *Critical Inquiry* 8 (4): 777–95.
Fox, Jonathan. 2007. *Accountability Politics: Power and Voice in Rural Mexico*. Oxford: Oxford University Press.
Fréitez, María Eugenia, and Alexandra Martínez. 2015. "Venezuela: Consejos comunales y comunas." In *¿Cómo transformar? Instituciones y cambio social en América Latina y Europa*, edited Miriam Lang, Belén Cevallos, and Claudio López, 191–218. Quito: Fundación Rosa Luxemburg/Abya-Yala.
Friedmann, Harriet. 1990. "The Origins of Third World Food Dependence." In *The Food Question: Profits versus People?* edited by Henry Bernstein, Ben Crow, Maureen Mackntosh, and Charlotte Martin, 13–31. London: Earthscan Publishers.
Fukuyama, Francis. 1992. *The End of History and the Last Man*. New York: Free Press.
Furtado, Celso. 1976. *Economic Development of Latin America: Historical Background and Contemporary Problems*. Cambridge: Cambridge University Press.
Gaceta Oficial. 2007a. No. 38.726, July 16, 2007, Caracas: rbv.
———. 2007b. No. 38.828, December 10, 2007, Caracas: rbv.
———. 2010a. No. 39.410, April 26, 2010, Caracas: rbv.
———. 2010b No. 39.494, August 24, 2010, Caracas: rbv.
———. 2011. No. 39.719, July 22, 2011, Caracas: rbv.
Gaceta Oficial Extraordinario. 2010. No. 6.011, December 21, 2010, Caracas: rbv.
———. 2015. No. 6.209, December 29, Caracas: rbv.
Gago, Verónica, and Diego Sztulwark. 2016. "The Temporality of Social Struggle at the End of the 'Progressive' Cycle in Latin America." *South Atlantic Quarterly* 115 (3): 606–14.
Gallas, Alexander. 2017. "Revisiting Conjunctural Marxism: Althusser and Poulantzas on the State." *Rethinking Marxism* 29 (2): 256–80.
Galli, Carlo. 2010. *Political Spaces and Global War*. Translated by Elisabeth Fay. Minneapolis: University of Minnesota Press.
Gamble, Andrew. 1988. *The Free Economy and the Strong State. The Politics of Thatcherism*. Basingstoke: Macmillan.
García, Marta Elena. 2017. "Reforma agraria en Nicaragua y sus efectos en la Cooperativa Agropecuaria Sandinista 'Leonel Valdivia Ortega,' Villa Chaguitillo del Minicipio de Sébaco, Matagalpa, 1937–2016." Masters thesis, Universidad Nacional Autónoma de Nicaragua.
Gardini, Gian Luca. 2010. *The Origins of MERCOSUR: Democracy and Regionalization in South America*. New York: Palgrave.
Gates, Leslie. 2010. *Electing Chávez: The Business of Anti-Neoliberal Politics in Venezuela*. Pittsburgh, Pa.: Pittsburgh University Press.
Gibson-Graham, J. K. 2002. "Beyond Global vs. Local: Economic Politics outside the Binary Frame." In *Geographies of Power: Placing Scale*, edited by A. Herod and M. W. Wright, 25–60. Malden, Mass.: Blackwell.
———. 2006. *The End of Capitalism (As We Knew It). A Feminist Critique of Political Economy*. Minneapolis: University of Minnesota Press.

Giddens, Anthony. 1984. *The Constitution of Society: Outline of the Theory of Structuration*. Cambridge: Polity Press.

Gilbert, A. 2004. "The Urban Revolution." In *Latin America Transformed: Globalization and Modernity*, edited by Robert N. Gwynn and Cristóbal Kay, 93–116. London: Hodder.

Gill, Bikrum Singh. 2023. "A World in Reverse: The Political Ecology of Racial Capitalism." *Politics* 43 (2): 153–68.

Ginn, Franklin. 2014. "Sticky Lives: Slugs, Detachment and More-than-Human Ethics in the Garden." *Transactions of the Institute of British Geographers* 39 (4): 532–44.

Giraldo, Omar Felipe, and Nils McCune. 2019. "Can the State Take Agroecology to Scale? Public Policy Experiences in Agroecological Territorialization from Latin America." *Agroecology and Sustainable Food Systems* 43 (7/8): 785–809.

Giunta, Isabella. 2014. "Food Sovereignty in Ecuador: Peasant Struggles and the Challenge of Institutionalization." *Journal of Peasant Studies* 46 (6): 1201–24.

Glenn, Evelyn Nakano. 2002. *Unequal Freedom: How Race and Gender Shaped American Citizenship and Labor*. Cambridge: Cambridge University Press.

Godek, Wendy. 2014. "The Institutionalisation of Food Sovereignty: The Case of Nicaragua's Law of Food and Nutritional Sovereignty and Security." PhD diss., Rutgers University.

———. 2015. "Challenges for Food Sovereignty Policy Making: The Case of Nicaragua's Law 693." *Third World Quarterly* 36 (3): 526–43.

———. 2021. "Food Sovereignty Policies and the Quest to Democratize Food System Governance in Nicaragua." *Agriculture and Human Values* 38:91–105.

Goldstein, Joshua S., and David P. Rapkin. 1991. "After Insularity: Hegemony and the Future World Order." *Futures* 23 (9): 935–59.

Golinger, Eva. 2007. *The Chávez Code: Cracking US Intervention in Venezuela*. London: Pluto.

Goodwin, Geoff. 2017. "The Quest to Bring Land under Social and Political Control: Land Reform Struggles of the Past and Present in Ecuador." *Journal of Agrarian Change* 17 (3): 571–93.

Gordon, Todd. 2019. "Capitalism, Neoliberalism, and Unfree Labour." *Critical Sociology* 45 (6): 921–39.

Gough, Jamie. 2004. "Changing Scale as Changing Class Relations: Variety and Contradiction in the Politics of Scale." *Political Geography* 23 (2): 185–211.

Graham, Nicole. 2011. *Lawscape: Property, Environment, Law*. London: Routledge.

Grajales, Inés Cárdenas. 2010. "El conocimiento tradicional y el concepto de territorio." *Núcleo de Estudios, Pesquisas e Projectos de Reforma Agrária*. February 2010, 1–12.

Gramsci, Antonio. 1971. *Selections from the Prison Notebooks*. Edited and translated by Quintin Hoare and Geoffrey Nowell Smith. New York: International Publishers.

———. 1977. *Selections from Political Writings (1910–1920)*. Edited by Quintin Hoare and translated by John Mathews. London: Lawrence and Wishart.

Grandin, Greg. 2007. *Empire's Workshop: Latin America, The United States, and the Rise of the New Imperialism*. New York: Holt.

———. 2019. *The End of the Myth: From the Frontier to the Border Wall in the Mind of America*. New York: Metropolitan.

Grinberg, Nicolas, and Guido Starosta. 2009. "The Limits of Studies in Comparative Development of East Asia and Latin America: The Case of Land Reform and Agrarian Policies." *Third World Quarterly* 30 (4): 761–77.

Grugel, Jean, and Pia Riggirozzi. 2012. "Post-Neoliberalism in Latin America: Rebuilding and Reclaiming the State after Crisis." *Development and Change* 43 (1): 1–21.

Gudynas, Eduardo. 2013. "Debates on Development and Its Alternatives in Latin America: A Brief Heterodox Guide." In *Beyond Development. Alternative Visions from Latin America*, edited by Miriam Lang and Dunia Morikani, 15–40. Amsterdam: Transnational Institute.

Gürcan, Efe Can. 2010. "New Regionalisms and Radical Identity Formation in Latin America: Towards an 'Alter-Global' Paradigm." *Journal of Social Research and Policy* 1 (2): 19–33.

——. 2014. "Cuban Agriculture and Food Sovereignty: Beyond Civil-Society-Centric and Globalist Paradigms." *Latin American Perspectives* 41 (4): 129–46.

Gürcan, Efe Can, and Onur Bakıner. 2015. "Post-Neoliberal Regional Integration in Latin America: Alianza Bolivariana para Los Pueblos de Nuestra América (ALBA)." In *Gramsci and Foucault: A Reassessment*, edited by David Kreps, 131–54. London: Routledge.

Gutiérrez, Alejandro S. 2015. "El sistema alimentario venezolano SAV: Evolución reciente, balance y perspectivas." *Agroalimentaria* 21 (40): 19–60.

Haas, Ernst B., and Philippe C. Schmitter. 1964. "Economics and Differential Patterns of Political Integration: Projections about Unity in Latin America." *International Organization* 18 (4): 705–37.

Halvorsen, Sam. 2019. "Decolonising Territory: Dialogues with Latin American Knowledges and Grassroots Strategies." *Progress in Human Geography* 43 (5): 790–814.

Hanke, Steve. 2019. "Venezuela's Hyperinflation Drags on for a Near Record—36 Months." *Forbes*, November 13, 2019. https://www.forbes.com/sites/stevehanke/2019/11/13/venezuelas-hyperinflation-drags-on-for-a-near-record36-months/?sh=1d304fee6b7b.

Hansen, Thomas Blom, and Stepputat, Finn. 2006. "Sovereignty Revisited." *Annual Review of Anthropology* 35: 295–315.

Harnecker, Marta. 2005. *Understanding the Venezuelan Revolution: Hugo Chávez Talks to Marta Harnecker*. New York: Monthly Review.

——. 2015. *A World to Build: New Paths toward Twenty-First Century Socialism*. New York: Monthly Review.

Harper, Kyle. 2011. *Slavery in the Late Roman World, A.D. 275–425*, Cambridge: Cambridge University Press.

Hart-Landsberg, Martin. 2013. *Capitalist Globalization: Consequences, Resistance, and Alternatives*. New York: Monthly Review.

Harvey, David. 2006. *The Limits to Capital*. London: Verso.

——. 2012. *Rebel Cities: From the Right to the City to the Urban Revolution*. London: Verso.

Hein, Wolfgang. 1980. "Oil and the Venezuelan State." In *Oil and Class Struggle*, edited by Peter Nore and Thomas Turner, 224–51. London: Zed.

Heffernan, Michael. 2003. "Fin de siecle, fin du monde?: On the Origins of European Geopolitics, 1890–1920." In *Geopolitical Traditions: A Century of Geopolitical Thought*, edited by Klaus Dodds and David Atkinson, 27–51. New York: Routledge.

Hellinger, Daniel. 2017. "Oil and the Chávez Legacy." *Latin American Perspectives* 44 (1): 54–77.

Henderson, Thomas Paul. 2017. "State–Peasant Movement Relations and the Politics of Food Sovereignty in Mexico and Ecuador." *Journal of Peasant Studies* 44 (1): 33–55.

———. 2018. "The Class Dynamics of Food Sovereignty in Mexico and Ecuador." *Journal of Agrarian Change* 18 (1): 3–21.

Hermann, Christoph. 2017. "Another 'Lost Decade'? Crisis and Structural Adjustment in Europe and Latin America." *Globalizations* 14 (4): 519–34.

Hernández, Juan Luis. 2009. "Evolución y resultatods del sector agroalimentaria en la V República." *Cuadernos del CENDES* 26 (72):67–100.

Herrera, Francisco F., Olga Domené-Painenao, and José Miguel Cruces. 2017. "The History of Agroecology in Venezuela: A Complex and Multifocal Process." *Agroecology and Sustainable Food Systems* 41 (3–4): 401–15.

Herrod, Andrew. 2011. *Scale*. London: Routledge.

Hesketh, Chris. 2016. "The Survival of Non-Capitalism." *Environment and Planning D: Society and Space* 34 (5): 877–94.

———. 2017. *Spaces of Capital/Spaces of Resistance*. Athens: University of Georgia Press.

Higginbottom, Anthony. 2013. "The Political Economy of Foreign Investment in Latin America: Dependency Revisited." *Latin American Perspectives* 190 (3): 184–206.

Hinsley, F. H. 1986. *Sovereignty*. Cambridge: Cambridge University Press.

Hoffman, Shirley. 2003. "Arawakan Women and the Erosion of Traditional Food Production in Amazonas Venezuela." In *Women and Plants: Gender Relations in Biodiversity Management and Conservation*, edited by Patricia L. Howard, 258–72. London: Zed Books.

Hoffmann, David L. 2011. *Cultivating the Masses: Modern State Practices and Soviet Socialism, 1914–1939*. Ithaca, N.Y: Cornell University Press.

Holt-Giménez, Eric. 2006. *Campesino a Campesino: Voices from Latin America's Farmer to Farmer Movement for Sustainable Agriculture*. Oakland, Ca.: Food First.

Houtart, François. 2014. "El desafío de la agricultura campesina para el Ecuador." In *La restauración conservadora del correísmo*, edited by Silvana González T., 167–77. Quito: Montecristi Vive.

Hozić, Aida. 2021. "Follow the Bodies: Global Capitalism, Global War, Global Crisis and Feminist IPE." *International Relations* 35 (1): 173–77.

Huambachano, Mariaelena. 2018. "Enacting Food Sovereignty in Aotearoa New Zealand and Peru: Revitalizing Indigenous Knowledge, Food Practices and Ecological Philosophies." *Agroecology and Sustainable Food Systems* 42 (9): 1003–28.

Huizer, Gerrit. 1973. *Peasant Rebellion in Latin America*. Harmondsworth: Penguin Books.

Humphrey, Caroline. 2007. "Sovereignty." In *A Companion to the Anthropology of Politics*, edited by David Nugent and Joan Vincent, 418–36. Malden, Mass.: Blackwell.

Hurtado, Karlys. 2016. "Trabajadores mantienen protesta en plantas de Arroz del Alba."

Ultima Hora, April 11, 2016. http://ultimahoradigital.com/2016/04/trabajadores-mantienen-protesta-en-plantas-de-arroz-del-alba/.
Iles, Alastair, and Maya de Wit Montenegro. 2015. "Sovereignty at What Scale? An Inquiry into Multiple Dimensions of Food Sovereignty." *Globalizations* 12 (4): 481–97.
Iturriza López, Reinaldo. 2016. *El Chavismo Salvaje*. N.p.: Trinchera.
Jackson, Robert. 2007. *Sovereignty: Key Concepts*. Cambridge: Polity Press.
Jakobsen, Jostein. 2021. "New Food Regime Geographies: Scale, State, Labour." *World Development* 145:2–7.
Jessop, Bob. 1985. *Nicos Poulantzas: Marxist Theory and Political Strategy*. London: Palgrave.
——.1991. "Accumulation Strategies, State Forms and Hegemonic Projects." In *The State Debate*, edited by Simon Clarke, 157–80. Basingstoke: Macmillan Press.
——.1999. "The Strategic Selectivity of the State: Reflections on a Theme of Poulantzas." *Journal of Hellenic Diaspora* 25 (1–2): 41–78.
——.2002. *The Future of the Capitalist State*. Cambridge: Polity.
Johnson, Lyman L., and Susan M. Socolow. 2002. "Colonial Centers, Colonial Peripheries, and the Economic Agency of the Spanish State." In Daniels and Kennedy, *Negotiated Empires*, 59–78.
Johnston, Hank, and Paul Almeida, eds. 2006. *Latin American Social Movements: Globalisation, Democratization, and Transnational Networks*. Oxford: Rowman and Littlefield.
Jones, M. R. 1997. "Spatial Selectivity of the State? The Regulationist Enigma and Local Struggles over Economic Governance." *Environment and Planning A* 29:831–64.
Kappeler, Aaron. 2013. "Perils of Peasant Populism: Why Redistributive Land Reform and 'Food Sovereignty' Can't Feed Venezuela." Paper presented at the "Food Sovereignty: A Critical Dialogue" international conference, Yale University, September 14–15, 2013.
——. 2015. "Sowing the State: Nationalism, Sovereignty, and Agrarian Politics in Venezuela." PhD diss., University of Toronto.
Katzenstein, Peter J. 2005. *A World of Regions: Asia and Europe in the American Imperium*. Ithaca, N.Y.: Cornell University Press.
Kay, Cristóbal. 1995. "Rural Latin America: Exclusionary and Uneven Agricultural Development." In *Capital, Power, and Inequality in Latin America*, edited by S. Halebsky and R. L. Harris, 21–52. Boulder: Westview Press.
——.2004. "Rural Livelihoods and Peasant Futures." In *Latin America Transformed: Globalization and Modernity*, edited by Robert N. Gwynne and Cristóbal Kay, 232–50. London: Hodder.
——.2008. "Reflections on Latin American Rural Studies in the Neoliberal Globalization Period: A New Rurality." *Development and Change* 39 (6): 915–43.
Kehoe, Dennis P. 2006. "Landlords and Tenants." In *A Companion to the Roman Empire*, edited by D. S. Potter, 298–311. Malden, Mass: Blackwell.
——. 2007. *Law and Rural Economy in the Roman Empire*. Ann Arbor: University of Michigan Press.
Keuchi, Keiichita. 2000. "Japanese Geopolitics in the 1930s and 1940s." In *Geopolitical*

Traditions: A Century of Geopolitical Thought, edited by Klaus Dodds and Atkinson, 72–92. New York: Routledge.

Kiely, Ray. 2005. *The Clash of Globalisations: Neo-Liberalism, the Third War and Anti-Globalisation*. Leiden: Brill.

Kimura, Mitsuhiko. 1995. "The Economics of Japanese Imperialism in Korea, 1910–1939." *Economics History Review* 48 (3): 555–74.

Kingsbury, Donald V. 2016. "From Populism to Protagonism (and Back?) in Bolivarian Venezuela: Rethinking Ernesto Laclau's on Populist Reason." *Journal of Latin American Cultural Studies* 25 (4): 495–514.

Knafo, Samuel. 2010. "Critical Approaches and the Legacy of the Agent/Structure Debate in International Relations." *Cambridge Review of International Affairs* 23 (3): 492–516.

———. 2017. "A Methodological Turn Long Overdue: Or, Why It Is Time for Critical Scholars to Cut Their Losses." In *What's the Point of International Relations?* edited by S. L. Dyvik, J. Selby, and R. Wilkinson, 242–52. London: Routledge.

Koerner, Lucas. 2016a. "Venezuela Combats Severe Drought with New Electricity Rationing Plan." *Venezuelanalysis*, April 25, 2016. https://venezuelanalysis.com/news/11947.

———. 2016b. "Venezuelan Businessman Replaces Leftist Sociologist as Economy Czar." *Venezuelanalysis*, February 16, 2016. https://venezuelanalysis.com/news/11855.

Kolers, Avery. 2009. *Land, Conflict, and Justice: A Political Theory of Territory*. Cambridge: Cambridge University Press.

Konings, Martijn. 2018. "The Logic of Leverage: Reflections on Post-Foundational Political Economy." *Finance and Society* 4 (2): 205–13.

Kornblihtt, Juan. 2015. "Oil Rent Appropriation, Capital Accumulation, and Social Expenditure in Venezuela during Chavism." *World Review of Political Economy* 6 (1): 58–74.

Kozarek, Katrina. 2017. "Venezuela's Communes: A Great Social Achievement." *Counterpunch*, November 24, 2017. https://www.counterpunch.org/2017/11/24/venezuelas-communes-a-great-social-achievement/.

———. 2018. "El Maizal Commune Leads by Example, Takes on Venezuelan State Superstructure." *Venezuelanalysis*, February 6, 2018. https://venezuelanalysis.com/video/13642.

Krasner, Stephen D. 1999. *Sovereignty: Organized Hypocrisy*. Princeton: Princeton University Press.

Krige, John. 2008. *American Hegemony and the Postwar Reconstruction of Science in Europe*. Cambridge, Mass.: MIT Press.

Krupa, Christopher, and David Nugent, eds. 2014. *State Theory and Andean Politics. New Approaches to the Study of Rule*. Philadelphia: University of Pennsylvania Press.

Kühnhardt, Ludger. 2010. *Region-Building*. Vol. 1, *The Global Proliferation of Regional Integration*. New York: Berghahn.

Kumar, Ashok. 2020. *Monopsony Capitalism: Power and Production in the Twilight of the Sweatshop Age*. Cambridge: Cambridge University Press.

Labaqui, I. 2014. "Who's Afraid of Reversing Neoliberal Reforms? Financial Statecraft in Argentina and Venezuela." In *The Financial Statecraft of Emerging Powers: Shield and

Sword in Asia and Latin America, edited by Leslie Elliot Armijo and Saori N. Katada, 21–46. New York: Palgrave.

La Botz, Dan. 2016. *What Went Wrong? The Nicaraguan Revolution: A Marxist Analysis.* Chicago: Haymarket Books.

Lacroix, Pierril, Christophe Chauveau, and Diana Taipe. 2013. "Soberanía alimentario y comercializatión campesina en Ecuador." In *Comercialización y soberanía alimentaria,* edited by Francisco Hidalgo, Pierril Lacroix, and Paola Román, 63–68. Quito: SIPAE.

Ladera, Marynés. 2014. "Crean los Consejos Presidenciales de Gobierno Popular." September 2, 2014. http://minci.gob.ve/2014/09/crean-los-consejos-presidenciales-de-gobierno-popular/.

Lahiff, Edward, Saturnino M. Borras, and Cristóbal Kay. 2007. "Market-Led Agrarian Reform: Policies, Performance and Prospects." *Third World Quarterly* 28 (8): 1417–36.

Lalander, Rickard. 2011. "Descentralización socialista? Reflexiones sobre democracia radical, participación política y el neoconstitucionalismo del siglo XXI en Bolivia, Ecuador y Venezuela." *Revista Politeia* 47 (34): 55–88.

Lampa, Roberto. 2016. "Crisis in Venezuela, or the Bolivarian Dilemma: To Revolutionize or to Perish? A Kaleckian Interpretation." *Review of Radical Political Economics* 49 (2): 198–218.

Lander, Edgardo, and Luis Fierro. 1996. "The Impact of Neoliberal Adjustment in Venezuela, 1989–1993." *Latin American Perspectives* 23 (3): 50–73.

La Razón. 2013. "La empresa alimentaria de Bolivia y Venezuela arrancará a finales de este año." October 25, 2013. http://www.la-razon.com/economia/alimentaria-Bolivia-Venezuela-arrancara-finales_0_1931207014.html.

Larner, Wendy, and William Walters. 2002. "The Political Rationality of 'New Regionalism': Toward a Genealogy of the Region." *Theory and Society* 31 (3): 391–432.

Larrabure, Manuel. 2013. "Human Development and Class Struggle in Venezuela's Popular Economy: The Paradox of 'Twenty-First Century Socialism.'" *Historical Materialism* 21 (4): 177–200.

Lavelle, Daniel Brian. 2013. "A Twenty-First Century Socialist Agriculture? Land Reform, Food Sovereignty and Peasant–State Dynamics in Venezuela." *International Journal of Sociology of Agriculture and Food* 21 (1): 133–54.

———. 2016. "Petro-Socialism and Agrarianism: Agrarian Reform, Food, and Oil in Chavista Venezuela." PhD diss., University of California, Berkeley.

Lawson, George, and Robbie Shilliam. 2009. "Beyond Hypocrisy? Debating the 'Fact' and 'Value' of Sovereignty in Contemporary World Politics." *International Politics* 46: 657–70.

Lebowitz, Michael. 2006. *Build It Now: Socialism for the Twenty-First Century.* New York: Monthly Review.

LeFeber, Walter. 1993. *Inevitable Revolutions: The United States in Central America.* New York: Norton.

Lefebvre, Henri. [1980] 2006. *La presencia y la ausencia: Contribución a la teoria de las representaciónes.* Mexico City: Fondo de la Cultura Económica.

———. 1991. *The Production of Space.* Oxford: Wiley-Blackwell.

Legler, Thomas. 2013. "Post-Hegemonic Regionalism and Sovereignty in Latin America: Optimists, Skeptics, and an Emerging Research Agenda." *Contexto Internacional* 35:325–52.

Leite, José Corrêa. 2005. *World Social Forum: Strategies of Resistance*. Chicago: Haymarket Books.

Lewis, Linden, ed. 2013. *Caribbean Sovereignty, Development and Democracy in an Age of Globalization*. New York: Routledge.

Li, Tania. 2007. *The Will to Improve: Governmentality, Development, and the Practice of Politics*. Durham, N.C.: Duke University Press.

Locke, John. 2003 [1689]. *Two Treatises of Government and A Letter Concerning Toleration*. Edited by Ian Shapiro. New Haven: Yale University Press.

Loick, Daniel. 2018. *A Critique of Sovereignty*. New York: Rowman and Littlefield.

Longa, Francisco, and Juan Wahren. 2009. "Venezuela." In *La tierra es nuestra, tuya y de aquel: La disputa por el territorio en América Latina*, edited by Norma Giarraca and Miguel Teubal, 99–131. Buenos Aires: Grupo de Estudio de los Movimientos Sociales de América Latina.

Long, Norman, and Bryan Roberts. 2005. "Changing Rural Scenarios and Research Agendas in Latin America in the New Century." In *New Directions in the Sociology of Global Development*, vol. 11, edited by Frederick Buttel and Philip McMichael, 57–90. Bingley: Emerald Group.

López, Liza Elena Aceves, and Guiseppe Lo Brutto. 2016. "Popular Power and Regional Integration: An Analysis of the ALBA-TCP." In *Popular Sovereignty and Constituent Power in Latin America*, edited by Emelio Betances and Carlos Figueroa Ibarra, 183–202. New York: Palgrave.

López Maya, Margarita. 2003. "The Venezuelan 'Caracazo' of 1989: Popular Protest and Institutional Weakness." *Journal of Latin American Studies* 35 (1): 117–37.

López-Sánchez, Roberto, and Carmen Hernández Rodríguez. 2014. "La lucha contra la impunidad de los crímenes políticos en Venezuela." *Historia Actual* 33:133–42.

Lorca, Sara. 2016. "Más del 90 % del sector privado está incorporado en la activación de los motores productivos." *Correo del Orinoco*, May 22, 2016. http://www.correo delorinoco.gob.ve/nacionales/mas-90-sector-privado-esta-incorporado-activacion-motores-productivos/.

Löwy, Michael. 1981. *The Politics of Combined and Uneven Development: The Theory of Permanent Revolution*. London: NLR.

Lubbock, Rowan. 2018. "From Magical State to Magical Region? Ecology, Labor and Socialism in ALBA." In *Understanding ALBA: Progress, Problems, and Prospects of Alternative Regionalism in Latin America and the Caribbean*, edited by A. K. Cusack, 195–210. London: ILAS.

———. 2020a. "The Hidden Edifice of (Food) Sovereignty: Rights, Territory, and the Struggle for Agrarian Reform in Venezuela." *Journal of Agrarian Change* 20 (2): 289–310.

———. 2020b. "Rights, Recognition and Norms in the Making of Latin American International Society: An Historical Materialist Interpretation." *Journal of International Relations and Development* 23:237–61.

———. 2020c. "Imperialism and the Geopolitics of COVID-19 in Venezuela." *Textos e Debates* 1 (34): 153–76.

———. 2022. "Capitalist Geopolitics and Latin America's Long Road to Regionalism." *Globalizations* 19 (4): 536–54.

LVC (La Vía Campesina). 1996. "Tlaxcala Declaration of the Vía Campesina." II International Conference of the Via Campesina, Tlaxcala, Mexico, April 18–21, https://viacampesina.org/en/ii-international-conference-of-the-via-campesina-tlaxcala-mexico-april-18-21/.

LVC et al. 2001. "Our World Is Not for Sale. Priority to Peoples: Food Sovereignty WTO Out of Food and Agriculture." https://www.citizen.org/documents/wtooutoffood.pdf.

———. 2007. Nyéléni Declaration, Nyéléni Village, Sélingué, Mali, February 27, 2007. https://nyeleni.org/IMG/pdf/DeclNyeleni-en.pdf.

LVC, Sofia Monslave, Peter Rosset, Saúl Vázquez, Jill Carino, and the West African Network of Peasant and Agricultural Producers' Organizations. 2006. "Agrarian Reform in the Context of Food Sovereignty, the Right to Food and Cultural Diversity: 'Land, Territory and Dignity." Paper prepared for the International NGO/CSO Planning Committee for Food Sovereignty (IPC), January 2006.

Macartney, Huw, and Stuart Shields. 2011. "Finding Space in Critical IPE: A Scalar-Relational Approach." *Journal of International Relations and Development* 14: 375–83.

Macleod, Andrew. 2018. *Bad News from Venezuela: Twenty years of Fake News and Misreporting*. New York: Routledge.

Macpherson, C. B. 2001. *The Political Theory of Possessive Individualism: Hobbes to Locke*. Don Mills, Ont.: Oxford University Press.

Macpherson, W. J. 1995. *The Economic Development of Japan, 1867–1941*. Cambridge, Cambridge University Press.

MAGAP-Heifer. 2014. *La agroecología está presente: Mapeo de productores agroecológicos y del estado de la agroecología en la sierra y costa ecuatoriana*. Quito: Heifer Ecuador.

Main, Alexander, and Codas, Gustavo. 2016. "The End of a Progressive Cycle?" *NACLA Report on the Americas* 48 (4): 381–84.

Malamud, Andrés. 2005. "MERCOSUR Turns 15: Between Rising Rhetoric and Declining Achievement." *Cambridge Review of International Affairs* 18 (3): 421–36.

Mann, Susan Archer. 1990. *Agrarian Capitalism in Theory and Practice*. Chapel Hill: University of North Carolina Press.

Marco, Daniel García. 2017. "Qué países de América Latina alimentan a la Venezuela de la crisis." BBC Mundo, May 28, 2017. http://www.bbc.com/mundo/noticias-america-latina-39995928.

Ma Rhea, Zane. 2017. *Frontiers of Taste: Food Sovereignty, Sustainability and Indigenous-Settler Relations in Australia*. New York: Springer.

Marín, Evaristo Marcano, and Steve Ellner. 2015. "It Is Necessary to Contextualize the Pragmatic and Populist Policies of the Chavista Government: An Interview with Steve Ellner." *Venezuelanalysis*, September 15, 2015. https://venezuelanalysis.com/analysis/11505.

Marquina, Cira Pasqual. 2019. "Campesinos Defending Chavez's Project: A Conversation with Andres Alayo." *Venezuelanalysis*, August 31, 2019. https://venezuelanalysis.com/analysis/14638.

———. 2020. "Venezuela's Oil Industry between Sanctions and Strategic Blunders:

A Conversation with Carlos Mendoza Potella." *Venezuelanalysis*, August 28, 2020. https://venezuelanalysis.com/analysis/14980.

Martí i Puig, Salvador, and Eduardo Baumeister. 2017. "Agrarian Policies in Nicaragua: From Revolution to the Revival of Agro-Exports, 1979–2015." *Journal of Agrarian Change* 17 (2): 381–96.

Martinez, Jenifer. 2013. "The ALBA-TCP Council of Social Movements: A Double-Turn in Counter-Hegemony." In Muhr, *Counter-Globalization and Socialism in the 21st Century*, 63–79.

Martínez Valle, Luciano. 2014. "La concentración de la tierra en el caso ecuatoriano: Impactos en el territorio." In *La concentración de la tierra: Un problema prioritario en el Ecuador contemporáneo*, edited by A. Berry, Luciano Martínez Valle, and L. North, 43–62. Quito: Ediciones Abya-Yala.

Martínez-Torres, María Elena, and Peter Rosset. 2014. "*Diálogo de Saberes* in La Vía Campesina: Food Sovereignty and Agroecology." *Journal of Peasant Studies* 41 (6): 979–97.

Marx, Karl. 1973. *Grundrisse: Introduction to the Critique of Political Economy*. Translated by Martin Nicolaus. New York: Vintage.

———. 1982. *Capital: Volume 1: A Critique of Political Economy*. London: Penguin.

———. 1991. *Capital: A Critique of Political Economy, Vol. 3*. New York: Penguin.

Marx, Karl, and Friedrich Engels. 1998. *The German Ideology*. New York: Prometheus.

Massabié, Germán. 2008. *Venezuela: A Petro-State Using Renewable Energies: A Contribution to the Global Debate about New Renewable Energies for Electricity Generation*. Wiesbaden: Verl. für Sozialwiss.

Massey, Doreen. 2009. "Concepts of Space and Power in Theory and in Political Practice." *Documents d'Anàlisi Geogràfica* 55:15–26.

Mato, Daniel. 2000. "Transnational Networking and the Social Production of Representations of Identities by Indigenous Peoples' Organizations of Latin America." *International Sociology* 15 (2): 343–60.

Matsumura, Wendy. 2016. "The Expansion of the Japanese Empire and the Rise of the Global Agrarian Question after the First World War." In *Cataclysm 1914: The First World War and the Making of Modern World Politics*, edited by Alexander Anievas, 144–73. Chicago: Haymarket.

Mazoyer, Marcel, and Laurence Roudart. 2006. *A History of World Agriculture: From the Neolithic age to the Current Crisis*. London: Earthscan.

McBeth, Brian Stuart. 2002. *Juan Vicente Gómez and the Oil Companies in Venezuela, 1908–1935*. Cambridge: Cambridge University Press.

McCormick, Thomas J. 1989. *America's Half-Century: United States Foreign Policy in the Cold War and After*. Baltimore: John Hopkins University Press.

McCune, Nils, Juan Reardon, and Peter Rosset. 2014. "Agroecological Formación in Rural Social Movements." *Radical Teacher* 98:31–37.

McKay, Ben. 2011. "Assessing the Impacts of Venezuela's State-Led Agrarian Reform Programme on Rural Livelihoods." Masters thesis, Saint Mary's University.

———. 2018. "The Politics of Agrarian Change in Bolivia's Soy Complex." *Journal of Agrarian Change* 18 (2) 406–24.

———. 2020. "Food Sovereignty and Neo-Extractivism: Limits and Possibilities of an Alternative Development Model." *Globalizations* 17 (8) 1386–404.

McKay, Ben, Ryan Nehring, and Marygold Walsh-Dilley. 2014. "The 'State' of Food Sovereignty in Latin America: Political Projects and Alternative Pathways in Venezuela, Ecuador and Bolivia." *Journal of Peasant Studies* 41 (6): 1175–200.
McMichael, Philip. 2009. "Global Citizenship and Multiple Sovereignties: Reconstituting modernity." In Atasoy, *Hegemonic Transitions*, 23–42.
———. 2014. "Historicizing Food Sovereignty." *Journal of Peasant Studies* 41 (6): 933–57.
McNeil, Kent. 2013. "Factual and Legal Sovereignty in North America: Indigenous Realities and Euro-American Pretensions." In *Sovereignty: Frontiers of Possibility*, edited by Julie Evans, Anne Genovese, Alexander Reilly, and Patrick Wolfe: 37–59. Honolulu: University of Hawai'i Press.
McNelly, Angus. 2022. "Harnessing the Storm: Searching for Constitutive Moments and a Politics of *Ch'ixi* after the Pink Tide." *Alternautas* 9 (1): 98–128.
McSherry, J. Patrice. 2005. *Predatory States: Operation Condor and Covert War in Latin America*. Lanham, Md.: Rowman and Littlefield.
Menéndez, Ricardo. 2013. "The Socialist Transformation of Venezuela." In *Spatial Politics*, edited by David Featherstone and Joe Painter, 224–34. Chichester: John Wiley.
Mészáros, István. 1995. *Beyond Capital: Toward a Theory of Transition*. New York: Monthly Review Press.
Metereau, Renaud. 2020. "Nicaraguan Peasant Cooperativism in Tension: Adaptive Strategy or Counter-Movement." *Third World Quarterly* 41 (5) 801–21.
Mezzadri, Alessandra. 2017. *The Sweatshop Regime: Labouring Bodies, Exploitation, and Garments Made in India*. Cambridge: Cambridge University Press.
Michelutti, Lucia. 2012. "Small-Scale Farmers under Socialist Governments: Venezuela and the ALBA People's Trade Agreement." London: IIED/HIVOS.
Milenky, Edward S. 1973. *The Politics of Regional Organization in Latin America: The Latin American Free Trade Association*. New York: Praeger.
MINPPAL. 2015. "Memoria y Cuenta 2015." January 2015. Caracas: rbv.
Mittal, Anuradha. 2009. "The Blame Game: Understanding the Structural Causes of the Food Crisis." In *The Global Food Crisis: Governance Challenges and Opportunities*, edited by Jennifer Clapp and Marc J. Coehen, 13–28. Ontario: Wilfrid Laurier University Press.
Modenessi, Massimo. 2019. *The Antagonistic Principle: Marxism and Political Action*. Translated by Larry Goldsmith. Leiden: Brill.
Modenessi, Massimo, ed. 2013. *Horizontes Gramscianos: Estudios en torno al pensamiento de Antonio Gramsci*. Mexico City: UNAM.
Modenessi, Massimo, and Maristella Svampa. 2016. "Posprogresismo y horizontes emancipatorios en América Latina." *America Latina en Movimiento*, August 10, 2016. https://latinta.com.ar/2016/08/posprogresismo-y-horizontes-emancipatorios-en-america-latina/.
Monsutti, Alessandro. 2012. "Fuzzy Sovereignty: Rural Reconstruction in Afghanistan, between Democracy Promotion and Power Games." *Comparative Studies in Society and History* 54 (3): 563–91.
Moore, Jason W. 2002. "Remaking Work, Remaking Space: Spaces of Production and

Accumulation in the Reconstruction of American Capitalism, 1865–1920." *Antipode* 34 (2): 176–204.

———. 2010a. "The End of the Road? Agricultural Revolutions in the Capitalist World-Ecology, 1450–2010." *Journal of Agrarian Change* 10 (3): 389–413.

———. 2010b. "Cheap Food and Bad Money: Food, Frontiers, and Financialization in the Rise and Demise of Neoliberalism." *Review* 33 (2/3): 225–61.

Moore, Margaret. 2001. *The Ethics of Nationalism*. Oxford: Oxford University Press.

Motta, Sara. C. 2014. "Latin America: Reinventing Revolutions, an 'Other' Politics in Practice and Theory." In *Rethinking Latin American Social Movements: Radical Action from Below*, edited by R. Stahler-Sholk, H. E. Vanden, and M. Becker, 21–44. Lanham, Md.: Rowman and Littlefield.

Movimientos Sociales del ALBA. 2007. "Declaración final de los Movimientos Sociales en la V Cumbre del ALBA." *Aporrea*, May 9, 2007. http://www.aporrea.org/tiburon/a34425.html.

———. 2008. "Carta de los Movimientos Sociales de las Américas." https://movimientos.org/node/13672?key=13672.

———. 2009. "Hacia la fundación del Consejo de Movimientos Sociales del ALBA-TCP." 1st Cumbre del Consejo Plurinacional Intercultural de los Movimientos Sociales de los Países del ALBA-TCP. Cochabamba, Bolivia, October 15–17, 2009. http://www.movimientos.org/es/albasi/show_text.php3%3Fkey%3D16072.

MPPAL (Ministerio del Poder Popular para la Alimentación). 2015. *Memoria y Cuenta 2015*. Vol. 1. Caracas: MPPAL.

MPPAT (Ministerio del Poder Popular de Agricultura y Tierras). 2007/8. Censo Agrario 2007/08, http://censo.mat.gob.ve/.

———. 2013. *Memoria 2012*. Caracas: MPPAT.

———. 2014. *Memoria 2013*. Caracas: MPPAT.

———. 2015. *Memoria 2014*. Caracas: MPPAT.

MPPAT/INDER (Ministerio del Poder Popular para la Agricultura y Tierras/Instituto Nacional de Desarrollo Rural). 2015. "Plan Nacional de Agricultura de Riego y Saneamiento de Tierras. Fase I (2015–2019)." Caracas: Venezuela.

MPPEU (Ministerio del Poder Popular para la Educación Universitaria). 2008. "Educación superior. Plan sectoral, 2008–2013." Caracas.

Muhr, Thomas. 2010. "Counter-Hegemonic Regionalism and Higher Education for All: Venezuela and the ALBA." *Globalisation, Societies and Education* 8 (1): 39–57.

———. 2011. *Venezuela and the ALBA: Counter-Hegemony, Geographies of Integration and Development, and Higher Education for All*. Saarbrucken: VDM Verlag.

———. 2013. *Counter-Globalization and Socialism in the 21st Century: The Bolivarian Alliance for the Peoples of Our America*. London: Routledge.

Muller, Hannah Weiss. 2017. *Subjects and Sovereign: Bonds of Belonging in Eighteenth-Century British Empire*. Oxford: Oxford University Press.

Muñoz, Heraldo. 2001. "Good-Bye U.S.A.?" In *Latin America in the New International System*, edited by J. S. Tulchin and R. H. Espach, 73–90. Boulder: Lynne Rienner.

Murphy, Craig. 2005. *Global Institutions, Marginalization, and Development*. London: Routledge.

Mutlu, Can E. 2015. "How (Not) to Disappear Completely: Pedagogical International Relations." *Millennium: Journal of International Studies* 43 (3): 931–41.
Myers, Natasha. 2017. "From the Anthropocene to the Planthroposcene: Designing Gardens for Plant/People Involution." *History and Anthropology* 28 (3): 297–301.
Nakatani, Paulo, and Rémy Herrera. 2008. "Structural Changes and Planning of the Economy in Revolutionary Venezuela." *Review of Radical Political Economics* 40 (3): 292–99.
Neeson, J. M. 1993. *Commoners: Common Rights, Enclosure and Social Change in England, 1700–1820*. Cambridge: Cambridge University Press.
Nelson, Marcel. 2015. *A History of the FTAA: From Hegemony to Fragmentation in the Americas*. New York: Palgrave.
———. 2019. "Walking the Tightrope of Socialist Governance: A Strategic-Relational Analysis of Twenty-First Century Socialism." *Latin American Perspectives* 46 (1): 46–65.
———. 2022. 'The Pacific Alliance: Regional Integration as Neoliberal Discipline," *Globalizations*, 19 (4): 571-86.
Neocleous, Mark. 2003. *Imagining the State*. Berkshire: Open University Press.
———. 2022. "The Pacific Alliance: Regional Integration as Neoliberal Discipline." *Globalizations* 19 (4): 571–86.
———. 2011. "War on Waste: Law, Original Accumulation and the Violence of Capital." *Science and Society* 75 (4): 506–28.
Ngai-Ling, Sum, and Bob Jessop. 2006. *Towards a Cultural Political Economy: Putting Culture in Its Place in Political Economy*. Cheltenham: Edward Elgar.
Noble, David F. 2011. *Forces of Production: A Social History of Industrial Automation*. London: Transaction Publishers.
North, Liisa L., and Timothy D. Clark, eds. 2018. *Dominant Elites in Latin America: From Neo-Liberalism to the "Pink Tide"*. New York: Palgrave.
Noticia al Dia. 2017. "Pérez Abad: Empresarios tienen derecho a participar en la Constituyente." May 19, 2017. http://noticiaaldia.com/2017/05/perez-abad-empresarios-tienen-derecho-a-participar-en-la-constituyente/.
Noticias de Venezuela. 2012. "Desmantelan planta de soya en El Tigre." April 6, 2012. https://noticierosvenezuela.wordpress.com/2012/06/04/desmantelan-planta-de-soya-en-el-tigre/.
O'Brien, Padraic. 2014. *Insurgent Planning in Venezuela and Brazil: The Case of the CRBZ and the MST*. Saarbrücken: *LAP LAMBERT*.
O'Connor, Sarah. 2013. "Amazon Unpacked." *Financial Times*, February 8, 2013. https://www.ft.com/content/ed6a985c-70bd-11e2-85d0-00144feab49a.
O'Donnell, Guillermo. 1973. *Modernization and Bureaucratic-Authoritarianism. Studies in South American Politics*. Berkley: University of California Press.
Olivares, Iván. 2015. "Albalinisa cobra US$189.3 millones a Venezuela." *Confidencial*, December 17, 2015. https://confidencial.com.ni/albalinisa-cobra-us189-3-millones-a-venezuela/.
Oliver, Lucio. 2013. "Gramsci y los cambios políticos recientes en América Latina." In Modenessi, *Horizontes Gramscianos*, 237–60.

———. 2017. "Gramsci y la noción de catarsis histórica: Su actualidad para América Latina." *Las Torres de Lucca: Revista Internacional de Filosofía Política* 6 (11): 29–42.

Olsen, Thomas. 2006. "The Zapatistas and Transnational Framing." In Johnston and Almeida, *Latin American Social Movements*, 179–96.

Ong, Aihwa. 2000. "Graduated Sovereignty in South-East Asia," *Theory, Culture and Society* 17 (4): 55–75.

OPEC. 2017. *Annual Statistical Bulletin*. www.opec.org/opec_web/static_files_project /media/.../ASB2017_13062017.pdf.

Orhangazi, Özgür. 2014. "Contours of Alternative Policy Making in Venezuela." *Review of Radical Political Economics* 46 (2): 221–40.

Ortiz, Mercedes, Patricia Carolina Ordaz Cañameras, and Vianna Esther Urbáez Malavé. 2016. "Nivel de desarrollo de los sistemas logísticos en el sector alimenticio de la zona norte del estado Anzoátegui, Venezuela." *Revista Espacios* 37 (11): 1–11. http://www .revistaespacios.com/a16v37n11/16371123.html.

Ortiz, Nelson. 2004. "Entrepreneurs: Profits without Power?" In *Unravelling of Representative Democracy in Venezuela*, edited by J. L. McCoy and D. J. Myers, 71–92. Baltimore: John Hopkins University Press.

Ortiz, Roberto José. 2014. "Agro-Industrialization, Petrodollar Illusions and the Transformation of the Capitalist World Economy in the 1970s: The Latin American Experience." *Critical Sociology* 42 (4–5): 599–621.

Otero, Gerardo. 2016. "Review of Philip McMichael's *Food Regimes and Agrarian Questions*." *Journal of World Systems Research* 22 (1): 299–305.

Ouviña, Hernán, and Mabel Thwaites Rey, eds. 2018. *Estados en disputa: Auge y fractura del ciclo de impugnación al neoliberalismo en América Latina*. Buenos Aires: CLACSO.

Page, Tiffany. 2010. "The Ambiguous Transition: Building State Capacity and Expanding Popular Participation in Venezuela's Agrarian Reform." PhD diss., University of California, Berkeley.

Palencia, Jannette Yépez. 2016. "En un 80% ha caído producción de la empresa estatal Arroz del ALBA." *Ultima Hora*. http://ultimahoradigital.com/2016/04/en-un-80-ha -caidoproduccion-de-la-empresa-estatal-arroz-del-alba/.

Palmer, Meredith Alberta. 2020. "Rendering Settler Sovereign Landscapes: Race and Property in the Empire State." *Environment and Planning D: Society and Space* 38 (5): 793–810.

Parker, Dick. 2008. "Chávez y la búsqueda de una seguridad y soberanía alimentarias." *Revista Venezolana de Economía y Ciencias Sociales* 14 (3): 121–43.

Parraguez-Vergara, Elvis, Beatriz Contreras, Neidy Clavijo, Vivian Villegas, Nelly Paucar, and Francisco Ther. 2018. "Does Indigenous and *Campesino* Traditional Ariculture Have Anything to Contribute to Food Sovereignty in Latin America? Evidence from Chile, Peru, Ecuador, Colombia, Guatemala and Mexico." *International Journal of Agricultural Sustainability* 16 (4–5): 326–34.

Pastor, Robert A. 2001. *Exiting the Whirlpool: U.S. Foreign Policy toward Latin America and the Caribbean*. Boulder: Westview Press.

Patel, Raj. 2009. "What Does Food Sovereignty Look Like?" *Journal of Peasant Studies* 36 (3): 663–706.

———. 2013. "The Long Green Revolution." *Journal of Peasant Studies* 40 (1): 1–63.
Paul, T. V., ed. 2012. *International Relations Theory and Regional Transformation*. Cambridge: Cambridge University Press.
Pearce, Stephanie. 2013. "Twenty-First Century Countertrade: The Case of Venezuela, 2004–2011." PhD diss., Queen Mary University.
Peck, James. 2010. *Ideal Illusions: How the U.S. Government Co-Opted Human Rights*. New York: Metropolitan.
Peña, Karla. 2016. "Social Movements, the State, and the Making of Food Sovereignty in Ecuador." *Latin American Perspectives* 43 (1): 221–37.
Perelman, Michael. 2000. *The Invention of Capitalism: Classical Political Economy and the Secret History of Primitive Accumulation*. Durham, N.C.: Duke University Press.
Perkins, John H. 1997. *Geopolitics and the Green Revolution: Wheat, Genes, and the Cold War*. Oxford: Oxford University Press.
Perla, Héctor, and Héctor Cruz-Feliciano. 2013. "The Twenty-First-Century Left in El Salvador and Nicaragua: Understanding Apparent Contradictions and Criticisms." *Latin American Perspectives* 40 (3): 83–106.
Perroux, François. 1983. *A New Concept of Development: Basic Tenets*. London: Croom Helm.
Petras, James, and Robert LaPorte Jr. 1970. "Modernization from Above versus Reform from Below: U.S. Policy toward Lain American Agricultural Development." *Journal of Development Studies* 6 (3): 248–66.
Petras, James, and Morris Morley. 1983. "Petrodollars and the State: The Failure of State Capitalist Development in Venezuela". *Third World Quarterly* 5 (1): 8–27.
Petras, James, and Henry Veltmeyer. 2002. "The Peasantry and the State in Latin America: A Troubled Past, an Uncertain Future." *Journal of Peasant Studies* 29 (3–4): 41–82.
Pezzola, Anthony A. 2018. "The Deep Roots of Protectionism in the Southern Cone: Constituent Interests and Mercosur's Common External Tariff." *Latin American Politics and Society* 60 (4): 69–92.
Phillips, Nicola. 2003. "The Rise and Fall of Open Regionalism? Comparative Reflections on Regional Governance in the Southern Cone of Latin America." *Third World Quarterly* 24 (2): 217–34.
———. 2004. *The Southern Cone Model: The Political Economy of Regional Capitalist Development in Latin America*. New York: Routledge.
Plaza, Galo. 1959. "For a Regional Market in Latin America." *Foreign Affairs* 37 (4): 607–16.
Ploeg, Jan Douwe van der, Ye Jingzhong, and Sergio Schneider. 2012. "Rural Development through the Construction of New, Nested, Markets: Comparative Perspectives from China, Brazil and the European Union." *Journal of Peasant Studies* 39 (1): 133–73.
Portes, Alejandro. 1985. "Latin American Class Structures: Their Composition and Change during the Last Decades." *Latin American Research Review* 20 (3): 7–39.
Portes, Alejandro, and Kelly Hoffman. 2003. "Latin American Class Structures: Their Composition and Change during the Neoliberal Era." *Latin American Research Review* 38 (1): 41–82.

Postel-Vinay, K. 2007. "The Historicity of the International Region: Revisiting the 'Europe and the Rest' Divide." *Geopolitics* 12 (4): 555–69.
Poulantzas, Nicos. 1975. *Classes in Contemporary Capitalism*. London: NLB.
———. 2014 [1978]. *State, Power, Socialism*. London: Verso Books.
Powell, John Duncan. 1971. "Venezuelan Agrarian Problems in Comparative Perspective." *Comparative Studies in Society and History* 13 (3): 282–300.
PROVEA. 2009. *Derecho a la tierra*. Caracas: PROVEA.
———. 2010. *Derecho a la tierra*. Caracas: PROVEA.
———. 2011. *Derecho a la tierra*. Caracas: PROVEA.
———. 2012. *Derecho a la tierra*. Caracas: PROVEA.
———. 2013. *Derecho a la tierra*. Caracas: PROVEA.
———. 2015. *Derecho a la tierra*. Caracas: PROVEA.
———. 2016. *Derecho a la tierra*. Caracas: PROVEA.
Przeworski, Adam. 1985. *Capitalism and Social Democracy*. Cambridge: Cambridge University Press.
Puntigliano, Andrés Rivarola. 2011. "'Geopolitics of Integration' and the Imagination of South America." *Geopolitics* 16 (4): 846–64.
Purcell, Thomas F. 2013. "The Political Economy of Social Production Companies in Venezuela." *Latin American Perspectives* 40 (3): 146–68.
———. 2017. "The Political Economy of Rentier Capitalism and the Limits to Agrarian Transformation in Venezuela." *Journal of Agrarian Change* 17 (2): 296–312.
Quastel, Noah. 2016. "Ecological Political Economy: Towards a Strategic-Relational Approach." *Review of Political Economy* 28 (3): 336–53.
Quevedo, Charles. 2019. "Revoluciones pasivas, cesarismo y transformismo: El ciclo progresista latinoamericano y las categorías de Gramsci." In *Gramsci: La teoría de la hegemonía y las transformaciones políticas recientes en América Latina—Actas del Simposio Internacional Asunción*. Asunción: Centro de Estudios Germinal, 128–44.
Rainey, Shirley A., and Glenn S. Johnson. 2009. "Grassroots Activism: An Exploration of Women of Color's Role in the Environmental Justice Movement." *Race, Gender and Class* 16 (3/4): 144–73.
Razavi, Shahra. 2009. "Engendering the Political Economy of Agrarian Change." *Journal of Peasant Studies* 36 (1): 197–226.
rbv. 1999. *Constitución de la República Bolivariana de Venezuela*. Caracas: rbv.
———. 2001a. "Decreto con fuerza de ley de tierras y desarrollo agrario." Caracas: rbv.
———. 2001b. "Líneas generales del plan de desarrollo económico y social de la nación 2001–2007." Caracas: rbv.
———. 2005. "Ley de reforma parcial del decreto con fuerza y rango de ley de tierras y desarrollo agrario." Caracas: rbv.
———. 2007. "Proyecto nacional Simón Bolívar primer plan socialista, 2007–2013." Caracas: rbv.
———. 2008a. "Ley orgánica de seguridad y soberanía agroalimentaria." July 31, 2008. Caracas: rbv.
———. 2008b. "Ley de salud agrícola integral." July 31, 2008, Caracas: rbv.
———. 2013. "Ley del plan de la patria: Segundo plan socialista de desarrollo económico y Social de la nación 2013–2019." December 4, 2013. Caracas: rbv.

Reardon, Simón Juan Alberto, and Reinaldo Alemán Pérez. 2010. "Agroecology and the Development of Indicators of Food Sovereignty in Cuban Food Systems." *Journal of Sustainable Agriculture* 34 (8): 907–922.

Rey, Juan Carlos. 1998. "Corruption and Political Illegitimacy in Venezuelan Democracy." In *Reinventing Legitimacy: Democracy and Political Change in Venezuela*, edited by Demarys Canache and Michael R. Kulishek, 13–36. Westport, Conn.: Greenwood Press.

Rey, Mabel Thawites. 2004. *La autonomía como búsqueda, el estado como contradicción*. Buenos Aires: Prometeo.

——— . 2010. "Después de la globalización neoliberal: ¿Qué estado en América Latina?" *Observatorio Social de América Latina* 11 (27): 19–43.

Rey, Mabel Thawites, ed. 2014. *El estado en América Latina: Continuidades y rupturas*. Buenos Aires: CLASCO.

Riggirozzi, Pía, and Diana Tussie, eds. 2012. *The Rise of Post-Hegemonic Regionalism: The Case of Latin America*. Dordrecht, New York: Springer.

Rioux, Sébastien, Genevieve LeBaron, and Peter J. Verovsek. 2020. "Capitalism and Unfree Labor: A Review of Marxist Perspectives on Modern Slavery." *Review of International Political Economy* 27 (3): 709–31.

Ripoll, Santiago. 2018. "As Good as It Gets? The New Sandinismo and the Co-option of Emancipatory Rural Politics in Nicaragua." Presentation at ERPI 2018 International Conference: Authoritarian Populism and the Rural World, March 17–18, 2018, The Hague.

Robertson, Ewan. 2013. "Law Limiting Costs, Prices and Profits Comes into Force in Venezuela." *Venezuelanalysis*, January 24, 2013. https://venezuelanalysis.com/news/10303.

——— . 2014. "Venezuelan Government Applies Law Limiting Costs, Prices and Profits." *Venezuelanalysis,* February 10, 2014. https://venezuelanalysis.com/news/10343.

Robinson, William I. 2004. *A Theory of Global Capitalism: Production, Class, and State in a Transnational World*. Baltimore: Johns Hopkins University Press.

——— . 2008. *Latin America and Global Capitalism: A Critical Globalization Perspective*. Baltimore: John Hopkins University Press.

Rodríguez, Jessica Torres. 2008. "Investigación Misión Zamora: Un compromiso con las campesinas y campesinos." In *Aun hay tiempo para el sol: Pobrezas ruales y programas sociales. Brasil, Venezuela, Guatemala. Una mirada desde lo local*, edited by Gabriela Scotto, 124–43. Rio de Janeiro: Act!onaid.

Roio, Marcos del. 2012. "Translating Passive Revolution in Brazil." *Capital and Class* 36 (2): 215–34.

Rojas, Ali Colina. 2006. "El nuevo cooperativismo venezolano: Una caracterización basada en estadísticas recientes." *Revista Venezolana de Economía Social* 12:227–48.

Roman-Alcalá, Antonio. 2016. "Conceptualising Components, Conditions and Trajectories of Food Sovereignty's 'Sovereignty.'" *Third World Quarterly* 37 (8): 1388–407.

Romero, Anibal. 1997. "Rearranging the Deck Chairs on the Titanic: The Agony of Democracy in Venezuela." *Latin American Research Review* 32 (1): 7–36.

Romero, Ignacio Ramirez. 2016. "La masacre de El Amparo no debe ser investigada nuevamente por la Corte Marcial sino por un tribunal penal ordinario." *Aporrea*, November 1, 2016. https://www.aporrea.org/ddhh/a236434.html.

Roncallo, Alejandra. 2014. *The Political Economy of Space in the Americas: The New Pax Americana*. London: Routledge.

Ross, Robert J. S. 2004. *Slaves to Fashion: Poverty and Abuse in the New Sweatshops*. Ann Arbor: University of Michigan Press.

Rosset, Peter M., Lia Pinheiro Barbosa, Valentín Val, and Nils McCune. 2022. "Critical Latin American Agroecology as a Regionalism from Below." *Globalizations* 19 (4): 635–52.

Rossi, Federico M. 2018. "Introduction to Part I: Social Movements and the Second Wave of (Territorial) Incorporation in Latin America." In Silva and Rossi, *Reshaping the Political Arena in Latin America*, 23–31.

Rossi, Federico, and Eduardo Silva. 2018. "Introduction: Reshaping the Political Arena in Latin America." In Silva and Rossi, *Reshaping the Political Arena in Latin America*, 3–22.

Rupert, Mark. 1995. *Producing Hegemony: The Politics of Mass Production and US Global Power*. Cambridge: Cambridge University Press.

Saguier, Marcelo I. 2010. "The Hemispheric Social Alliance and the Free Trade Area of the Americas Process: The Challenges and Opportunities of Transnational Coalitions against Neo-liberalism." *Globalizations* 4 (2): 251–65.

Santos, Boaventura de Sousa. 2010. *Para descolonizar Occidente: Más allá del pensamiento abismal*. Buenos Aires: CLASCO.

———. 2015. *Epistemologies of the South: Justice against Epistemicide*. London: Routledge.

Sassen, Saskia. 2006. *Territory, Authority, Rights: From Medieval to Global Assemblages*. Princeton: Princeton University Press.

Schaposnik, Carmen Rosa, and Eugenia Candelaria Pardo. 2015. "ALBA-TCP: Hacia nuevos mecanismos de participación de la economía social y solidaria." *Cooperativismo & Desarrollo* 23 (106): 35–44.

Schavelzon, Salvador. 2015. "The End of the Progressive Narrative in Latin America." *Open Democracy*, September 15, 2015. https://www.opendemocracy.net/en/democraciaabierta/end-of-progressive-narrative-in-latin-america/.

Schiavoni, Christina. 2015. "Competing Sovereignties, Contested Processes: Insights from the Venezuelan Food Sovereignty Experiment." *Globalizations* 12 (4): 466–80.

———. 2017. "The Contested Terrain of Food Sovereignty Construction: Toward a Historical, Relational and Interactive Approach." *Journal of Peasant Studies* 44 (1): 1–32.

Schiavoni, Christina, and William Camacaro. 2009. "The Venezuelan Effort to Build a New Food and Agriculture System." *Monthly Review* 61 (3): 129–41.

Schincariol, Vitor Eduardo. 2018. *Society and Economy in Venezuela: An Overview of the Bolivarian Period (1998–2018)*. New York: Springer.

Scott, James C. 1998. *Seeing Like a State: How Certain Schemes to Improve the Human Condition Have Failed*. New Haven: Yale University Press.

SELA. 2013. "ALBA-TCP as a Mechanism for Cooperation with a Regional Scope." Thirty-ninth Regular Meeting of the Latin American Council, Caracas, Venezuela, October 27–29. SP/CL/XXXIX.O/Di No 4-13: 3–29.

Selva, Simone. 2017. *Before the Neoliberal Turn: The Rise of Energy Finance and the Limits of US Foreign Economic Policy*. New York: Palgrave.

Serulnikov, Sergio. 2003. *Subverting Colonial Authority: Challenges to Spanish Rule in Eighteenth-Century Southern Andes.* Durham, N.C.: Duke University Press.

Settembrino, Yanina. 2012. "Tensiones en los movimientos sociales en Venezuela." *Cuadernos de Antropología Segunda Epoca*, Número Especial: 85–94.

Shaikh, Anwar. 2007. *Globalization and the Myths of Free Trade: History, Theory and Empirical Evidence.* London: Routledge.

Silva, Eduardo. 2009. *Challenging Neoliberalism in Latin America.* Cambridge: Cambridge University Press.

———. 2013. *Transnational Activism and National Movements in Latin America: Bridging the Divide.* New York: Routledge.

Silva, Eduardo, and Federico Rossi. 2018. *Reshaping the Political Arena in Latin America: From Resisting Neoliberalism to the Second Incorporation.* Pittsburgh, Pa.: University of Pittsburgh Press.

Silver, Beverly. J. 2003. *Forces of Labor: Workers Movements and Globalization since 1870.* Cambridge: Cambridge University Press.

Simpson, Gerry. 2004. *Great Powers and Outlaw States: Unequal Sovereigns in the International Legal Order.* Cambridge: Cambridge University Press.

Skonieczny, Amy. 2001. "Constructing NAFTA: Myth, Representation, and the Discursive Construction of U.S. Foreign Policy." *International Studies Quarterly* 45 (3): 433–54.

Smallwood, Stephanie E. 2019. "Reflections on Settler Colonialism, the Hemispheric Americas, and Chattel Slavery." *William and Mary Quarterly* 76 (3): 407–16.

Smith, Neil. 2003. *American Empire: Roosevelt's Geographer and the Prelude to Globalization.* Berkeley: University of California Press.

Smith, Tony. 1991. "The Alliance for Progress: The 1960s." In *Exporting Democracy: The United States and Latin America*, edited by Abraham F. Lowenthal, 71–89. Baltimore: Johns Hopkins University Press.

Smith, Woodruff D. 1980. "Friedrich Ratzel and the Origins of Lebensraum." *German Studies Review* 3 (1): 51–68.

Snipstal, Blain. 2015. "Repeasantization, Agroecology and the Tactics of Food Sovereignty." *Canadian Food Studies / La Revue Canadienne des Études sur L'alimentation* 2 (2): 164.

Solórzano Cavalieri, I. G. 2012. "Modelo juridico aplicable a las Empresas Grannacional." M.A. thesis. Caracas: UBV.

Spalding, Rose J. 2008. "Neoliberal Regionalism and Resistance in Mesoamerica: Foro Mesoamericano Opposition in Plan Puebla-Panama and CAFTA." In *Latin American Social Movements in the Twenty-First Century*, edited by Richard Stahler-Sholk, Harry E. Vanden, and Glen David Kuecker, 323–36. Boulder: Rowman and Littlefield.

Spanakos, Anthony, and Dimitris Pantoulas. 2017. "The Contribution of Hugo Chávez to an Understanding of Post-Neoliberalism." *Latin American Perspectives* 44 (1): 37–53.

Spronk, Susan. 2013. "Neoliberal Class Formation(s): The Informal Proletariat and 'New' Workers" Organizations in Latin America." In *The New Latin American Left: Cracks in the Empire*, edited by Jeffery R. Webber and Barry Carr, 75–94. Boulder: Rowman and Littlefield.

Stevenson, Hayley. 2014. "Representing Green Radicalism: The Limits of State-Based

Representation in Global Climate Governance." *Review of International Studies* 40 (1): 177–201.

Street, James H. 1987. "The Technology Frontier in Latin America: Creativity and Productivity." In *Latin America's Economic Development: Institutionalist and Structuralist Perspectives*, edited by J. L. Dietz and James H. Street, 200–16. Boulder: Lynne Rienner.

Strønen, Iselin. 2017. *Grassroots Politics and Oil Culture in Venezuela*. New York: Palgrave.

Suggett, James. 2008. "ALBA Summit in Venezuela Responds to World Food Crisis and Bolivian Crisis." *Venezuelanalysis*, April 24, 2008. https://venezuelanalysis.com/news/3380

———. 2009a. "ALBA Trade Bloc Forms Joint Food Company at Summit in Venezuela." *Venezuelanalysis*, February 3, 2009.https://venezuelanalysis.com/news/4165.

———. 2009b. "Venezuela Expropriates Cargill Rice Plant That Evaded Price Controls." *Venezuelanalysis*, March 5, 2009. https://venezuelanalysis.com/news/4267.

Sunkel, Osvaldo. 1993. "From Inward-Looking Development to Development from Within." In *Development from Within: Toward a Neostructuralist Approach for Latin America*, edited by Osvaldo Sunkel, 23–60. Boulder: Lynne Rienner.

Sutherland, Manuel. 2016a. "La peor de las crisis económicas, causas, medidas y crónica de una ruina anunciada." February 17, 2016. https://alemcifo.wordpress.com/2016/02/17/2016-la-peor-de-las-crisis-economicas-causas-medidas-y-cronica-de-una-ruina-anunciada/.

———. 2016b. "Crítica a la política económica del 'socialismo del siglo XXI': apropiación privada de la renta petrolera, política de importaciones y fuga de capitales." *Nueva Epoca* 38 July–December: 39–63.

———. 2018. "La ruina de Venezuela no se debe al 'socialismo' ni a la 'revolución.'" *Nueva Sociedad*, March–April. http://nuso.org/articulo/la-ruina-de-venezuela-no-se-debe-al-socialismo-ni-la-revolucion/.

Svampa, Maristella. 2013. "'Consenso de los Commodities' y lenguajes de valoración en América Latin." *Nueva Sociedad* 244 (March–April). https://nuso.org/articulo/consenso-de-los-commodities-y-lenguajes-de-valoracion-en-america-latina/.

Swyngedouw, Erik. 1997. "Excluding the Other: The Production of Scale and Scaled Politics." In *Geographies of Economies*, edited by R. Lee and J. Wells, 167–77. London: Routledge.

Tapia, Luis. 2011. *El etado de derecho como tiranía*. La Paz: CIDES-UMSA.

Tarrow, Sidney. 2005. *The New Transnational Activism*. Cambridge: University of Cambridge Press.

Telesur. 2018. "Ecuador anuncia su salida del ALBA-TCP." August 23, 2018. https://www.telesurtv.net/news/ecuador-salida-alba-tcp-jose-valencia-20180823-0038.html.

Telesur English. 2018. "Venezuela: Region Shifts Right, Maduro Calls for Stronger ALBA." *Venezuelanalysis*, November 5, 2018. https://venezuelanalysis.com/news/14132.

———. 2020. "ALBA Members to Relaunch Food Plan Amid COVID-19: Venezuela FM." June 29, 2020. https://www.telesurenglish.net/news/ALBA-Members-To-Relaunch-Food-Plan-Amidst-COVID-20200629-0014.html.

Teschke, Benno. 2003. *The Myth of 1648: Class, Geopolitics and the Making of Modern International Relations.* London: Verso.

———. 2011. "Decisions and Indecisions: Political and Intellectual Receptions of Carl Schmitt." *New Left Review* 67:61–95.

Teubal, Miguel. 2009. "Agrarian Reform and Social Movements in the Age of Globalization: Latin America at the Dawn of the Twenty-first Century." *Latin American Perspectives* 36 (4): 9–20.

Thomas, Peter D. 2011. "Conjuncture of the Integral State?: Poulantzas' Reading of Gramsci." In *Reading Poulantzas*, edited by Alexander Gallas, Lars Bretthauer, John Hannankulam, and Ingo Stutzle, 277–92. London: Merlin Press.

Thompson, E. P. 1975. *Whigs and Hunters: The Origin of the Black Act.* New York: Pantheon.

Thompson, Merisa S. 2019. "Still Searching for (Food) Sovereignty: Why Are Radical Discourses Only Partially Mobilised in the Independent Anglo-Caribbean?" *Geoforum* 101: 90–99.

Tilley, Lisa, and Robbie Shilliam. 2018. "Raced Markets: An Introduction." *New Political Economy* 23 (5): 534–43.

Tilzey, Mark. 2018. *Political Ecology, Food Regimes, and Food Sovereignty: Crisis, Resistance, and Resilience.* New York: Palgrave.

———. 2019. "Authoritarian Populism and Neo-Extractivism in Bolivia and Ecuador: The Unresolved Agrarian Question and the Prospects for Food Sovereignty as Counter-Hegemony." *Journal of Peasant Studies* 46 (3): 626–52.

Tomlins, Christopher L. 1993. *Law, Labor, and Ideology in the Early American Republic.* Cambridge: Cambridge University Press.

Tooze, Adam. 2008. *The Wages of Destruction: The Making and Breaking of the Nazi Economy.* New York: Penguin.

Townsend, Kenneth W. 2019. *First Americans. A History of Native Peoples.* New York: Routledge.

Trauger, Amy. 2014. "Toward a Political Geography of Food Sovereignty: Transforming Territory, Exchange and Power in the Liberal Sovereign State." *Journal of Peasant Studies* 41 (6): 1131–52.

———. 2017. *We Want Land to Live: Making Political Space for Food Sovereignty.* Athens: University of Georgia Press.

Tuck, Richard. 1979. *Natural Rights Theories. Their Origin and Development.* Cambridge: Cambridge University Press.

Tzeiman, Andrés. 2013. "Estado y desarrollo en América Latina: Dilemas y debates de las ciencias sociales latinoamericanas en el posneoliberalismo (2006–2012)." *Programa Becas. Informe de Investigación.* Buenos Aires: CLACSO. http://biblioteca.clacso.edu.ar/clacso/becas/20131016123041/Tzeimaninformeoctubre2013trabajofinal.pdf.

Val, Valentin, Peter M. Rossett, Carla Zamora Lomelí, Omar Felipe Giraldo, and Dianne Rocheleau. 2019. "Agroecology and La Via Campesina I: The Symbolic and Material Construction of Agroecology through the Dispositive of 'Peasant-to-Peasant' Processes." *Agroecology and Sustainable Food Systems* 43 (7–8): 872–94.

van der Pijl, Kees. 2006. *Global Rivalries: From the Cold War to Iraq.* London: Verso.

———. 2014. *The Discipline of Western Supremacy: Modes of Foreign Relations and Political Economy.* Vol. 3. London: Pluto Press.
Vaz, Ricardo. 2018a. "'Pueblo a Pueblo': Building Food Sovereignty in Venezuela." *Venezuelanalysis*, June 7, 2018. https://venezuelanalysis.com/analysis/13862.
———. 2018b. "Production and Conflict in El Maizal Commune." *Venezuelanalysis*, September 7, 2018. https://venezuelanalysis.com/analysis/14038.
———. 2018c. "Interview with Angel Prado (Part I): 'The Commune Holds the Solution to the Crisis.'" *Venezuelanalysis*, August 16, 2018. https://venezuelanalysis.com/analysis/14005.
Vega, Xavier Léon. 2017. "Agroindustria y soberanía alimentaria en Ecuador." *El futuro de la alimentación y retos de la agricultura para el siglo XXI: Debates sobre quién, cómo y con qué implicaciones sociales, económicas y ecológicas alimentará el mundo* April 2017, 1–20.
Velasco, Alejandro. 2010. "'A Weapon as Powerful as the Vote': Urban Protest and Electoral Politics in Venezuela, 1978–1983." *Hispanic American Historical Review* 90 (4): 661–95.
Veltmeyer, Henry, and Edgar Záyago Lau, eds. 2021. *Buen Vivir and the Challenges to Capitalism in Latin America.* London: Routledge.
Venezuelanalysis. 2017. "In Detail: The Deaths So Far." June 11, 2017. https://venezuelanalysis.com/analysis/13081.
Vergara-Camus, Leandro. 2014. *Land and Freedom: The MST, the Zapatistas and Peasant Alternatives to Neoliberalism.* London: Zed Books.
Vergara-Camus, Leandro, and Cristóbal Kay. 2017. "The Agrarian Political Economy of Left-Wing Governments in Latin America: Agribusiness, Peasants, and the Limits of Neo-developmentalism." *Journal of Agrarian Change* 17 (2): 415–37.
VTV. 2020. "Creado fondo unificado para financimiento del desarrollo agrícola, comunal y agrourbano." January 16, 2020. https://www.vtv.gob.ve/creado-fondo-unico-para-financiamiento-de-agricultura-urbana/
Wallerstein, Immanuel. 2011. *The Modern World-System IV: Centrist Liberalism Triumphant, 1789–1914.* Berkeley: University of California Press.
Walton, J., and D. Seddon 1994. *Free Markets and Food Riots: The Politics of Global Adjustment.* Oxford: Blackwell.
Weaver, John C. 2003. *The Great Land Rush and the Making of the Modern World, 1650–1900.* Montreal: McGill-Queen's University Press.
Webber, Jeffrey R. 2010. "Venezuela under Chávez: The Prospects and Limitations of Twenty-First Century Socialism, 1998–2009." *Socialist Studies/Études Socialistes* 6 (1): 11–44.
———. 2017a. *The Last Day of Oppression and the First Day of the Same: The Politics and Economics of the New Latin American Left.* Chicago: Haymarket.
———. 2017b. "Evo Morales, *Transformismo*, and the Consolidation of Agrarian Capitalism in Bolivia." *Journal of Agrarian Change* 17 (2): 330–47.
Weis, Tony. 2003. "Agrarian Decline and Breadbasket Dependence in the Caribbean: Confronting Illusions of inevitability." *Labor, Capital and Society/Travail, capital et société* 36 (2): 174–99.

———. 2007. "Small Farming and Radical Imaginations in the Caribbean Today." *Race and Class* 49 (2): 112–17.
Weis, W. Michael. 2001. "The Twilight of Pan-Americanism: The Alliance for Progress, Neo-Colonialism, and Non-Alignment in Brazil, 1961–1964." *International History Review* 23 (2): 322–44.
Weisbrot, Mark, and Jeffrey Sachs. 2019. "Punishing Civilians: U.S. Sanctions on Venezuela." *Challenge* 62 (5): 299–321.
Weisbrot, Mark, and Luis Sandoval. 2007. "The Venezuelan Economy in the Chávez Years." Washington, D.C.: Center for Economic and Policy Research.
Werz, Nikolaus. 1990. "State, Oil and Capital Accumulation in Venezuela." In *The State and Capital Accumulation in Latin America*, vol. 2, *Argentina, Bolivia, Colombia, Ecuador, Peru, Uruguay, Venezuela*, edited by Christian Anglade and Carlos Fortin, 182–210. Basingstoke: Macmillan.
Wilson, Bradley R. 2015. "Reclaiming the Worker's Property: Control Grabbing, Farmworkers and the Las Tunas Accords in Nicaragua." *Journal of Peasant Studies* 42 (3-4): 747–63.
Wilson, Marisa. 2016. "Cuban Exceptionalism? A Genealogy of Postcolonial Food Networks in the Caribbean." In *Postcolonialism, Indigeneity and Struggles for Food and Sovereignty: Alternative Food Networks in Subaltern*, edited by Marisa Wilson, 146–74. New York: Routledge.
Wittman, Hannah. 2009. "Reworking the Metabolic Rift: La Vía Campesina, Agrarian Citizenship, and Food Sovereignty." *Journal of Peasant Studies* 36 (4): 805–26.
Wood, Ellen M. 1981. "The Separation of the Economic and the Political in Capitalism." *New Left Review* 1 (127): 66–95.
———. 1995. *Democracy Against Capitalism: Renewing Historical Materialism*. London: Verso.
———. 2008. *Citizens to Lords: A Social History of Western Political Thought from Antiquity to the Middle Ages*. London: Verso.
———. 2012. *Liberty and Property: A Social History of Western Political Thought from Renaissance to Enlightenment*. London: Verso.
Yaffe, Helen. 2015. "Venezuela: Building a Socialist Communal Economy?" *International Critical Thought* 5 (1): 23–41.
Yarrington, Doug. 1997. *A Coffee Frontier: Land, Society, and Politics in Duaca, Venezuela, 1830–1936*. Pittsburgh, Pa: University of Pittsburgh Press.
Yashar, Deborah. 1999. "Democracy, Indigenous Movements, and the Postliberal Challenge in Latin America." *World Politics* 52 (1): 76–104.
Yelling, J. A. 1977. *Common Field Enclosure in England 1450–1850*. London: Macmillan.

INDEX

Locators in italics indicate a figure. Locators in bold indicate a table.

absolute *versus* abstract space, 32
absolutist sovereignty, 27
Acción Democrática, 74
agrarian capital and rational industrial management, 35
"agrarian question," 51–52
agricultural production volumes, 142–5, *144*
agriculture in Venezuelan economy, 5, 74–75, 122, 142–5. *See also* ALBA (Alianza Bolivariana para los Pueblos de Nuestra América); Venezuela
agrochemical use in Venezuela, 145–6
agroecology, 3, **41**, 42, 93, 127–8
Agropatria, 120
Alayo, Andres, 121
ALBA (Alianza Bolivariana para los Pueblos de Nuestra América): accumulation regime of, 96–97, *98;* agricultural production volumes, *144;* agriculture value added (percentage of GDP) in, *91;* centrality of Venezuela in, 15, 73, 97–100, 164–5; Chávez on formation of, 84–85; Council of Social Movements in, 85–88, *86,* 100; development of, 2, 21; domestic capture of ground rent and, 69–70; Empresa Mixta Socialista del, 94; entanglement and, 6; "Eulalia Ramos" and, 94; factories and, 18–19; failures of, 13, 166–167; food exporters to Venezuela, *91;* Food Grandnationals in Venezuela, 99; food sovereignty and, 2, 3–4, 165; global governance and, 96–97; Grandnational Concept and, 88–93, 132; hegemonic project of, 97–98, *98;* institutional materiality of, *86,* 93–100; knowledge-power and antagonism within, 113; "magical region" and, 99; mode of regulation of, 46, 97, *98;* oil wealth, food sovereignty, and, 46; Pesquera Industrial del, 120; policy issues within, 113; regional imports/exports and, 90–91; regional "strategic terrain" of, 12–13; socialist internationalism and, 162; sovereignty and, 10, 97–98, *98,* 100, 165; state power and, 12; "strategic relational" approach and, 13, *98;* strategic selectivity and politics of scale in, 44–47; threat to Indigenous and subaltern communities of, 69; traditional workplace hierarchies in, 83
ALBA-Arroz: Annual Project results and, **142–3**; bureaucratic corruption and, 120; deficit of raw materials and, 142–3; distribution issues and, 148–150; establishment of, 133–4; fate of, 159; focus on, 19; food sovereignty and, 141–6; hierarchical structure and conflicts within, 136–7; occupation of, 18, 19, 132; Payara mayor's office and, 147–8; Point and Circle initiative and, 146–7; politics of production at, 157, 158, 165–6; production capacity issues of, 134<n8; self-management and, 138–140; socialism and, 166; sustainability of, 156; workers and, 21–22, 155–7
ALBA Caruna (Caja Rural Nacional), 95
ALBA de Nicaragua, S.A. (ALBANISA), 95–96, 99
ALBA-Food, **90**, 90–91, 95–99

Index

Alliance for Progress, 55–56
Amazon warehouses, 35
Anderson, Perry, 27
Aponte, Arturo, 132
Argimiro Gabaldón (Venezuela), 110, 126
Arreaza, Jorge, 166, 167
Arrighi, Giovanni, 45
authoritarian statism, 73, 76–77, 83, 99–100
autogestión (self-management), 138–40

Barkan, Joshua, 8
Barrio Adentro program, 1–2
Bauman, Zygmunt, 4
Berlant, Lauren, 7
Betancourt, Rumulo, 74
Beveridge, Albert Jeremiah, 5
Bhandar, Brenna, 30
Bidet, Jacques, 9, 24–25, 33, 42, 163
Blomley, Nicolas, 103
Bodin, Jean, 28
Bolívar, Simón, 49, 84, 169n5
Bolivarian Alternative for the People of Our America (ALBA), 1
bolivarianismo, 78–81, 83–84
Bolivarian Republic of Venezuela, 14, 21, 165. See also Venezuela
Bolivarian Revolution, 4, 80
Bolivarian state: ALBA and, 12–13, 19, 99; authoritarian statism and, 97; bolivarianismo and, 79, 83; chavismo and, 14; FTAA and, 84; magical region and, 46; peasant relations with, 105–106, 118–9
Bolivia: CCCs in, 124; EMSA in, 94–95; "hybridized agrarian citizenship" and, 114; land reform in, 113–4; vertical territoriality in, 113–4
Bolshevik revolution, 160
Bonilla, Yarimar, 6
Bowman, Isaiah, 53
Brazil, 65–66
British Empire, 29–30, 50
Burawoy, Michael, 157–8
bureaucracy and ALBA-Arroz, 137–8
bureaucratic corruption in Venezuela, 119–21
bureaucratic despotism, 157–8

CADIVI (Comisión de Administración de Divisas), 91
Caldera, Rafael, 75
Campesino-a-Campesino movements, 68–69

CANEZ (Coordination Agraria Nacional Ezequiel Zamora), 109
capital: Atlantic, 64; controls, 77, 81; corporate, 3, 107; finance, 60; flight, 80; landed, 34–35, 68, 117; sovereign power of; 33, 171n3; revolution of the productive forces and, 70; rural-urban migration of, 52; territory and, 34–35; transnationalization of, 69, 115
capitalism: abstract space and, 32; compartmentalization and, 24; dawn of era of, 28; exclusion and sovereignty in, 47; "modern" sovereignty and, 9; sovereign power and, 31, 51; violent charade of, 32
capitalist geopolitics, development of, 49
capitalist state, 36–37, 42–43, 164
capitalist world economy, 70–71
caracazo riots, 77–78
Cargill, 133
Caribbean Energy Cooperation Agreement, 46
Caribbean subregion, 6–7, 102
Carmona, Pedro, 79
Castañeda, Jorge, 160
Castro, Akalapeizime, 152
Castro, Fidel, 1
Castro Soteldo, Wilmar, 132
CCC (*circuitos cortos de comercialización*), 123–4
Cely, Nataly, 114–5
Centro Técnico Productive Socialista Florentino, 122
Chávez, Hugo: ALBA and, 1, 84–85, 89, 93–94, 162; anti-neoliberal regionalism of, 84; on Bolivarian state, 117; on capitalism, 2; challenges for, 21; chavismo and, 14, 73, 80, 146, 158–9, 168; *economía social* of, 81–83; food sovereignty and, 142; Gran Misión AgroVenezuela of, 112; as "man of destiny," 78; on necessity of unity, 85; Point and Circle initiative and, 132–3; rise of, 14
chavismo, 14, 73, 80, 146, 158–9, 168
Chibber, Vivek, 153
Chile and neoliberal experimentation, 60
Ciccariello-Maher, 108–109
circuitos cortos de comercialización (CCC), 123–4
class struggle and "strategic terrain": differential "distances" and, 38; knowledge-power and, 123; "Point and Circle" initiative and, 146; Poulantzas on, 11–12; property-power and,

104, 112; transformation of Venezuelan state and, 76, 80–81
Cohen, Morris R., 33
Cold War imperialism, 50
colonialism: British Empire and, 29–30; consequences of "eliminatory" mode of, 30; global food politics and, 16; possessive individual in North American, 31; Spanish Empire and, 28–29
competency, 36
Comprehensive Cooperation Agreement, 46
Confederación de Nacionalidades Indígenas del Ecuador, 107
Consejos de Poder Ciudadano, 116
continental history, 20, 49–51, 65–67
conuco, 5, 169n2
cooperative advantage (Grandnational Concept), 89–92
cooperatives, agrarian, 82–83, 121–2, 130
Coordinadora Democrática, 79
Coronil, Fernando, 46, 72
Correa, Rafael, 104, 107, 112
Correinte Revolucionaria Bolívia y Zamora (CRBZ), 118
COSEP (Consejo Superior de la Empresa Privada), 108
Council of Social Movements (ALBA), 3, 85–88, 86, 100; social movements and, 85–88, 100
COVID-19 pandemic, 166
Crosby, Alfred, 34
Cuba, 1–2, 90–91, 94, 101–102, 134, *142–143*
Cuban revolution, 55
CVAL (Corporación Venezolana de Alimentos), 94, 96, 126, 133–134, 155

Davis, Mike, 34
Davis, Sasha, 7
"democratic road to socialism," 11–12, 39, 43, 48, 87
"dialogue of knowledges," 40, 41
Draper, Hal, 161

economía social (Chávez), 81–83
Economic Space of the ALBA-TCP (ECOALBA), 92–93
Ecuador: CCCs and, 124; food sovereignty and, 114–6; land reform in, 107; peasant/Indigenous movements in, 107, 112, 115; vertical territoriality in, 114–6

Edelman, Marc, 38
Elden, Stuart, 24
El Maizal, 126–127, 131, 168
EMSA (Empresa Mixta Socialista del ALBA), 13, 94–96, 133–4
endogenous development, 92–93, 97, 98, 169–70n6
Enríquez, Laura, 172n8
Estado Major (Venezuela), 150
"Eulalia Ramos" Soy Processing Plant (Venezuela), 94
expansionism: German, 51–52; Japanese, 52; North American, 70; World War II and, 51
exploitation, 35
EZLN (Ejército Zapatista de Liberación Nacional), 67

Fabricant, Nicole, 114
FEDECAMARAS, 79
FEDEINDUSTRIAS, 152
FENOCIN (Confederación Nacional de Organizaciones Campesinas, Indígenas y Negras), 107
Fernández, Albert Noguera, 104
feudalism, 27–28
fieldwork, use of, 17–19
Fifth Republic (Chávez), 100
First Continental Encounter of Agroecology Trainers of LVS, 40
FNCEZ (Frente Nacional Campesina Ezequiel Zamora), 106, 108
Food and Nutritional Sovereignty and Security (FNSS), 105
food crisis of 2007–2008, 2
food distribution, 147–50
food regimes, 12
food sovereignty: agroecology and, 128–129; aims of principles of, 4–5; ALBA and legislation on, 102; ALBA-Arroz and, 141–6; ALBA failures and, 162; Bolivia's "Productive Revolution" and, 113–4; building of participatory food regime for, 4; Caribbean subregion and, 102; central parameters of, 20; challenges of state apparatus and, 159; chavismo and, 146–7; class-relational reading of, 9; Cuba and, 101–2; fragmented politics and, 100; goals of, food sovereignty 3; IALA and, 123; industrial food production and, 129; industrial processing and, 21–22; integration between farmers and factories

food sovereignty (*continued*)
for, 141–142; Misión Mercal and, 125; property- and knowledge-power in, 103–4, 130; regionalization and, 93; rights and role of peoples in, 39; "strategic terrain" approach to, 13; vertical territoriality and, 113–8

food sovereignty legislation: Bolivia and, 104, 106–7; Ecuador and, 104; horizontal scaling and, 127–8; Landless Peasant Movement and, 104; land reform and, 130; Nicaragua and, 105, 107–8; Venezuela and, 105–6, 108–9

food sovereignty movements, 16, 40, 162

food sovereignty politics: ALBA and, 16, 21, 101; challenge to property- and knowledge-power in, 164; forms of organization in, 41–42; method for approaching, 15–18; "multiple sovereignties" in, 42, 43; regionalism and, 17

food sovereignty scholarship: diversity of, 16–17; historical boundedness of, 8; "modernity" and, 47; "sovereignty problem" in, 6, 23, 38, 162–163

foreign monopolization of agriculture, 145

Foro Mesoameicano network, 67

Foucault, Michel, 11

"Four Policemen," 53

fragmentation and sovereignty, 31

FTAA (Free Trade Area of the Americas), 1, 64, 67, 73, 84

Fukuyama, Francis, 160

Gago, Verónica, 167
García, Ambar, 88, 167
García, Marta Elena, 116
García, Tirso, 132
gardening state, 4–5
German expansionism, 51–52
Gibson-Graham, J. K., 44
Giraldo, Omar Felipe, 128
global governance and postwar order, 53–54
globalization, 49
global scale, problems with, 44
Global South, 54, 55, 59, 76, 150
Gramsci, Antonio, 10–11, 78, 169n4
Grandin, Greg, 31
Grandnational Concept, 88–93, 100, 132
Grandnational Enterprises (GNE), 2, 88–89, 92–94, 162

Grandnational production chain (food), **90**
Grandnational Projects (GNP), 88
Gran Misión AgroVenezuela (Chávez), 112
grassroots as term, 5
Great Depression (1870s), 50
Green Revolution, 55–56, 57, 68–69, 70
Großraum, 52
Grugel, Jean, 9
Gualán, Romelio, 115
Guerrero, Nerson, 106

Harnecker, Marta, 84
hegemony, 10, 25, 36, 43. *See also* Gramsci, Antonio; "strategic-relational" approach; United States
Hemispheric Social Alliance, 67
Herrera Campíns, Luis, 77
hidden abode of production, 32–33
Higginbottom, Anthony, 69
horizontal scaling: CCCs and, 123–6; El Maizal and, 126–7; food sovereignty and, 127–8, 130–1; peasant movements and, 123–9
Hozić, Aida, 32

identity formation and territoriality, 40
Iles, Alistair, 23
imports and settler colonial state-spaces, 50
import substitution industrialization (ISI), 55, 92, 153–4
Indigenous communities, violence against, 29, 69
Indigenous knowledge, 3
Indigenous land claims in North America, 29–30
Indigenous movements in Latin America, 30, 40, 41, 67, 104, 107. *See also* peasant movements
individualism, 30
industrial food production, 21–22, 129
Instituto Universitario Latinoamericano de Agroecología (IALA), 123
integration theory, 53
international loans, 60
international regional institutions, 45, 49
ISI (import substitution industrialization), 55, 92, 153–154
Iturriza, Reinaldo, 168

Jakobsen, Jostein, 12
Japanese expansionism, 52

Jaua, Elías, 118
Jessop, Bob, 12, 25, 43, 44, 164

Kennedy, John F., 55
Knafo, Samuel, 16
knowledge-power: abstraction and, 34, 38; capitalist production and, 11, 25; capitalist territory of, 9, 35–36; food sovereignty and, 21, 103, 130; Green Revolution and, 56; sovereignty and, 163; use in framework of, 9, 11, 21
Krasner, Stephen D., 6

labor and sovereignty, 8
labor-state relation, 158
Lagos, Gustavo, 57, 63
Land Law of 2001 (Venezuela), 5
Landless Peasant Movement (Movimiento sin Tierra), 104
land redistribution, 107, 109–10
land reform and ALBA, 104–12
latifunda (Roman), 26, 27
Latin America: 1980s agrarian spaces in, 60–61; agriculture *versus* industry in, 56–57; agro-chemical use in, 56; Alliance for Progress and, 56; end of progressive cycle in, 166–8; expansion of exports from, 60; Green Revolution in, 56; "lost decade" in, 61; need for regional market in, 56–57; neoliberalism and, 50–60, 62–63; "Nontraditional Agricultural Exports" and, 61; participatory democracy in, 43; political realignment of, 167–168; political technology and, 41; postwar integration initiatives in, 54; radical social forces in, 168; regionalism and, 49–50, 58–59, 70; revolutionary politics in, 55; rural-urban migration in, 66; socialist internationalism in, 161–2; structural adjustments in, 59; transnational activism in, 67–68; "vertical territoriality" in, 40–41
Latin American Common Market (LACM), 58
Latin American Free Trade Association (LAFTA), 58
Latin American Left: hegemonic project of, 10; neoliberalism and, 50; return of the state and, 113; rise of "new social movements" in, 66–68; socialism and, 160–1
Lebensraum, 51–53
Lefebvre, Henri, 8, 25, 32
Legler, Thomas, 17

Lenin, Vladimir, 42–43
Li, Tania, 4
liberal democracy, 160–1
literacy and Petrocaribe, 2
Locke, John, 29–30
Lodge, Henry Cabot, 55
López, Héctor, 132
Loyo, Juan Carlos, 118
Luce, Henry, 53
LVC (La Vía Campesina): discourse of, 39, 69; food sovereignty and, 3; prominence of, 68; state alliance of, 69; territory and, 40

Macleod, Alan, 19
Maduro, Nicolás, 125, 150, 152, 159, 167–8
Martínez-Torres, María Elena, 40
Marx, Karl, 8, 24, 26, 28, 32–33
Massacre of Amparo, 105
"material condensation" of capitalist state, 37–38
McCormick, Thomas J., 56
McCune, Nils, 128
McMichael, Philip, 41, 42, 43
MERCOSUR (Southern Common Market), 20, 63–65, 71
Mesa Agraria, 115
methodology 15–18
Mexico, 60, 64, 67. *See also* North American Free Trade Agreement (NAFTA)
Miami Summit, 64
Ministerio de la Economía Familiar, Comunitaria, Cooperative y Asociativa (MEFCCA), 116
Misión Mercal (Venezuela), 125
Modenessi, Massimo, 10
modernity, 8–9, 20, 25, 47, 163
monetarists, 60
Monroe Doctrine, 54, 64
Monsanto, 145
Montenegro de Wit, Maywa, 23
Morales, Evo, 104, 106, 113
Motta, Sara, 161
Movimiento V República (MVR), 78
multiple sovereignties, 41, 42, 43, 48
Murphy, Craig, 53
Mutlu, Can, 17–18
Myers, Natasha, 5

NAFTA (North American Free Trade Agreement), 45, 63–64, 67
national bourgeoisie, 153

Index

nation-state, 36–37
Neeson, J. M., 113
neoliberal discipline, 59–60, 61–63, 71
neoliberalism: EZLN response to, 67; fragmentation of state and, 61–62; NGOs and, 62; political technologies of, 62–63; reign of, 160–161
neoliberal state, 62
new constitutionalism in Latin America, 104
"New Economic Model," 60
Newman, Simeon, 172n8
new map of goods (Grandnational Concept), 89–92
Nicaragua, 90–91, 95, 107, 112, 116–7, 130
Nixon, Richard, 58
non-governmental organizations (NGO), 61–62
Nontraditional Agricultural Exports (NTAE), 61
North American Free Trade Agreement (NAFTA), 45, 63–64, 67

oil: ALBA and, 13–15, 46, 85, 90, 97, 134; authoritarian statism and, 72–75; Barrio Adentro program and, 1–2; diplomacy and, 83–85; Venezuela and, 19–21, 77–81, 97–99, 98, 164–5
oil crisis of 1973, 59
open regionalism, 63
Operation Condor, 60
"organic crisis" in Venezuela, 78
Organic Law of Food Security and Sovereignty (Venezuela), 127
Organic Law of Lands and Agricultural Development (Venezuela), 105–6
Organic Law of the Food Sovereignty Regime (Ecuador), 104
Organic Law of the Supreme Tribunal of Justice (Venezuela), 108
Organic Law of Work (Venezuela), 159
Ortega, Daniel, 95, 105
outline of book, 20–22

Pacto de Punto Fijo, 13, 74, 78
Paraqueima, Jesús, 94
parcelization of sovereignty, 27
passive revolution, 10
Payara, Venezuela, 22, 132, 146–151, 154, 166
Payara plant (ALBA-Arroz), 141, 147–9, 151, 154
Payara Socialista (commune), 149–51, 159
PDVSA (Petróleos de Venezuela, S. A.), 75, 79–80, 95

peasant movements: ALBA states and, 129–30; Bolivarian state and, 117–8; Bolivia and fragmentation of, 114; boundary between rights in, 39; CCCs and, 123–4; coffee workers in Nicaragua and, 172n1; Ecuador and, 107; FNCEZ and, 106; food sovereignty and, 3; Green Revolution and, 68–69; horizontal scaling and, 123–9; identification of, 170n8; knowledge-power and, 117; Latin American, 104–12; "local petty sovereigns" and, 109; methods of production and, 109–10; rise of, 67–68; Venezuela and, 108–9; violence toward, 108–9. *See also* EZLN (Ejército Zapatista de Liberación Nacional); La Vía Campesina (LVC)
Peña, Karla, 115
Peoples' Trade Treaty (ALBA), 90–91, 169n1
Perdomo, Juan Vicente, 159
Pereira, Ruben, 85, 168
Pérez, Carlos Andrés, 14, 75–77
Pérez Abad, Miguel, 152, 154
Pesquera Industrial del ALBA (Pescalba), 120
Petrocaribe energy agreement, 2
PETRONIC, 95
Pink Tide, 1, 12, 50
Píritu I plant (ALBA-Arroz), 136, 139
Píritu II plant (ALBA-Arroz), 132–5
Píritu III plant (ALBA-Arroz), 137–40
Plan Tierras (Ecuador), 107
Plaza, Galo, 57–58
"Point and Circle" initiative, 22, 132–133, 146–51, 159
"political surplus value," 36
political technology, 24, 26–27, 30, 43
politics of production, 11
politics of scale, 44
possessive individual, 31
Poulantzas, Nicos: on competency, 36; on democratic road to socialism, 87; on feudal territory, 27–28; on Global South, 76; on "material condensation," 37; on misreading of capitalist state, 42–43; politics of production and, 11–12; relational theory of capitalist state of, 25, 47–48, 163–4; on Roman Empire, 26; on state personnel, 119; on theory and practice, 15–16
Powell, John Duncan, 74
Prado, Ángel, 168
precapitalist society, 25–26, 32

primitive accumulation, 28–29
private property: dispossession and, 30; feudalism and, 27; peasant holding of, 109; property-power and, 25, 36, 165; Roman Empire and, 26; separation of political and economic under rise of, 28; territory and, 35; transformation of rights and, 32, 34, 154
"Productive Revolution" (Bolivia), 113
profit caps, 153
property-power: ALBA-Arroz and, 159; capital and, 24; class struggle and, 104–12; edifice of sovereignty and, 9, 21; exclusion and, 34; "existential sovereignty" and, 36; food sovereignty and, 103; Green Revolution and, 56; instrumentalization of, 33; knowledge-power and, 11; land reform and, 130; nature of, 33–34; private property and, 25, 36, 165; sovereignty and, 163
Proyecto de Alianzas Rurales (PAR), 114

Ramírez, Mareli, 119, 126, 129
Ratzel, Friedrich, 51–52
regime of accumulation, 50
regional integration, 53–54, 63–65
regionalism in Latin America, 17, 20, 49–52, 70–71, 164
regional markets, 57
regional spaces and expansionism, 51–53
relational theory of capitalist state (Poulantzas), 25, 37–38, 73
revolutionary democracy, 1
Riggirozzi, Pia, 9
rights, formal and informal, 39
rights and territory: British colonization and, 29; capitalist transformation of, 9; edifice of sovereignty as, 9, 24, 47, 162; Indigenous modes of political organization and, 30; neoliberal sovereignty and, 62; precapitalist, 25; racial/ethnic differences as foundation of, 30–31; representative democracy and, 37; role of, 162–3
Rockefeller, Nelson A., 58
Roman-Alcalá, Antonio, 23
Roman Empire, 26–27
Roosevelt, Franklin Delano, 53
Rosset, Peter M., 40
Rostow, Walt, 54, 55
Royama, Masamichi, 52
rural populations, 60–61, 102, 104

scales of accumulation, 45
Schiavoni, Christina, 23, 125
Schmitt, Carl, 52
Scott, James C., 4
second-order condensations, 45
self-management (*autogestión*), 138–40, 158
settler sovereign landscapes, 31
Silva, Lula da, 65–66
social economy (*economía social*), 81–83
socialism: Latin American project of, 6; need for democratic road toward, 43; struggle for, 160–161; two souls of, 161
socialist geopolitics, 1
socialist internationalism in Latin American, 161–162
socialist production units (SPUs), 134
social movements, 21, 66–69, 84–88, 115–6, 161. *See also* Council of Social Movements (ALBA); peasant movements
Social Production Companies, 83
sovereign clarity of politics, 25
sovereignty: as absolute preserve of state, 28; absolutist state and, 28; Caribbean subregion and, 102; character of, 23; effects of modernity on, 24; forms of, 6–8; fragmentation of, 26–27, 31; framework for state and capitalist, 37; issues with, 6–8; nation-state and capital in edifice of, 36–37; "organized hypocrisy" of, 6; precapitalist societies and, 24; "problem" of, 6–8, 23–25, 162–163; property- and knowledge-power as, 47–48; racial/ethnic difference as foundation of, 30–31; rights and territory as, 9, 47, 162–163; Spanish bureaucracy, exploitation, and, 28–29; state-capital nexus in, 38–39; "strategic essentialism" and, 39
sovereignty problem: addressing the, 6–8; food sovereignty studies and, 162–163; framework for analyzing, 23–25
spatial selectivity, 45, 58, 63, 69, 84, 99–100
Spanish Empire, 28–29
state: rebuilding and reclaiming of, 9–10; as "strategic field and process," 38; as "strategic field of struggle," 11; untangling of, 17
State, Power, Socialism (Poulantzas), 11, 15–16
state-capital relations, 151–5
state-capital nexus, 9, 21, 25, 38
strategic-relational approach: ALBA and, 93–99, 98; elements of, 44; extending scale with, 25, 164; strategic and spatial selectivity in, 48

strategic selectivity: ALBA and, 98–99, 100; Bolivarian state and, 84; bottom-up form of, 69; Jessop and, 12; Latin American integration and, 58; materiality of capitalist state and, 37; neoliberalism and, 62–63; policymaking and, 44–45, 80; Poulantzas and, 171n 4; "social economy" and, 21
Strønen Iselin, 72
"structuration theory," 16
Sumak Kawsay, 3
Sunacoop, 82
surplus-value, 170n2
sweatshop labor, 35
Sztulwark, Diego, 167

territorial basis of society, 24
territoriality, 8, 40, 41, 103–104
Teschke, Benno, 27
Thomas, Peter, 169no.4
Thompson, Merisa S., 102
trade agreements, 63–66
transgenics, 143, 145
transnational activism, 67–68
Tratado de Montevideo, 58
Trauger, Amy, 23
triple subsidy (check), 143
typology of industrial regimes, 157–8

United States: continental history and, 20, 49; "continent-sized island" of, 51; economic Lebensraum of, 53, 55; foreign policy of, 53–55, 70; hegemony of, 50–51, 70; organizational transformations within, 51; response to recession by, 59
U.S. dollar, 59
U.S. imperialism, 53–54
U.S.-Latin American relations, 54, 58. *See also* neoliberalism

Venezuela: agrarian reform in, 5; agricultural policy in, 74–75; ALBA and, 97–100, 164–165; ALBA and role of, 13; ALBANISA and, 95–96; alliance with private sector in, 151–155; authoritarian statism in, 76–78, 168, 174n1; Barrio Adentro program and, 1; as Bolivarian Republic, 14, 21, 165; Bolivarian Revolution and, 4, 80; "bosses' strike" in, 79; bureaucratic corruption in, 119–20, 146–51; *caracazo* riots and "organic crisis" in, 77–78; CCCs in, 124–126; Chávez and, 14–15, 78–79; chavismo and exchange controls in, 80; communal councils (*consejos comunales*) in, 82–83, 117, 170n6; 173n16; coup d'etat in, 79; distribution of rural labor regimes in, 111–2; *economía social* in, 81–83; economic crisis in, 15; EMSAs in, 96; endogenous development and, 92–93; energy entities and, 135–6; "exceptional democracy" of, 13–15; falling ground rent and, 134–5; flagship products and, 122; focus on, 19, 20–21; food distribution issues and, 149–50; food sovereignty and, 127–128, 131, 141; foreign monopolization of agriculture in, 145; inflation in, 135, 135–136, 154; international policy and oil wealth of, 84; ISI policies and, 153–154; knowledge-power and, 117; labor unrest and nationalization of oil in, 75; land distribution in, 110; land reform in, 110–111, 112; land rescued/regularized in, 111; "magical state" of, 46; Misión Mercal and, 125; multiple sovereignties and, 117–118; oil and, 19–21, 72–74, 77–81, 97–99, 98, 164–5; Payara Socialista and, 159; peasant movements in, 117–8, 121; Pérez and, 14; pricing issues in, 151–154, 156; profit caps in, 153; regime of austerity in, 77; regional trade and, 90–91; rural cooperatives and, 121–2; social economy in, 166; territorial infrastructure in, 128; trajectory of politics in, 74; U.S. imperial strategy and, 19; vertical territoriality in, 117–23; *Vuelta al Campo* and, 121. *See also* Bolivarian state
vertical scaling, 113–23
vertical territoriality in Latin America, 40–41
violent abstractions, 32
Vuelta al Campo (Venezuela), 121

willful state, 4
world regions, formation of, 49
World Social Forum (WSF), 68

Yo Sí Puedo literacy campaign, 2

Zapatistas (EZLN), 67

GEOGRAPHIES OF JUSTICE AND SOCIAL TRANSFORMATION

1. *Social Justice and the City*, rev. ed.
   BY DAVID HARVEY
2. *Begging as a Path to Progress: Indigenous Women and Children and the Struggle for Ecuador's Urban Spaces*
   BY KATE SWANSON
3. *Making the San Fernando Valley: Rural Landscapes, Urban Development, and White Privilege*
   BY LAURA R. BARRACLOUGH
4. *Company Towns in the Americas: Landscape, Power, and Working-Class Communities*
   EDITED BY OLIVER J. DINIUS AND ANGELA VERGARA
5. *Tremé: Race and Place in a New Orleans Neighborhood*
   BY MICHAEL E. CRUTCHER JR.
6. *Bloomberg's New York: Class and Governance in the Luxury City*
   BY JULIAN BRASH
7. *Roppongi Crossing: The Demise of a Tokyo Nightclub District and the Reshaping of a Global City*
   BY ROMAN ADRIAN CYBRIWSKY
8. *Fitzgerald: Geography of a Revolution*
   BY WILLIAM BUNGE
9. *Accumulating Insecurity: Violence and Dispossession in the Making of Everyday Life*
   EDITED BY SHELLEY FELDMAN, CHARLES GEISLER, AND GAYATRI A. MENON
10. *They Saved the Crops: Labor, Landscape, and the Struggle over Industrial Farming in Bracero-Era California*
    BY DON MITCHELL
11. *Faith Based: Religious Neoliberalism and the Politics of Welfare in the United States*
    BY JASON HACKWORTH
12. *Fields and Streams: Stream Restoration, Neoliberalism, and the Future of Environmental Science*
    BY REBECCA LAVE
13. *Black, White, and Green: Farmers Markets, Race, and the Green Economy*
    BY ALISON HOPE ALKON
14. *Beyond Walls and Cages: Prisons, Borders, and Global Crisis*
    EDITED BY JENNA M. LOYD, MATT MITCHELSON, AND ANDREW BURRIDGE
15. *Silent Violence: Food, Famine, and Peasantry in Northern Nigeria*
    BY MICHAEL J. WATTS
16. *Development, Security, and Aid: Geopolitics and Geoeconomics at the U.S. Agency for International Development*
    BY JAMEY ESSEX
17. *Properties of Violence: Law and Land-Grant Struggle in Northern New Mexico*
    BY DAVID CORREIA
18. *Geographical Diversions: Tibetan Trade, Global Transactions*
    BY TINA HARRIS
19. *The Politics of the Encounter: Urban Theory and Protest under Planetary Urbanization*
    BY ANDY MERRIFIELD
20. *Rethinking the South African Crisis: Nationalism, Populism, Hegemony*
    BY GILLIAN HART
21. *The Empires' Edge: Militarization, Resistance, and Transcending Hegemony in the Pacific*
    BY SASHA DAVIS
22. *Pain, Pride, and Politics: Social Movement Activism and the Sri Lankan Tamil Diaspora in Canada*
    BY AMARNATH AMARASINGAM
23. *Selling the Serengeti: The Cultural Politics of Safari Tourism*
    BY BENJAMIN GARDNER
24. *Territories of Poverty: Rethinking North and South*
    EDITED BY ANANYA ROY AND EMMA SHAW CRANE
25. *Precarious Worlds: Contested Geographies of Social Reproduction*
    EDITED BY KATIE MEEHAN AND KENDRA STRAUSS
26. *Spaces of Danger: Culture and Power in the Everyday*
    EDITED BY HEATHER MERRILL AND LISA M. HOFFMAN
27. *Shadows of a Sunbelt City: The Environment, Racism, and the Knowledge Economy in Austin*
    BY ELIOT M. TRETTER
28. *Beyond the Kale: Urban Agriculture and Social Justice Activism in New York City*
    BY KRISTIN REYNOLDS AND NEVIN COHEN

29. *Calculating Property Relations: Chicago's Wartime Industrial Mobilization, 1940–1950*
BY ROBERT LEWIS

30. *In the Public's Interest: Evictions, Citizenship, and Inequality in Contemporary Delhi*
BY GAUTAM BHAN

31. *The Carpetbaggers of Kabul and Other American-Afghan Entanglements: Intimate Development, Geopolitics, and the Currency of Gender and Grief*
BY JENNIFER L. FLURI AND RACHEL LEHR

32. *Masculinities and Markets: Raced and Gendered Urban Politics in Milwaukee*
BY BRENDA PARKER

33. *We Want Land to Live: Making Political Space for Food Sovereignty*
BY AMY TRAUGER

34. *The Long War: CENTCOM, Grand Strategy, and Global Security*
BY JOHN MORRISSEY

35. *Development Drowned and Reborn: The Blues and Bourbon Restorations in Post-Katrina New Orleans*
BY CLYDE WOODS
EDITED BY JORDAN T. CAMP AND LAURA PULIDO

36. *The Priority of Injustice: Locating Democracy in Critical Theory*
BY CLIVE BARNETT

37. *Spaces of Capital / Spaces of Resistance: Mexico and the Global Political Economy*
BY CHRIS HESKETH

38. *Revolting New York: How 400 Years of Riot, Rebellion, Uprising, and Revolution Shaped a City*
GENERAL EDITORS: NEIL SMITH AND DON MITCHELL
EDITORS: ERIN SIODMAK, JENJOY ROYBAL, MARNIE BRADY, AND BRENDAN O'MALLEY

39. *Relational Poverty Politics: Forms, Struggles, and Possibilities*
EDITED BY VICTORIA LAWSON AND SARAH ELWOOD

40. *Rights in Transit: Public Transportation and the Right to the City in California's East Bay*
BY KAFUI ABLODE ATTOH

41. *Open Borders: In Defense of Free Movement*
EDITED BY REECE JONES

42. *Subaltern Geographies*
EDITED BY TARIQ JAZEEL AND STEPHEN LEGG

43. *Detain and Deport: The Chaotic U.S. Immigration Enforcement Regime*
BY NANCY HIEMSTRA

44. *Global City Futures: Desire and Development in Singapore*
BY NATALIE OSWIN

45. *Public Los Angeles: A Private City's Activist Futures*
BY DON PARSON
EDITED BY ROGER KEIL AND JUDY BRANFMAN

46. *America's Johannesburg: Industrialization and Racial Transformation in Birmingham*
BY BOBBY M. WILSON

47. *Mean Streets: Homelessness, Public Space, and the Limits of Capital*
BY DON MITCHELL

48. *Islands and Oceans: Reimagining Sovereignty and Social Change*
BY SASHA DAVIS

49. *Social Reproduction and the City: Welfare Reform, Child Care, and Resistance in Neoliberal New York*
BY SIMON BLACK

50. *Freedom Is a Place: The Struggle for Sovereignty in Palestine*
BY RON J. SMITH

51. *Loisaida as Urban Laboratory: Puerto Rico Community Activism in New York*
BY TIMO SCHRADER

52. *Transecting Securityscapes: Dispatches from Cambodia, Iraq, and Mozambique*
BY TILL F. PAASCHE AND JAMES D. SIDAWAY

53. *Non-Performing Loans, Non-Performing People: Life and Struggle with Mortgage Debt in Spain*
BY MELISSA GARCÍA-LAMARCA

54. *Disturbing Development in the Jim Crow South*
BY MONA DOMOSH

55. *Famine in Cambodia: Geopolitics, Biopolitics, Necropolitics*
BY JAMES A. TYNER

56. *Well-Intentioned Whiteness: Green Urban Development and Black Resistance in Kansas City*
BY CHHAYA KOLAVALLI

57. *Urban Climate Justice: Theory, Praxis, Resistance*
EDITED BY JENNIFER L. RICE, JOSHUA LONG, AND ANTHONY LEVENDA

58. *Abolishing Poverty: Toward Pluriverse Futures and Politics*
BY VICTORIA LAWSON, SARAH ELWOOD, MICHELLE DAIGLE, YOLANDA GONZÁLEZ MENDOZA, ANA GUTIÉRREZ GARZA, JUAN HERRERA, ELLEN KOHL, JOVAN LEWIS, AARON MALLORY, PRISCILLA MCCUTCHEON, MARGARET MARIETTA RAMÍREZ, AND CHANDAN REDDY

59. *Outlaw Capital: Everyday Illegalities and the Making of Uneven Development*
BY JENNIFER LEE TUCKER

60. *High Stakes, High Hopes: Urban Theorizing in Partnership*
BY SOPHIE OLDFIELD

61. *The Coup and the Palm Trees: Agrarian Conflict and Political Power in Honduras*
BY ANDRÉS LEÓN ARAYA

62. *Cultivating Socialism: Venezuela, ALBA, and the Politics of Food Sovereignty*
BY ROWAN LUBBOCK

www.ingramcontent.com/pod-product-compliance
Lightning Source LLC
Chambersburg PA
CBHW021756230426
43669CB00006B/100